PENGUIN BOOKS

THE BURNING OF BRIDGET CLEARY

Angela Bourke is Senior Lecturer in Irish at University College Dublin, National University of Ireland. She has been a visiting professor at Harvard University and the University of Minnesota, and writes, lectures, and broadcasts regularly on Irish oral tradition and literature. She is the author of one short-story collection, *By Salt Water*.

Praise for *The Burning of Bridget Cleary*

"[A] tightly constructed and authentically dramatic account. . . . [A] powerful reconstruction of the crime."
—*The New York Times Book Review*

"Historian Bourke brings to life the schism between modern, literate thinking and traditional oral folk beliefs, showing how each can express and conceal unspeakable impulses and acts."
—*Entertainment Weekly*

"This historian is also an accomplished storyteller who uncovers everyday details that transport us to Ballyvadlea, Tipperary, in 1895. With the economical skill of a thriller writer, Bourke heightens the suspense . . . [and] offers credible explanations. Cooly academic in the best sense, *The Burning of Bridget Cleary* is social history at its most imaginative." —*Newsday*

"Flowing and ethereal."
—*The Baltimore Sun*

"Bourke fills her narrative with meticulous research on the social, economic, and religious customs that prevailed in rural Ireland, as well as the Clearys' domestic circumstances—their childless marriage, rumored infidelities, and laborer's heritage—which elevates the book from the lurid crime story to a historically rich and heady tale. . . . It is chilling to read at the end of this fascinating book that the Clearys' house is still referred to by the locals as 'the fairy cottage' and 'the place where they burned the witch.'"
—*Elle*

"Bourke . . . exhibits a . . . balanced grasp of the story and a[n] . . . intimacy with the culture. . . . Because Bridget's murder offers a window into the changing world of Irish peasantry in the late nineteenth century, her tragic but fascinating story will interest many."
—*Library Journal*

"This is a fascinating story and a horrific one. Bourke has taken the kind of history exemplified in Le Roy Ladurie's *Montaillou*, wherein historical narrative is given heft and depth and the scent of every day from the driest and minutest details of legal proceedings and newspaper reports. Bourke illuminates the exquisite tensions between the lively Bridget, who made her own money as a milliner, and her husband, a cooper also educated and prosperous but resentful of his wife's independence. That power and control, not superstition and ignorance, lay at the center of why Bridget Cleary was killed and holds us mesmerized till the end."
—*Booklist*

"From the feathers on her hat, to Dotey the cat who climbed on her shoulders, to her pitiable last words as her husband closed in for the kill—every detail of Bridget Cleary's world and life is represented here with passionate sympathy, disciplined by a wealth of scholarship and enlivened by subtle intelligence. A wonderful, wonderful book."
—Nuala O'Faolain, author of *Are You Somebody?*

The Burning of Bridget Cleary

Bridget and Michael Cleary's
Wedding Portrait
1887

ANGELA BOURKE

THE BURNING

OF

BRIDGET

CLEARY

A True Story

PENGUIN BOOKS

PENGUIN BOOKS
Published by the Penguin Group
Penguin Putnam Inc., 375 Hudson Street,
New York, New York 10014, U.S.A.
Penguin Books Ltd, 27 Wrights Lane, London W8 5TZ, England
Penguin Books Australia Ltd, Ringwood, Victoria, Australia
Penguin Books Canada Ltd, 10 Alcorn Avenue,
Toronto, Ontario, Canada M4V 3B2
Penguin Books (N.Z.) Ltd, 182–190 Wairau Road,
Auckland 10, New Zealand

Penguin Books Ltd, Registered Offices:
Harmondsworth, Middlesex, England

First published in the United States of America by Viking Penguin,
a member of Penguin Putnam Inc. 2000
Published in Penguin Books 2001

3 5 7 9 10 8 6 4

Frontis photo courtesy of Margaret Rossiter

THE LIBRARY OF CONGRESS HAS CATALOGED
THE HARDCOVER EDITION AS FOLLOWS:
Bourke, Angela.
The burning of Bridget Cleary : a true story / Angela Bourke.
p.   cm.
Includes bibiographical references (p.) and index.
ISBN 0-670-89270-X (hc.)
ISBN 0 14 10.0202 6 (pbk.)
1. Cleary, Bridget, ca. 1869–1895   2. Murder—Ireland—Tipperary
(Country)—Case studies.   3. Tipperary (Ireland : Country)—
Social conditions—19th century.   I. Title.
HV6535.1742 T563   2000
364.15'23'094192—dc21   00–026891

Printed in the United States of America
Set in Bembo
Designed by Francesca Belanger

For Louis
and in memory of Adele Dalsimér
1939–2000

CONTENTS

Family Tree: Clearys, Bolands, and Kennedys

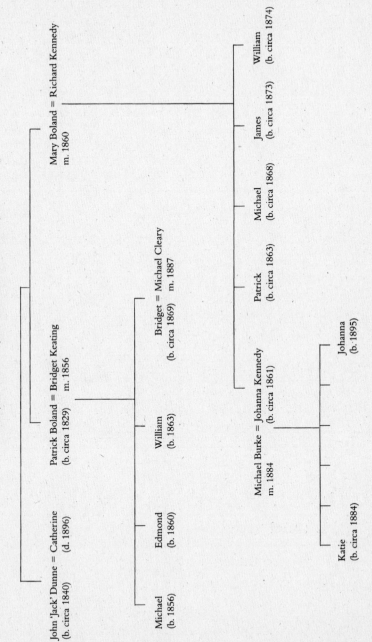

John 'Jack' Dunne = Catherine
(b. circa 1840)   (d. 1896)

Patrick Boland = Bridget Keating
(b. circa 1829)   m. 1856

Mary Boland = Richard Kennedy
                      m. 1860

Michael
(b. 1856)

Edmond
(b. 1860)

William
(b. 1863)

Bridget = Michael Cleary
(b. circa 1869)   m. 1887

Michael Burke = Johanna Kennedy
m. 1884   (b. circa 1861)

Patrick
(b. circa 1863)

Michael
(b. circa 1868)

James
(b. circa 1873)

William
(b. circa 1874)

Katie
(b. circa 1884)

Johanna
(b. 1895)

CHRONOLOGY
March–July 1895

Monday, March 4

Tipperary: Bridget Cleary walks from Ballyvadlea to John Dunne's house in Kylenagranagh with eggs. Catches cold.

London: First reading of Land Law (Ireland) Bill.

Tuesday, March 5

Tipperary: Bridget Cleary at home in Ballyvadlea, confined to bed with "a raging pain in her head."

Thursday, March 7

Tipperary: Bridget Cleary's illness continues.

London: Oscar and Constance Wilde, Lord Alfred Douglas attend *The Importance of Being Earnest*.

Saturday, March 9

Tipperary: Patrick Boland walks to Fethard; asks Dr. William Crean to call on his daughter.

London: Opening of Oscar Wilde's libel case against the Marquess of Queensberry.

Monday, March 11

Tipperary: Dr. Crean has not yet visited Bridget Cleary. Michael Cleary walks to Fethard to summon him.

Wednesday, March 13

Tipperary: Michael Cleary walks to Fethard again. Dr. Crean calls to Cleary's house, A.M.; Johanna Burke, Mary Kennedy, Jack Dunne visit Bridget Cleary. Fr. Cornelius Ryan calls, administers last rites, P.M. Michael Cleary doses his wife with herbs obtained from "a woman in Fethard."

Thursday, March 14

Tipperary: Fr. Ryan refuses to visit Bridget Cleary a second time. Michael Cleary walks to Kyleatlea to consult herb doctor Denis Ganey. Relatives and neighbors visit Bridget Cleary; force her to swallow herbs boiled in new milk; carry her to and from fire. News of Michael Cleary's father's death. Kennedy brothers and Patrick Boland go to wake. Others stay till 6:00 A.M.

Friday, March 15

Tipperary: Michael Cleary fetches Fr. Ryan, early A.M.; mass in Bridget Cleary's room. Neighbors visit during day and evening. Bridget dressed, sitting by fire. Argument about fairies. Michael Cleary knocks his wife to the floor; she burns to death. Husband and Patrick Kennedy bury body.

Saturday, March 16

Tipperary: Rumors about Bridget Cleary's disappearance; mention of fairies. Cleary, Dunne, and Michael Kennedy walk to Drangan, meet priests. Royal Irish Constabulary begins search for missing woman.

Sunday, March 17

Tipperary: Micheal Cleary tries to borrow William Simpson's gun. Keeps vigil at Kylenagranagh Fort with other men.

Monday, March 18

Tipperary: William Simpson swears "information" before William W. Tennant JP. Police search continues. Michael Cleary keeps second night's vigil at Kylenagranagh.

London: Grand Jury returns true bill against Marquess of Queensberry for criminal libel.

Tuesday, March 19

Tipperary: Johanna Burke swears "information." Cleary at Kylenagranagh again.

London: Whitehall denies reports that Prime Minister Lord Rosebery is seriously ill.

Wednesday, March 20

Tipperary: Further informations sworn. Nine arrest warrants issued. First newspaper reports of Bridget Cleary's disappearance, Clonmel.

Thursday, March 21

Tipperary: Prisoners arrested, charged at Town Hall, Clonmel.

Friday, March 22

Tipperary: Charred body of Bridget Cleary found in shallow grave. Johanna Burke arrested; released soon after.

London: Reports of Lord Rosebery's sleeplessness continue.

Saturday, March 23

Tipperary: Coroner's inquest, Cloneen. Verdict: death by burning.

Sunday, March 24

Tipperary: Fr. Con Ryan denounces "outrage" at mass in Cloneen. RIC find spade and shovel at Clearys' house.

Monday, March 25

Tipperary: Prisoners before magistrates, Clonmel courthouse. Direct examination of Johanna Burke, Crown witness.

Tuesday, March 26

Tipperary: Examination of Johanna Burke continues; deposition of her daughter Katie. Constable Thomas McLoughlin, Kilkenny, takes photographs in Ballyvadlea. *Cork Examiner* reporter visits house.

Wednesday, March 27

Tipperary: RIC buries Bridget Cleary under cover of darkness, Cloneen.

Dublin: Unionist and nationalist newspapers publish editorials about the case.

Thursday, March 28

Tipperary: William Simpson shows *Cork Examiner* reporter around Cleary's house.

London: Newspapers report "Lord Rosebery's progress very slow." Sir Edward Grey demands that French clarify their position in Africa; fear of war with France.

Sunday, March 31

New York: *New York Times* picks up story of Bridget Cleary: "barbarous episode near Fethard."

Monday, April 1

> Tipperary: Prisoners put forward on remand charged with willful murder. Evidence of William Simpson and Fr. Con Ryan.

Tuesday, April 2

> Tipperary: Hearing continues, Clonmel; Cleary's clothing produced in court.

> London: Second Reading of Land Law (Ireland) Bill moved by Chief Secretary John Morley, opposed by Edward Carson.

Wednesday, April 3

> Tipperary: Fair day in Clonmel; no court sitting. *Clonmel Chronicle* publishes tabloid supplement: "The Appalling Tragedy in Ballyvadlea."

> London: *Regina* v. *Queensberry* opens, Old Bailey. Edward Carson cross-examines Oscar Wilde.

Thursday, April 4

> Tipperary: Hearing continues, Clonmel; evidence of Acting Sergeant Patrick Egan. *Daily Graphic* publishes sketches of Fr. Ryan, Mary Kennedy, William Simpson, and the nine men accused.

> London: *Regina* v. *Queensberry,* cross-examination by Carson continues until after lunch; Carson's speech for the defense begins, 3:00 P.M.

Friday, April 5

> Tipperary: Hearing continues; Denis Ganey discharged; medical evidence heard.

> London: Carson's speech continues, Old Bailey. Verdict: Not guilty. Oscar Wilde arrested.

Saturday, April 6

> Tipperary: Statements by prisoners, Clonmel. Nine prisoners committed for trial.

> London: Oscar Wilde charged with offenses under Criminal Law Amendment Act, 1885.

Thursday, May 2

> Tipperary: Meeting of Cashel Poor Law Guardians discusses letter regarding Dr. Crean sent by Local Government Board,

April 9, to Dispensary Management Committee, Fethard. Suggests that "a caution . . . will meet the case."

Friday, May 10

Tipperary: Dr. Crean deemed to have resigned May 2. Fethard Dispensary Management Committee resolves to advertise his job.

Wednesday, May 15

Tipperary: *Nationalist* reports William Simpson making money from guided tours of Clearys' cottage.

Friday, June 21

London: Lord Rosebery's Liberal Government resigns.

Wednesday, July 3

Tipperary: Grand Jury sworn, Clonmel. Kennedys' house burned down.

Thursday, July 4

Tipperary: Mr. Justice William O'Brien opens July assizes, Clonmel; Grand Jury finds true bill for murder against Michael Cleary and four others, true bill for wounding against all nine accused; testimony of Johanna Burke.

Friday, July 5

Tipperary: Trial of Michael Cleary: further testimony of Johanna Burke; testimony of Katie Burke; judge puts issue paper to jury—prisoner found guilty of manslaughter. William Ahearne discharged. Other prisoners found guilty of wounding; sentences handed down. Mary Kennedy released.

Friday, July 12

Tipperary: Prisoners Michael Cleary, Jack Dunne, Patrick Kennedy, transferred to Mountjoy Prison, Dublin.

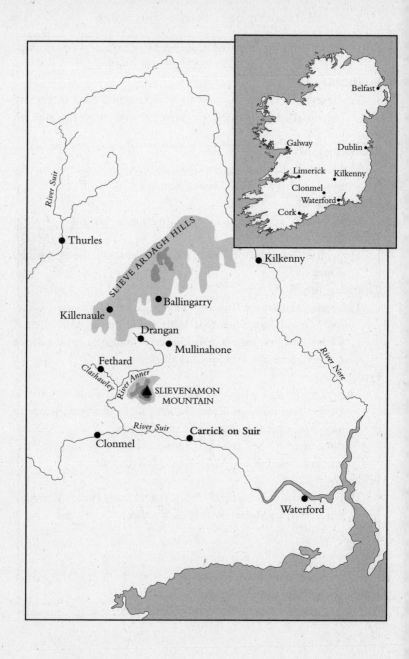

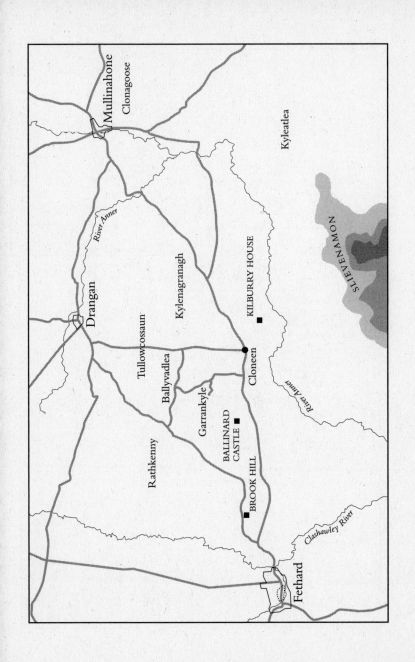

There was a woman one time taken by the fairies. She was married. They took [her] away from the husband and left him another old yoke [thing] instead of her. The husband was in a terrible way over it, and he didn't know what he had best do to get her back. He went to a fairyman that lived somewhere in the County Kilkenny and he told him his story. The fairyman told him that [the fairies] would be passing by the end of his house on a certain night and that he'd see them—he gave him some herbs so that he could see them—and that his wife would be riding on a grand grey horse; and when she'd be passing him to seize and hold on to her, that if he missed her he'd never see her again. He came home, and on this certain night he went out to the end of the house, and he was no length there when the fairies came on, and they galloping. He saw the wife on the white horse and the minute she came up to him he grabbed her and held her. He put some herbs he was after getting from the fairyman into her hand, so that she'd stay with him, and begob he had his wife back again. When they went back into the house, the other yoke was gone off with herself.

Told by Mrs. John Carroll (65), Assegart, Foulksmills, Co. Wexford, December 1937, and written down by Tomás Ó Ciardha (IFC 437: 106–7). Used by kind permission of the Head of Department of Irish Folklore, University College Dublin.

Laborers, Priests, and Peelers

THE WINTER OF 1894/95 was exceptionally hard, with February 1895 the coldest yet recorded in many parts of Ireland and Britain. Farm work was seriously delayed, and agricultural laborers in Ireland were facing unemployment and destitution. In mid-March, though, both weather and economic prospects improved. It was a time of record keeping and centralized bureaucracy. At Birr Castle Observatory in King's County, as Offaly was then called, Robert Jacob kept scrupulous twice-daily weather records, which he entered by hand on large printed sheets supplied by the Meteorological Office in London. On April 2, 1895, in accordance with instructions printed on the form, he folded his March return four times to make a letter-sized packet, stuck on a red halfpenny stamp showing the head of a younger Queen Victoria, and sent it off. The back of the form had already been printed with the address: 63 Victoria Street, London. It arrived there on April 4, postmarked "Parsonstown 6.50 Ap 2 95."

According to Jacob's records, the temperature at Birr Castle at nine o'clock in the morning, Wednesday, March 13, had been 37.4 degrees Fahrenheit; twenty-four hours later it had risen to 50.5. By 9 o'clock on Thursday evening the weather was still mild and dry, with a temperature of 46.8. Fifty miles away, on a farm at Kishogue, near the village of Drangan, County Tipperary, Michael Kennedy asked his employer, Edward Anglin, for his wages, and set out on a three-mile walk along dark roads to give the money to his widowed mother. Mary Kennedy lived in a tiny, mud-walled, thatched house beside Ballyvadlea bridge, where Michael and his brothers and sister had grown up. When he got there, however, she was on her way out. Her twenty-six-year-old niece Bridget Cleary had been ill for several days, and Mary Kennedy was going to visit her for the second or third time. Michael Kennedy decided to follow his mother to his cousin's house, across the bridge and up the hill. Bridget lived only half a mile away, with her husband, Michael Cleary, a cooper, and her father, who was Mary Kennedy's brother.

The Clearys lived in a slate-roofed laborers' cottage, built a few years earlier; though modest, it was a much better house than Mary Kennedy's, or indeed than many others in the area. When Michael Kennedy arrived there on the night of Thursday, March 14, it was full of people and activity. His cousin's illness seemed to have reached some kind of crisis. In the kitchen, where a group of neighbors waited, some green stumps of whitethorn were burning slowly in the fire grate, and a large oil lamp stood on the table. Just off the kitchen, Bridget Cleary lay in the front bedroom, where the only light came from a candle. Her bed almost filled the tiny room, but several men were standing around it, holding her down; another was lying across her legs.

Most of the men in the bedroom were Bridget Cleary's relatives, among them Michael Kennedy's brothers, Patrick, James, and William. The others were her husband Michael, her father Patrick Boland, and a cousin of his called Jack Dunne. A teenage boy, William Ahearne, was with them, holding the candle. The men were trying to make Bridget Cleary swallow herbs boiled in new milk—Michael Cleary was holding a saucepan and a spoon—but she was resisting them. Again and again, as though they doubted her identity, they demanded, in the name of God, that she say whether or not she was indeed Bridget Cleary, daughter of Patrick Boland and wife of Michael Cleary. The men were shouting as they questioned her and forced the mixture into her mouth. Eventually they lifted her out of bed and carried her through the door to the kitchen fire, about twenty feet away. There they questioned her again, holding her over the smoldering wood as they demanded that she answer her name. The neighbors who were in the kitchen heard them talk about witches and fairies.

When Bridget Cleary's death was being investigated in the weeks that followed, Michael Kennedy claimed not to remember much about the events of that evening. In Clonmel Prison, seven months later, it was noted that he had been tubercular ("phthisical") for years. He may also have had epilepsy, for he told the court that he was susceptible to fits, and that he had lost consciousness in the crowded and noisy house. When he woke up, he said, he was lying in bed in the second small bedroom at the back of the house, where his uncle, Patrick Boland, usually slept. He believed he had been unconscious for at least half an hour.

The house was quiet again by the time he woke. Bridget Cleary was in bed, and apparently resting, but at some point during the evening word had come that her husband's father had died. Michael Cleary was not from Ballyvadlea, but from Killenaule, about eight miles away, and several of the men were preparing to walk there to attend his wake. Wakes were all-night affairs, and major social events for the rural working class, with storytelling, games, and other amusements; they were prime occasions for the exchange of terrifying legends about ghosts and fairies, and for young men and women to meet. Patrick, James, and William Kennedy had wanted to go earlier—they had spent part of the evening shaving each other in the back bedroom in preparation—but Michael Cleary had delayed them by demanding that they stay and assist him with his wife's treatment until after midnight. Michael Cleary himself might have been expected to go to Killenaule, if only to see his bereaved mother, but he insisted on staying at home with his wife. Old-style wakes were increasingly frowned on by respectable society, and Michael Cleary was better educated than most of his wife's relatives; still, his decision not to attend his own father's wake was surprising.

Michael Kennedy's older brother Patrick was thirty-two, Michael himself was twenty-seven, James was twenty-two, and William twenty-one. All were farm laborers and unmarried, and only the younger two could read or write. They left the house in Ballyvadlea together at about one o'clock in the morning to walk to Killenaule. Eight miles was a considerable distance, but the night was fine and men of their class were used to walking. The moon had been full three nights earlier, and had been up for over an hour by the time they set out, so they would have had no difficulty in finding their way. Several women and a few of the other men remained in the house for the rest of the night, carrying drinks to Bridget Cleary as she called for them. It was not unusual for people to stay up very late like this, talking and swapping stories, when they visited neighbors: the Irish word *airneán,* which has no precise equivalent in English, means just this sort of gathering.

The moon was high in the sky at about three in the morning when the Kennedys arrived at the wake. Their sixty-six-year-old un-cle, Patrick Boland, joined them there even later. After a few hours, he returned to Ballyvadlea, where his daughter still lay ill, but the four Kennedys stayed all the next day in Killenaule. They walked back together as far as Drangan on Friday evening, then Patrick, James, and William continued home to their mother's house at Bally-vadlea bridge, while Michael returned to Anglin's farm at Kishogue.

Saturday, March 16, was warm and sunny, but as Michael Kennedy walked from Kishogue back into Drangan village, a shock awaited him. Thirty-six hours earlier, he had seen his cousin Bridget Cleary ill in bed in Ballyvadlea, but now he was told that she had dis-appeared from her home. More disturbing still was the suggestion that she had gone across the fields with two men in the middle of the previous night, wearing only her nightdress. Some people were even saying plainly that the fairies had taken her away.

Despite his protestations about having fainted in his cousin's house, Michael Kennedy must have known something of the treat-ment she had received on Thursday evening. According to the kind of stories often told at firesides and at wakes, certain illnesses were supposed to be the work of the fairies, who could abduct a healthy young person and leave a sickly changeling instead: herbal medicines and ordeals by fire were both said to be ways of banishing such a changeling.

In Drangan, Michael Kennedy spent a while outside Feelys' gro-cery shop and spoke to two men named Burke and Donovan, but he could get no further information. He had begun to walk back toward Anglin's farm when he met the two men most likely to know the truth, Michael Cleary and Jack Dunne. Dunne had been one of the men gathered around Bridget Cleary's bed on Thursday night. He was Mary Kennedy and Patrick Boland's first cousin, and lived near Ballyvadlea, in the townland of Kylenagranagh.

Cleary and Dunne were both agitated when Michael Kennedy met them in the street, a little after midday. In fact Michael Cleary seemed distraught. He was wearing a suit of light gray tweed—jacket, waistcoat, and trousers—and a navy-blue cap, but his clothes had greasy marks and hung loosely, as though they were too big for him, and when Kennedy spoke to him he made no answer. Ignoring the younger man's questions, he kept on walking toward the large Catholic church in the center of the village, while Jack Dunne limped along behind. Dunne, according to his own later account, was gravely concerned about Cleary. Cleary had been talking wildly about strange men, and burning, and had threatened to cut his own throat, so Dunne had persuaded him to come to Drangan to talk to the priest. When Michael Kennedy could get no reply from either of the men, he turned and followed them, and together the three entered the chapel yard.

Drangan is a quiet village in the beautiful and fertile green rolling farmland of County Tipperary's South Riding, about fifteen miles northeast of Clonmel, and seven from the medieval walled town of Fethard. When the census was taken in 1891, it had 34 houses, and a population of 127. The village has one street, which begins where the road from Fethard enters from the southwest. Mullinahone is four miles to the east, but the main road between the two towns passes farther south, through the village of Cloneen. Drangan lies surrounded by hills, on the edge of the Slieve Ardagh range, roughly at the center of a quadrangle of major roads whose northern corners are at Killenaule and Ballingarry. It is a natural meeting place for a scattered rural population, at the head of a small valley which runs down to Mullinahone, but its importance is strictly local.

By far the most imposing building in Drangan is the chapel, as Catholic churches are usually called in rural Ireland. It stands on the north side of the main street, squarely in the center of the village, surrounded by graves dating from the nineteenth and twentieth centuries. High iron railings and gates separate it from the street outside, and a plaque announces its dedication in 1850 to the Immaculate Conception of the Virgin Mary.

In the years following Catholic Emancipation in 1829, "big chapels" like this one steadily replaced the humble buildings in which Catholics had previously worshipped. The earliest were rectangular and strictly functional, but by 1895, large, costly, and elaborately decorated cruciform buildings in towns and villages proclaimed the social and economic importance of the Catholic Church and its clergy. Drangan chapel was built of cut stone between 1850 and 1853, and Drangan, whose shops and houses flank it and look up to it, is a classic example of what has been called a "chapel-village," where the construction of a big chapel in the countryside in the nineteenth century generated the growth of other services, including the state apparatus of police station and post office.[1]

When Michael Kennedy, Michael Cleary, and Jack Dunne entered the chapel yard at about one o'clock, Michael McGrath, the fifty-nine-year-old parish priest of Cloneen and Drangan, was in the church. The Synod of Thurles in 1850 had laid down rules for the administration and regulation of Catholic practice in Ireland, reinforcing the Church's control of its members' daily lives. The Synod was the first formal meeting of the Irish bishops since 1642, and many of its prescriptions were designed to centralize religious activity in church buildings, and put an end to the tradition of administering the sacraments in private homes. The Synod had decreed that confessions should be heard regularly in all churches, and the faithful encouraged to attend the sacrament weekly; so on March 16, 1895, Fr. McGrath was hearing confessions. His curate, or coadjutor, Cornelius Fleming Ryan, known as "Father Con," was also in the chapel. Not only was this the day before St. Patrick's Day, it was a feast of the Immaculate Conception of the Virgin Mary, to whom the building was dedicated.

Jack Dunne went into the building alone. Like Michael Kennedy and his brothers, he was a farm laborer. A short, fat, gray-haired man, who walked with a pronounced limp, he was described in contemporary accounts as old, although records show that he was fifty-five in 1895. The same pattern emerges again and again among the documents of this story, as people in their fifties and sixties, if they belong to the laboring class, are described as "old." Accounts of their physical appearance reflect the hardships and privations of working-class life in nineteenth-century Ireland, especially for those born before the Famine of 1845–49. Jack Dunne could read, but not write. He was missing several teeth; his eyesight was poor, and a fracture had left his right leg shorter than his left.[2]

Michael Kennedy stayed in the yard with the still-agitated Michael Cleary, while Dunne went into the chapel. Cleary, bearded and balding, looked older than his thirty-five years. He was easily the most educated of the three, able to read and write, and possessor of a skilled trade, for he was a cooper, a maker of the casks and barrels in which commodities of all kinds, both wet and dry, were stored and transported. Before coming to live with his wife and her father, Michael Cleary had worked for several years in Clonmel, and he had built up a lucrative trade of his own since moving to Ballyvadlea. As he waited outside the chapel, however, he was weeping and distressed. Michael Kennedy stood awkwardly beside him.

In the chapel, Jack Dunne made his way to where Fr. McGrath was hearing confessions.[3] When Fr. McGrath had listened to Dunne's story, he told him to send Michael Cleary in at once to speak to him.

Michael Cleary, still crying, went into the chapel, but instead of going to speak to Fr. McGrath, he approached the altar. There the younger of the parish's two priests, Fr. Con Ryan, found him kneeling, tearing out his hair and, as he put it later, behaving like a madman. Cleary seemed to be suffering, Fr. Ryan said, from remorse for something he had done, and wanted to go to confession, but the curate did not think he was "in a fit state to receive the sacrament" and asked him instead to come into the vestry. Fr. Ryan began to feel afraid of him then, however, and coaxed him back out into the yard, where Jack Dunne and Michael Kennedy were waiting. Cleary was still crying loudly.

Fr. Ryan moved toward Dunne, gesturing to Michael Cleary to leave him. "Go on," he said, according to Dunne's memory; "'tis this man I want to be talking to." Throughout the evidence given later to the magistrates at Clonmel Petty Sessions, and again before a judge and jury at the summer assizes, witnesses who could not write told their stories with considerable dramatic use of direct speech.

The priest addressed Jack Dunne as Michael Kennedy took Cleary aside. "What's up with him?"

Dunne told him that Cleary had claimed to have burned his wife the previous night, and that three or four people had buried her. "I've been asking them all morning to take her up and give her a Christian burial."

Fr. Ryan had visited Bridget Cleary in her home only the day before. He was horror-struck: "How could three or four of them go out of their minds simultaneously?" he wondered in his evidence. His impression, he said, had been that Michael Cleary's mind was going astray. "He's in a bad way," he told Dunne. "It would be better to see after him [to do something about him]. We'll see the parish priest."

Fr. McGrath had come out of the chapel into the yard, and the younger priest went to speak to him. Jack Dunne watched the two priests talking, then both he and Michael Kennedy saw Fr. Ryan cross the street and go into the constabulary barracks.

In 1895, as now, Drangan's architecture proclaimed the importance of Catholicism in the life of rural Ireland, its centrality in the village, and the authority of its priests. In 1895, it also demonstrated the delicate balance between the church and a very different, equally centralized authority.

The "Peelers," called after their founder, Sir Robert Peel, lived and worked in the Royal Irish Constabulary barracks in Drangan. RIC men were the eyes, ears, and often the arms, of the British administration, based in Dublin Castle. Their training and discipline were military and, unlike other police forces in the United Kingdom, they were armed. They were engaged in surveillance of known or suspected subversives, but also had considerable civil and local government responsibility, to the extent that by the end of the nineteenth century their duties had become "more akin to house-keeping than to peace-keeping," and they rarely carried firearms. Their position could still be ambiguous, however: their work did not endear them to the tenant farmers and shopkeepers, who constituted the increasingly nationalist Irish Catholic middle class, even though over 70 percent of the men recruited to the force after 1861 were Catholic. In the 1880s, members of the RIC were boycotted in County Tipperary, especially during the operation of the repressive "coercion" legislation, during and after the Land War of 1879–82.[4]

With a history of nationalist politics and agrarian conflict, County Tipperary's South Riding had the highest police presence of any county in Ireland in the 1890s: 47 per 10,000 of population, compared with the lowest figure of 12 each in the northern counties of Derry and Down, or 34 and 38 in North Tipperary and Meath respectively. According to the census of 1891, 7 district inspectors, 10 head constables, and 454 sergeants, acting sergeants, and constables comprised the force in South Tipperary.

A road guide published in 1893 for the use of members of the constabulary gives a flavor of the world in which the RIC was operating.[5] The agrarian disturbances and "outrages" that had characterized the Land War and its aftermath had largely ceased, although occasional incidents were still reported. Members of the constabulary had leisure to become proficient riders of bicycles: a new sport and mode of transport until recently available only to the gentry. The author acknowledges the help he has received from all ranks of the RIC, including "the junior constable, who, perhaps an enthusiastic cyclist, did his utmost to place his local knowledge at the service of the public." The book includes, among advertisements for corn cures, fishing tackle, insurance, and whiskey, several for bicycles, pneumatic tires, and cycling clothes, as well as for publications devoted to cycling. Intended for "the overcoat pocket, or the hand-bag of the tourist," this work was undertaken "with the view of supplying a great want of the Royal Irish Constabulary, and of kindred public services; and also of providing a 'Road Book' of a reliable and comprehensive character, for the use of cyclists and tourists, of Irish travellers and others of the public who may desire to travel through our beautiful island."

"Each Police Barrack in Ireland," the guidebook begins, "is the centre of a circle of 'Circumjacent' Stations. Each Police Station has sent in a return, on identical lines, giving similar information as regards itself and circumjacent neighbouring Police Barracks which are printed in uniform style and sequence." Reduced to a system of abbreviations, each entry details the facilities available in the vicinity of a barracks: post, telegraph, and money-order offices, with their opening hours and times of delivery and collection; horse-drawn "post-cars" for hire; nearest railway station; markets, court sittings, and places of interest or beauty, if any. (None is listed for Drangan or Cloneen, although Fethard has several.) Directions to each of the "circumjacent" stations are given as part of every entry, with distances calculated to within a quarter of a mile. Every road mentioned is classified from A ("level broad roads, on which two four-wheeled vehicles can trot abreast") to D ("up and down hill, and narrow"), with a description of its condition, ranging from G[ood] or F[air], to I[ndifferent] or R[ocky and rutty].

Standardization and uniformity were hallmarks of nineteenth-century official thinking, gradually imposed throughout the countryside: police officers, soldiers, railway employees, and postmen wore uniform clothing, which immediately identified them; works of literature were published in identical bindings in uniform editions; administrators at every level of society filled out printed forms and returned them by post to central offices for filing; trains ran according to printed timetables, and standard time was gradually adopted even in the most remote areas. In Ireland, as elsewhere in Europe, these were the symptoms of profound cultural change. As the English language replaced Irish throughout most of the country during the same period, oral tradition gave way to print. A whole world of wakes, herbal cures, stories of kings and heroes, and legends of the fairies—the culture of those who had not learned to read and write— became increasingly marginal. Jack Dunne, Michael Kennedy, his older brother Patrick, and several others in this story, were among those people. They still lived in a symbolic universe very different from the one mapped by the RIC: centralization and uniformity had little relevance to their daily lives.

Even priests wore uniform in late-nineteenth-century Ireland. By decree of the Synod of Thurles, and partly as a strategy for safe-guarding clerical celibacy, black clerical garb, including the Roman collar, had become standard for Catholic priests, who were also ordered to avoid undue familiarity with women.[6] The Catholicism the priests propounded in the towns and chapel villages of County Tipperary was modern minded, outward looking, literate, and essentially middle class. It sternly opposed attendance at wakes, and had no time whatever for stories about fairies. Highly centralized, with priests reporting to bishops, and bishops reporting to Rome, the church in Ireland was strongly influenced by Continental practice, especially the Marian devotions favored increasingly by the papacy in this period. The dedication of Drangan Chapel to the Immaculate Conception, four years before Rome defined that doctrine as dogma, was typical. Since 1870, the church hierarchy's authority had been strengthened by the declaration of papal infallibility, but such teaching had little effect on the landless, or on their oral culture. Folk religion was centered on holy wells, local saints, the kin-group, and the home, rather than on church buildings, and its teachings were transmitted through traditional prayers, songs, and stories, not through printed catechisms. Well into the twentieth century, this kind of uncentralized Catholicism, which sat more easily with unofficial traditions about a fairy supernatural than the official version could, was still strong in places where Irish was spoken.[7]

Most Catholic priests in Tipperary in the late nineteenth century were drawn from the increasingly prosperous class of English-speaking tenant farmers. Many held leases on farms of their own, and lived at least as well as the better-off farmers to whom they ministered.[8] Although the five, seven, or more years they spent in seminary training could not be described as a liberal education, it equipped them to take the lead in a society where schooling and literacy were steadily advancing. Many were involved in the politics of the Land League (1880–81), and of the Irish National League that succeeded it: most of the National League's ninety-six branches were centered on Catholic chapels.[9]

The RIC monitored the activities of the Land League and the National League, and reported regularly on the movements of the many priests known to be politically active. By 1895, the political power of priests was less than it had been, and land agitation had died down, but Michael McGrath, parish priest of Drangan, had a history of political involvement, and his activities were still of interest to the members of the constabulary stationed across the street from his church.[10]

Cornelius Fleming Ryan, the priest who walked into the RIC barracks on Saturday afternoon, March 16, 1895, was a member of a prominent Catholic family from Murroe, in nearby County Limerick. He had been ordained at the Irish College in Rome in 1885, and had worked for some time in London before coming to Drangan. Several of his close relatives held important positions in the Cashel Diocese, but Con Ryan remained a curate until his death in 1916.[11] A tall ringed cross memorial above his grave in Drangan chapel yard records that "His charity and zeal endeared him to the people to whom he ministered for twenty-two years." In 1895, he was thirty-seven and had been in the parish for just two years. The provisions of the Synod of Thurles had generally had the effect of insulating the clergy from the lives of their ordinary parishioners, but Fr. Ryan knew the Clearys. Care of the sick was specifically mentioned as a reason for priests to visit parishioners in their homes, and on the previous Wednesday, and again on Friday morning, Fr. Ryan had visited Bridget Cleary, at her husband's request.[12]

In the barracks, Fr. Ryan met the acting sergeant, Patrick Egan. He told the policeman that "he thought Michael Cleary was off his head, and that it would be well to see him home and keep him under observation." He also mentioned that he suspected foul play, and suggested that Jack Dunne might be able to give the police more information.

Acting Sergeant Egan had probably already heard the same story as Michael Kennedy had about Bridget Cleary's mysterious disappearance from her home; he certainly knew that extraordinary stories were circulating. He accompanied Fr. Ryan out of the barracks, and together they watched as Cleary, Dunne, and Kennedy set off back down the street toward Cloneen.

Michael Kennedy's account of that Saturday is the sketchiest: his bewilderment and agitation show clearly in the short, disjointed sentences in which he later gave his evidence in court. He simply says that he thought Michael Cleary was out of his mind, so that, instead of returning to his employer's farm at Kishogue, he went with him and Jack Dunne back to Ballyvadlea. On the way he several times asked Cleary, "What about Bridget?" but received no reply. Jack Dunne, for his part, reported that Michael Cleary spent the journey trying to persuade him to go with him to Kylenagranagh, to rescue his wife from the fairies. Kylenagranagh was the name of the townland where Dunne himself lived. There was a big house there, whose deserted outbuildings he had helped Cleary to search that morning, but there was also a ringfort. Ringforts—roughly circular embankments—are known to archaeology as the remains of early medieval dwelling places; despite their name, few of them are thought to have had any defensive purpose. Long deserted, they were commonly referred to in their localities as places where the fairies lived. This was often suggested tongue in cheek, however, and Dunne insisted he had had no intention of going to the "fort" of Kylenagranagh. "It was only moonshine," he told the court.

Acting Sergeant Egan and another policeman followed Michael Cleary, Jack Dunne, and Michael Kennedy along the Fethard road as far as the turn for Cloneen. The policemen wore dark-green uniform caps, tunics, and trousers, with boots and belts of highly polished leather. A handcuff case and a baton hung from each of their belts; each man's whistle was ready on its chain.[13] The afternoon was fine: at almost 60 degrees Fahrenheit, it was unusually warm for March. After the turning, the two policemen walked on the opposite side of the road from the men, to keep them in sight as the road twisted and turned. According to details supplied for the RIC road book by Sergeant Patrick Furey of Cloneen, this was a B-class road (level and narrow), in "fair" condition; (the Drangan return, however, gave its condition as "indifferent"). Two miles from Drangan, the men reached Mary Kennedy's small cottage near Ballyvadlea bridge. At that point, Acting Sergeant Egan approached Michael Cleary and asked him about the extraordinary rumors concerning his wife's disappearance.

Cleary did not answer. He appeared, according to Egan, to be "in very deep trouble." Acting Sergeant Egan asked the question several times, and when Cleary still did not reply, followed him up the hill to his home, one of the laborers' cottages recently built by the Guardians of the Cashel Poor Law Union, under the terms of the Labourers (Ireland) Act of 1883.[14]

It was late afternoon, between four and five o'clock, when Egan reached the house. Again he asked Cleary about his wife. "She left about twelve o'clock last night," Michael Cleary replied, adding that he had not seen her going. He had been in bed, he said. He had not slept for the last seven or eight nights because of his wife's illness, but he had gone to bed the previous night before twelve.

As he came out of the house, Acting Sergeant Egan met Cleary's father-in-law, Patrick Boland, distressed and weeping. "My daughter will come back to me," he heard him cry, over and over.

Back at Ballyvadlea bridge, Michael Kennedy had not been long at his mother's house when he saw four more policemen. "There was crowds of people," he said later in court, "labouring boys and police also, searching rivers, dykes and lakes, and everything around, and I assisted them." There are no lakes as such in the vicinity of Bally-vadlea, although after the wet weather of early March there would have been deep pools and flooded fields. A number of small streams flow through the area, and the fields are divided from each other and from the roads by thick, tall hedgerows with drainage ditches running along them. The policemen whom Michael Kennedy saw near his mother's house were from the Cloneen barracks. Word had reached them that the missing woman had been ill-treated in her home on the night of March 14, and a search had been instituted.

The originator of this complaint was almost certainly William Simpson, who lived only a few hundred yards from the Clearys, be-tween their house and Mary Kennedy's. Simpson was their neighbor, and, according to some reports, their friend; he and his wife had been in the Clearys' house on Thursday night when Michael Kennedy had followed his mother there, and had stayed until six o'clock the fol-lowing morning. But his circumstances and background were very different from those of either the Clearys or Kennedys. An artist from the London illustrated paper the *Daily Graphic,* who sketched him two weeks later as he gave evidence in Clonmel courthouse, showed Simpson with hair carefully parted, wearing a wing-collared shirt and a neatly trimmed mustache; by contrast, Michael Cleary and the Kennedy brothers were shown standing in the dock, unkempt, wearing shirts without collars.

William Simpson described himself in a sworn statement as a "caretaker," employed by Mr. Thomas Lindsay of Passage West, County Cork, but, so soon after the Land War, this word was a euphemism. Thomas Lindsay is listed in Thom's *Directory* for 1895 as owning 2,397 acres in County Tipperary, with a rateable valuation of £1,663. "Caretakers," also known as property defense protectors, but colloquially called "emergencymen," were deeply unpopular; RIC reports, even as late as 1895, mention many attacks made on them and detail the protection afforded them by the police. William Simpson and his family occupied a farm from which Lindsay had evicted the earlier tenants some years previously. They paid a special low rent, for no local person would have taken up the lease on such a farm.

A William Simpson, almost certainly the same man, turns up again in the 1901 census. He has moved to Garrangyle, the next townland to Ballyvadlea, where he describes himself as a "Land Steward," living in a two-room house, the property of Paul M. Lindsay. Paul Lindsay lives alone in a much larger house in the same townland; he is thirty-six and unmarried and is also listed as the owner of several houses in Ballyvadlea. Lindsay describes himself as a farmer, and gives his birthplace as County Cork: evidently he is the heir of Simpson's former employer, Thomas Lindsay. In 1901, William Simpson gave his age as thirty, and his religion as Protestant Episcopalian. His wife, Mary, also a Protestant Episcopalian, was ten years older, and they had two daughters, Margaret, aged eleven, and Mary, nine. This would make him twenty-four at the time of Bridget Cleary's death; it also suggests a certain precocity, for his older daughter must have been conceived when he was eighteen and his wife twenty-eight.

"Emergencyman" was the term used by local farmer Patrick Power in 1997 to describe William Simpson. Evictions by landlords, especially during and after the Land War of 1879–82, left lasting bitterness in the countryside. Although the poorest tenants had been evicted in large numbers earlier in the nineteenth century, many of those evicted toward its end were substantial farmers—often those who had refused to pay rent increases which seemed to them unreasonable—and the political reaction was correspondingly more intense. The term "boycott" was coined by a priest in County Mayo from a land agent's surname in 1880, when social and commercial ostracism became the standard—and highly effective—weapon of an outraged tenantry. In the same year in County Tipperary, Henry Meagher and his wife were evicted from a large farm at Kilburry, just south of Cloneen, for refusing to pay an increase in their annual rent from £300 to £500. A huge public meeting was held in protest, and several branches of the Land League were founded immediately in South Tipperary. Tension between farmers and agricultural laborers increased when laborers worked for landlords and their agents, but "land-grabbers," and emergencymen in particular, were especially detested, and frequently boycotted.[15] In July 1894, for instance, all fifty-four children were withdrawn from a school near Tullamore, King's County, when an emergencyman's children turned up there. And in June 1895, the RIC reported:

> Thomas Jordan of Brackleagh, Newport Dist[rict, County Mayo], surrendered the evicted farm which he had taken to the landlord last month for the following reasons:—viz—the refusal of the clergy to church his wife after her confinement, or to receive any dues from him while he held the farm.

In 1890, in Clonagoose, Mullinahone, less than eight miles from Ballyvadlea, complaints were made that an emergencyman's younger brother had been ill treated in the school.[16] William Simpson's daughters, aged five and three in 1895, would probably not yet have been sent to school, but local tradition around Ballyvadlea says that shopkeepers in Cloneen would not serve him.

When the search for Bridget Cleary got under way on Saturday, March 16, 1895, the day after her disappearance, it was not quite two weeks since the Liberal government had introduced a new Land Law Bill for Ireland. William Gladstone had retired as prime minister the previous year after the defeat of his second Home Rule Bill, but it finally seemed as though the grievances of Irish tenants were about to be effectively redressed under his successor, Lord Rosebery. John Morley, the chief secretary for Ireland, had moved the Land Bill's first reading in the House of Commons on March 4. The bill was wide ranging and comprehensive in its provisions, and despite strong opposition from the unionists, was expected to succeed. Farmers in Tipperary, as elsewhere in Ireland, were looking forward to its passage.

Meanwhile, spectator sports, rather than political meetings, were what attracted crowds. The Gaelic Athletic Association, founded in 1884, was part of an international phenomenon facilitated by railway travel: sport as entertainment for the masses. Sunday, March 17, St. Patrick's Day, was another fine day. In Mullinahone, a large crowd was expected to watch "a great display of hurling and football," sponsored by the GAA.[17] The Clonmel Emeralds football team would play Drangan at two o'clock, and other matches would follow. A notice in the *Nationalist and Tipperary Advertiser*, published in Clonmel on March 13, exhorted its readers to attend:

> All lovers of the Gaelic sports are expected to assemble in their thousands and show by their presence that they appreciate the fine old manly pastimes of their forefathers . . .
> God Save Ireland!

On the same night, also in Mullinahone, the death occurred of Thomas J. Kickham, draper, brother of Charles Joseph Kickham, the political activist and writer, whose 1879 novel, *Knocknagow, or the Homes of Tipperary,* had done much to propagate an ideal of rural Irish life. "No more ardent, or truer Irish nationalist breathed," according to Thomas Kickham's obituary in the *Freeman's Journal* of Thursday, March 21, which also noted that the Reverend Con Ryan had been among the several priests who attended his funeral on Tuesday, March 19.

William Simpson would hardly have been welcome at either the GAA tournament or the funeral, while the Clearys and the Kennedys would not have been expected. Neither Clearys nor Kennedys belonged to the class of tenant farmers who founded and supported the GAA, whose sons became priests and who attended the funerals of "ardently nationalist" shopkeepers. Their origin was among the landless laborers: the working class of rural Ireland, whose poverty until relatively recently had been squalidly abject, and whose contribution to the rhetoric of emergent nationalism was quite minimal. Nevertheless, the crowds that assembled in Mullinahone on Sunday and Tuesday would have begun to hear their names, for as the search continued for the missing woman, sensational rumors were circulating. The story that Bridget Cleary had gone away with the fairies had acquired a vividly memorable form: people were saying now that she would soon reappear, riding a white horse.

Mary Simpson, known as Minnie, lived with her husband William and their two small daughters in the farmhouse a few hundred yards from the Clearys. On Saturday morning, Patrick Boland had told her that his daughter had gone away. Minnie Simpson had visited the house later, probably while Michael Cleary was in Drangan with Jack Dunne, but had found only the old man, who had refused to leave his bed. Early on St. Patrick's Day she heard the missing woman's husband talk explicitly about the fairies: "I heard it said by Michael Cleary on Sunday morning that his wife was up at Kylenagranagh Fort, and that they would go for her on Sunday night, and that she would be on a gray horse, and they would have to cut the cords—the cords that were tying her on the horse, and that she would stay with them if they were able to keep her." Cleary had already mentioned Kylenagranagh Fort to Jack Dunne on the walk back from Drangan on Saturday. (The ringfort no longer exists, but it is clearly marked as an enclosure on the sites and monuments map of the area.)[18]

It was certainly odd for Michael Cleary to have spoken about his missing wife in these terms, but the imagery of a woman taken by the fairies and later seen riding a white or gray horse is quite common in the oral legends of the Irish countryside. To Minnie Simpson, however, a Protestant and an outsider in Ballyvadlea, it may have been unfamiliar as well as exotic. She told the magistrates in Clonmel that, although she had heard of the "fairy fort" of Kylenagranagh, less than a mile from her home, she had never seen it.

Kylenagranagh had another significance for local people, and for the police, as a place where illicit activities were sometimes carried out unobserved. Thirty years earlier, when revolutionary nationalism was at its height after the American Civil War, the RIC had penetrated some of the hill's secrets. Between June and October 1865, an Irish American named James Lynch, a private in the American army, lived at Cloneen. He was observed by the Mullinahone RIC drilling Fenians (members of the Irish Republican Brotherhood) on Kylenagranagh Hill on Sundays and holidays. The RIC kept him under observation until he returned to America in the spring of 1866.

Eighteen years later, the police again patrolled the hill, this time in connection with National League activities. Kilburry, the farm from which Henry Meagher and his wife had been evicted in 1880, was just south of Kylenagranagh. The Meaghers continued to live locally, and were known to consort with Michael Cusack, secretary of the National League in Drangan. Cusack was himself under constant police observation, having recently returned from America where he had learned how to manufacture explosives.[19] The farm at Kilburry had been taken over by a man named Bayley, from County Cork, who was described as "very obnoxious" (i.e., unpopular), and given police protection. Mrs. Meagher had been heard to say that she would personally shoot anybody who took over the farm, and the RIC were watching her closely. They set up a "protection post" with two constables in temporary residence at Kilburry, and in July 1884 Sergeant James Madden of Mullinahone reported:

> Mrs Maher [sic] sometimes carries a black handbag, but as she is reputed to be addicted to drink, I am informed that its contents is almost invariably a teacup and a bottle of whiskey. In my opinion she is too cautious to carry any compromising documents or weapons about with her.

The following October, Madden received orders from District
Inspector J. B. Lopdell in Carrick on Suir:

> You will see that the two const[ables] at Kilburry P[rotection]
> P[ost] thoroughly understand what they are to do—also see that
> they are comfortable, and visit the post occasionally to keep
> everything regular—the party at Cloneen can patrol in that di-
> rection and through Kylenagranagh in particular, and also of
> course through the rest of the subDistrict.[20]

The fairy legends of oral tradition marked Kylenagranagh as important. The RIC mapped the territory differently, but in both systems Kylenagranagh was a significant reference point: the vernacular
map of traditional narrative agreed with the police designation of the
hill as a place apart from normal human habitation and legitimate interests. Anyone seen there could be suspected of being up to no
good; anyone desiring privacy might seek it out.[21]

It was almost dark by seven o'clock on Sunday evening, St.
Patrick's Day, when Michael Cleary went back along the road to the
farmhouse where the Simpsons lived. He asked William Simpson for
the loan of his revolver. Possession of such a weapon underlines
Simpson's vulnerability and unpopularity as an emergencyman, but
the Clearys had apparently taken no part in boycotting him. They
were frequently in his house and he in theirs.

Simpson did not lend Cleary the gun. Cleary told him he wanted
it in order to force some others to go with him to Kylenagranagh. He
explained to Simpson that these others had convinced him that his
wife had gone with the fairies, but that now they were refusing to
come with him to rescue her. Cleary said that his wife had told him
she would ride out of the fort on a white horse on the Sunday night,
and that if he could cut the ropes that tied her to the saddle and keep
her, she would stay with him.

Later that evening, William Simpson said, he saw Michael Cleary
going toward Kylenagranagh with a big table knife in his pocket.
James and William Kennedy were among a "crowd" he had gathered
to go with him to the fort; they too had been told that Bridget

Cleary was to appear there on a white horse. Jack Dunne did not go with them. On Sunday, Monday, and again on Tuesday night, the young men went to Kylenagranagh Fort, but saw nothing, and on Wednesday they refused to go again. By Wednesday, however, James Kennedy and Michael Cleary were among nine people for whom arrest warrants had been issued. Alfred Joseph Wansbrough, the RIC District Inspector based in Carrick-on-Suir, had heard of Bridget Cleary's disappearance. He had ordered a full-scale search by police from Drangan, Cloneen, and Mullinahone, and had himself already visited the house in Ballyvadlea and taken notes.

On Monday, March 18, William Simpson swore "an information" before W. Walker Tennant, a justice of the peace, of Ballinard Castle near Cloneen, to the effect that he had seen Bridget Cleary ill-treated in her home on the previous Thursday night, and naming the people responsible. On Tuesday, a woman called Johanna Burke swore "an information" before the same magistrate, and the next day at Fethard, DI Wansbrough himself swore before Tennant and the resident magistrate from Clonmel, Colonel Richard Evanson, as follows:

> I have just and reasonable grounds for believing that the ill-treatment which Bridget Cleary was subjected to was in administering to her herbs prepared for her by Denis Ganey, of Kyleatlea, and that it was by his instruction she was placed over a fire, and wounded, and otherwise ill-treated. I charge Denis Ganey with causing Bridget Cleary to be ill-treated, and great actual bodily harm done to her.

Denis Ganey, known locally as a "herb-doctor" or "quack-doctor," was the ninth person arrested on March 21. The others were Michael Cleary; Patrick Boland; his sister Mary Kennedy; their cousin John (Jack) Dunne; Mary Kennedy's sons Patrick, Michael, and James; and sixteen-year-old William Ahearne, who had held the candle in Bridget Cleary's bedroom on March 14. The youngest Kennedy brother, twenty-one-year-old William, was arrested the next day.

Johanna Burke (sometimes spelled Bourke), who swore an information on March 19, was Mary Kennedy's daughter and Bridget Cleary's first cousin. She was to become one of the most important figures in the story as it unfolded. She had visited the sick woman almost daily during her illness, and her sworn account of what had happened on the night of March 15 was transcribed to be read in court:

> I was at the house on the night of the 15th inst.; Bridget Cleary was raving; after some time she got up, dressed, and sat at the fire; she afterwards went to bed; I went out for some sticks; when I returned I met her at the doorway going out against me with her nightdress. I endeavoured to hold her and failed; since that time I have not seen her; her husband followed her for some time, and returned; he did not see her; she is missing ever since.

As it happened, Johanna Burke was lying: she knew that her cousin was dead.

On the same day as Burke swore her information, the midweek editions of Clonmel's two newspapers carried reports of Bridget Cleary's disappearance. In the unionist paper, the *Clonmel Chronicle,* read by the landlord class and its supporters, the Wednesday evening report was headed "Gone with the Fairies":

> A good deal of excitement has been caused in the district about Drangan and Cloneen by the "mysterious disappearance" of a labourer's wife, who lived with her husband, a farm labourer, in that part of the country. The poor woman had been ill for some time, and a few days ago she told her husband that if he did not do something for her by a certain time "she would have to be going." An old woman who had been nursing the sick woman was sitting up with her as usual one night last week, and, as she puts it, the invalid was "drawn" away. Search has been made everywhere and the police have been communicated with, but up to this afternoon no trace of the missing woman has been discovered. The country people entertain the opinion that she has "gone with the fairies!"

Evidently two competing narratives were at work in the countryside around Ballyvadlea, as some people stuck to their story of fairy abduction while the RIC conducted its methodical search. The *Chronicle*'s account is short on detail, and inaccurate. Michael Cleary was a cooper, not a farm laborer, while Johanna Burke, who had given evidence about nursing Bridget Cleary before her disappearance, was no older than thirty-four.

The *Nationalist* for the same day is notably more accurate in its description of people and places, but its first account of Bridget Cleary's disappearance reminds us that in 1895 the Irish Revival was at its height, and that the reading public knew something of fairies. New books on fairies, and new editions of old ones, like Robert Kirk's *The Secret Common-Wealth of Elves, Fauns and Fairies,* appeared throughout the 1890s to satisfy the appetite of a reading public which was reacting against industrialization and urbanization. The young poet William Butler Yeats had published his *Fairy and Folk Tales of the Irish Peasantry* in 1888, and three more books on similar themes since then. Lady Augusta Gregory, widowed and living at Coole Park in County Galway, had read his *Celtic Twilight,* stories from Sligo folklore, in 1893. They had made her "jealous for Galway" and eager to match them with her own collecting.[22] The two had met briefly in 1894, although their famous collaboration would not begin until 1896. Yeats had also begun to publish the poems that would appear in *The Wind Among the Reeds* (1899), blending folk beliefs with the aristocratic magic of medieval Irish texts recently edited by scholars and helping to make Irish fairies fashionable among the reading public.

The language used by the *Nationalist*'s correspondent in his opening phrases is borrowed from romantic nationalism, especially the use of "Erin" as the name of the country.

MYSTERIOUS DISAPPEARANCE OF A YOUNG WOMAN
The Land of the Banshee and the Fairy

What would read as a kin to the fairy romances of ancient times in Erin, is now the topic of all lips in the neighbourhood of Drangan and Cloneen. It appears that a young woman named

Cleary, wife of a cooper, living with her father and husband in a labourer's cottage in the townland of Ballyvadlea, took ill a few days ago, was attended by priest and doctor, and believed to have been suffering from some form of nervous malady, she suddenly disappeared on last Friday night, and has not since been heard of. Her friends who were present assert that she had been taken away on a white horse before their eyes, and that she told them when leaving, that on Sunday night they would meet her at a fort on Kylenagranagh Hill, where they could, if they had the courage, rescue her. Accordingly, they assembled at the appointed time and place to fight the fairies, but, needless to say, no white horse appeared. It has transpired that her friends discarded the doctor's medicine, and treated her to some fairy quackery. However the woman is missing, and the rational be-lief is that in the law courts the mystery shall be elucidated. I need not say that the authorities have their own notions of the matter, but I shall reserve further comments until events more clearly develop themselves.

In the same edition, another correspondent, possibly a local per-son in Fethard or Mullinahone, wrote as follows:

A comparatively young couple, married and without a family, lived on a farm belonging to Mr Michael Quirke, T. C., Clon-mel, in the Cloneen district, the wife being about 30 years of age.[23] She complained of illness some ten days ago, and got gradually worse, and ultimately the priest was sent for. Seeing the state the woman was in he anointed her, and prepared her for death. Last Thursday she called her husband, and solemnly informed him she was "going," and detailed certain events which she told him would take place the following night, but regarding which I do not think it necessary to tax the credulity of your readers. One event did take place, which has produced all the sensation—the woman did disappear at the hour and time specified, although her husband and father were within a few yards of where she had been lying ill, and, as far as I can as-certain, up to the present, notwithstanding the exertions of the police and numerous search parties, no account of her, alive or dead, has been found. Of course at the evening firesides wild stories of ghosts, fairies, and "good people" are, under the circumstances, devoured with an avidity that only a mysterious occurrence of this kind can produce. Possibly the appearance of the woman in the flesh, by-and-bye, may rob the case of all the romance. For this reason I purposely avoid giving names at present.

This writer, undoubtedly a Catholic, is familiar with fireside stories about "the good people," as the fairies of Irish oral tradition are generally called, but certainly gives them no credence.

On Thursday, March 21, the day after these newspaper reports appeared, nine people were brought under arrest to the Town Hall in Clonmel. Eight of them were charged with "assaulting and ill-treating Bridget Cleary" on March 14, 1895, "causing her actual bodily harm"; the ninth, Denis Ganey, the herb doctor, was charged with having caused the offense to be committed.

According to the *Cork Examiner,* Denis Ganey was a middle-aged man, somewhat stout, with a red-yellow beard and a slight limp. The *Daily Graphic* artist, a little over a week later, drew him as a tall man with high cheekbones, longish hair, and a full beard, standing straight and dignified, a little apart from the other defendants. Described as a farmer, and as able to read and write, he lived in a "thatched cabin" in Kyleatlea. This is a townland on the northern slope of Slievenamon, four miles from Ballyvadlea in the opposite direction from Fethard. As its name—in Irish *Coill an tSléibhe,* the wood on the mountain—suggests, the land around Kyleatlea is poorer than that around Drangan and Ballyvadlea. Ganey was certainly not wealthy, but the crucial difference between his position and that of most of the other accused was that he was a farmer, not a landless laborer. Evidently his physical condition was superior to theirs too, for although at fifty-eight he was three years older than Jack Dunne, journalists described him as middle-aged, not old.

Denis Ganey, or Gahan, who may never have met Bridget Cleary, would have to spend a further two weeks in Clonmel Prison, accused of being an accessory to her ill-treatment. Newspapers would refer to him as a "medicine-man" and a "witch-doctor," and spin fantastic but tenacious theories about his part in Bridget Cleary's story. He was angry and indignant when DI Wansbrough's sworn information about him was read out. "Did he see me?" he demanded. "Does he say that I assisted in doing away with the woman?" Ganey's was perhaps the reputation worst injured, with least cause, by Bridget Cleary's death. The magistrates, when the case came before them, found no case against him, and promptly discharged him on April 5.

In Clonmel Town Hall, Patrick Boland still insisted that his daughter was alive and well: "I have three more persons," he said, "and they can say that she was strong the night she went away. She got up and dressed." But there was still no sign of Bridget Cleary. The male prisoners were remanded to Clonmel Prison, while the missing woman's aunt, Mary Kennedy, was sent by train to the nearest women's prison in Limerick, forty-nine miles away.

Bridget Cleary's body was found the next day, March 22. Guided by William Simpson, the RIC searched an area of swampy land in the townland of Tullowcossaun. In the corner of a field about a quarter of a mile from the Clearys' house, Sergeant Patrick Rogers of Mullinahone noticed broken bushes and freshly disturbed earth. Constables Somers and O'Callaghan helped him to dig, and soon, in a hole about eighteen inches deep, wrapped in a sheet, they uncovered a woman's body. It was badly burned, and lay in a crouched position, the knees drawn up and the arms folded across the breast. The head was covered in a sack, and was undamaged; there was a gold earring in the left ear. The only clothing, apart from some scraps of rag which were stuck to the body, was a pair of black stockings.

2

Fairies and Fairy Doctors

WHAT DID PEOPLE MEAN when they said that Bridget Cleary had left her home and gone to the fairy fort of Kylenagranagh? What were the herbs given to her on the night of Thursday, March 14? Why did the men carry her back and forth from her bed to the kitchen hearth that night, and why did she die of burns twenty-four hours later? The rest of this book is an attempt to answer these questions and others by untangling the various strands of narrative that survive about the death of Bridget Cleary. To understand the narratives' terms of reference, it will be useful to know something of Irish fairy legend, for in Ireland in 1895, just out of sight of the solid new Catholic chapels with their paved yards and stout iron railings and underneath the orderly grid of print which Victorian officials and administrators were conscientiously laying over every corner of the island, another world continued to exist whose ways of thinking were based on oral tradition, not on the printed word.

Oral cultures were found all over the world until well into the twentieth century, but in the heyday of European colonialism they were overwhelmingly interpreted, in the light of Darwinian ideas, as primitive and childish—charming, perhaps, but certainly incapable of any discriminating engagement with reality. Literacy had become the essential key to participation in the modern world. By the end of the twentieth century, however, a high standard of literacy has become less essential for economic survival. New technologies rely more and more on the manipulation of icons and images; voice transmission becomes steadily easier and cheaper, and perhaps for these reasons, the linear and hierarchical ways of thinking that flourished in the nineteenth century have become less dominant: it is easier than it used to be to imagine a system of thought that does not rely on writing. Meanwhile, since the nineteenth century, scholars on all continents have been working with the intellectual and aesthetic content of oral traditions.

In the Arts Building of the National University of Ireland's campus at Belfield, on Dublin's southside, is the archive of the Department of Irish Folklore. Here, at the end of a corridor hung with portraits of storytellers and collectors, is a large room whose walls are lined with shelves. Most of the floor is occupied by metal card-index cabinets, and the shelves are filled with thick, bound volumes, almost all handwritten, though parts of some are typed. A number is stamped on the leather spine of each. These are the manuscripts of the Irish Folklore Collection, assembled and catalogued since 1927 by a dedicated team of professional and part-time collectors and scholars.

In 1927, the Irish Free State was five years old. Its civil service and administrative infrastructure had been inherited from the British, but its guiding spirit was strongly influenced by ideas of Ireland's cultural uniqueness. Douglas Hyde, son of a Protestant clergyman from County Roscommon, would be elected first president of Ireland under the new constitution ten years later. On the foundation of the Irish Free State he was Professor of Modern Irish at the National University, a post he had held since the university's foundation in 1908. His writings and lectures had been immensely influential in the cultural revival. *Beside the Fire* (1890) was a collection of folktales from Hyde's native County Roscommon; in 1892, Hyde's lecture to the National Literary Society, "On the Necessity for Deanglicizing Ireland," spelled out the implications of colonization for Irish society;[1] in 1893, his *Love-Songs of Connacht/Abhráin Ghrádh Chúige Connacht,* a collection of oral poetry in Irish with English translations, attracted enthusiastic praise from the young William Butler Yeats; in the same year, Hyde cofounded, and became president of, Connradh na Gaedh-ilge, the Gaelic League. Its goal was to revive Irish as a spoken and written language, and it soon had branches all over Ireland.

One of Hyde's students, and later his assistant at the university, was a young man born in County Antrim in 1899, James Hamilton Delargy. In 1923, Hyde sent him to learn Irish from native speakers in County Kerry. In Cill Rialaigh, near Ballinskelligs at the southernmost tip of the Iveragh peninsula, Irish-language activist Fionán Mac Coluim directed Delargy to the gifted storyteller, Seán Ó Conaill (1853–1931), who could neither read nor write, who knew no English, and who had never traveled farther from his home than Killorglin, thirty-five miles away. In the years that followed, Ó Conaill introduced Delargy to an intellectual life he had thought lost since the Middle Ages, and incidentally provided him with a design for his life's work.[2]

Delargy soon began to use the Irish version of his name, Séamus Ó Duilearga. In 1926, with Mac Coluim and others, he founded the Irish Folklore Society, and a year later became editor of its journal, *Béaloideas,* which was to be a vehicle for the publication of Irish folklore in both Irish and English; in 1935, three years after Éamon de Valera's Fianna Fáil government came to power, he became director of the new, state-funded Irish Folklore Commission. The commission had an annual grant of £3,200, and was given three rooms on the top corridor of the university building on Earlsfort Terrace (now the National Concert Hall), as office and archive space (it later moved to 82 St. Stephen's Green, and then to Belfield). A full-time staff was appointed, including six specially trained collectors.[3]

Delargy's focusing on oral storytelling was timely. The tradition was dying out, with fewer, smaller, and less discerning audiences available on whom a talented storyteller might test his or her art. Meanwhile, the new Irish state, led by de Valera, born in New York in 1882 but brought up in County Limerick, was forging a distinctive national cultural identity whose ethos would be strongly rural.[4] In other parts of Europe too, newly emergent nation-states were looking to oral tradition for a sense of their past, which would be independent of the narratives imposed by their colonizers. Delargy went to the universities of Lund and Uppsala in Sweden to learn more about the collecting and classification of oral traditions. In Ireland, the nineteenth-century romantic nationalism that had caused the newly founded GAA to present its games as "the fine old manly pastimes" of its members' forefathers, and to find the roots of these pastimes in the pages of medieval sagas, also inspired the scholars who edited the sagas, and the founders of the Abbey Theatre who drew on them. Elsewhere, Finland's national epic, the *Kalevala,* published in 1835, was just one example of the sort of work constructed of oral materials in response to the demands of similar movements.[5]

The Scandinavian countries and Finland were at the forefront in the new discipline of folklore. To be sure, the name had been coined as early as 1846 in England, by William Thoms, but throughout the nineteenth century it was essentially an antiquarian, and an amateur, pursuit. Yeats and Lady Gregory, visiting cottages in the west of Ireland and writing down the stories told to them in English by deferential country people, were typical of the gentlefolk who interested themselves in such matters. Many of them joined the Folk-Lore Society, founded in London in 1878, and published their findings in the *Folk-Lore Journal.* The material the members of this and similar societies gathered and published was voluminous, and continues to be valuable, but it followed no scientific pattern, and they established no central archive or cataloging system.[6]

The system adopted by the Irish Folklore Commission for organizing and classifying the material recorded by its collectors is still used by its successor, the Department of Irish Folklore, in Belfield. Based on the Swedish model, and set out in Seán Ó Súilleabháin's *A Handbook of Irish Folklore* (1942), it divides the material into fourteen large categories. The first two, Settlement and Dwelling, and Livelihood and Household Support, reflect the great wealth of craft and domestic traditions in Scandinavia. In the Irish archive, however, by far the greatest concentrations of material are in the sections on Mythological Tradition and Popular Oral Literature. The Great Famine of the mid-nineteenth century had had a devastating effect on ordinary people's material culture, but storytelling and patterns of behavior had survived well into the twentieth century, along with music and song.

Under Popular Oral Literature, in the *Handbook,* as in the IFC archive, we find the international folktales and hero tales that are the pride of Irish oral tradition: long, episodic narratives, most of them in Irish, telling of bravery and magic in a world long ago. Here too are legends—stories purporting or seeming to be true, although their claims may be preposterous and their patterning may show the method of their making—along with songs and other oral poetry.

Under Mythological Tradition, Ó Súilleabháin's *Handbook* describes the features of fairy belief in Ireland by means of fifteen closely printed pages of sample questions designed to be put to informants by collectors. Thick bundles of index cards in the IFC archive's catalogue attest to the responses gathered over seventy years. Similar traditions are found in Scotland and, with variations, across much of Europe. From Ireland and Scotland they have been extensively transplanted to the Atlantic provinces of Canada, where immigrants found a landscape not unlike the one they had left, while people of Irish or Scottish ancestry all over the world are familiar with their broad outlines.[7]

Fairies are normally invisible, but they are there. They live in the air, under the earth, and in water, and they may be just a little smaller than humans, or so tiny that a grazing cow blows hundreds of them away with every breath. They had their origin when the rebellious angel Lucifer and his followers were expelled from Heaven, and God the Son warned God the Father that Heaven would soon be empty. Like figures in a film that is suddenly stopped, the expelled angels falling toward Hell halted where they were: some in mid-air, others in the earth, and some in the ocean, and there they remain.[8] They are jealous of Christians, and often do them harm, but are not totally malevolent since they still hope to get back to Heaven one day. To do so, however, they must have at least enough blood in their veins to write their names, and so far they have not even that much.

Fairies are not human, but they resemble humans and live lives parallel to theirs, with some significant differences: they keep cows, and sell them at fairs; they enjoy whiskey and music; they like gold, milk, and tobacco, but hate iron, fire, salt, and the Christian religion, and any combination of these mainstays of Irish rural culture serves to guard against them. Sometimes it is said that there are no women among the fairies. In any case, they steal children and young women, and occasionally young men, and leave withered, cantankerous changelings in their place. They can bring disease on crops, animals, and humans, but by and large, if treated with neighborly consideration, they mind their own business and even reward favors.

Questions about fairies, if asked in the Ireland of today, may be greeted with amusement or derision, but if not accompanied by too much earnestness, they will still often elicit answers. It is rare, and perhaps always has been, to meet people who unequivocally believe that a race of supernatural beings lives invisibly alongside humans and shares their landscape. It is much less rare, however, for stories to be told about such beings, or for features of the environment, both physical and social, to be explained by reference to them. Quite hard-headed people may sometimes be seen to observe precautions that seem tacitly to acknowledge the existence, however marginally, of fairies.

Fairies belong to the margins, and so can serve as reference points and metaphors for all that is marginal in human life. Their mostly underground existence allows them to stand for the unconscious, for the secret, or the unspeakable, and their constant eavesdropping explains the need sometimes to speak in riddles, or to avoid discussion of certain topics. Unconstrained by work and poverty, or by the demands of landlords, police, or clergy, the fairies of Irish legend inhabit a world that is sensuously colorful, musical, and carefree, and as writers from Yeats to Irish-language poet Nuala Ní Dhomhnaill have observed, legends about them richly reflect the imaginative, emotional, and erotic dimensions of human life.

Legends of the fairies, told by skilled storytellers like James Delargy's friend Seán Ó Conaill, are complex works of art, often taking up several pages of manuscript or print when written down. Not everybody who tells them is such an artist, however, and most fairy legends are short. As Danish folklorist Bengt Holbek remarks: "What matters is not their artistic impact, but their function as arguments about reality . . . Legends *debate* the relation between our daily reality and some kind of possibly real 'otherworld.'"[9] One feature that makes fairy legends so tenacious in a changing cultural environment is the concision and vivid memorability of their central themes. Another is their connection to real, named people and to real places in a known landscape. Yet another reason why they survive is that their narratives interact so intimately with the practicalities and the emotional realities of daily life.

Viewed as a system of interlocking units of narrative, practice, and belief, fairy legend can be compared to a database: a premodern culture's way of storing and retrieving information and knowledge of every kind, from hygiene and child care to history and geography. Highly charged and memorable images like that of a woman emerging on a white horse from a fairy dwelling are the retrieval codes for a whole complex of stored information about land and landscape, community relations, gender roles, medicine, and work in all its aspects: tools, materials, and techniques. Stories gain verisimilitude and storytellers keep their listeners' attention by the density of circumstance they depict, including social relations and the technical details of work. Most stories, however, are constructed around the unexpected and therefore memorable happenings in people's lives. Encounters with or interference by the fairies in these stories reminds listeners (and readers) of everything in life that is outside human control. It is not surprising, then, that death and illness are among the preoccupations of fairy legends.

Almost any death, other than a gentle and gradual departure in old age, is open to interpretation as the work of the fairies. A person who spends some time in their company may waste away and die after returning home. Or they may abduct happy, healthy humans, whether children or able-bodied adults, and replace them with withered, sickly, evil-tempered or taciturn changelings, which either live for a while, or appear already dead. The changeling is usually an elderly member of the fairies' own community, and may sometimes even be substituted for an abducted farm animal. The events spoken of may be tragic, but they are presented in entertaining, often grimly humorous, stories. In this way, cautions against eating carrion, *feoil thubaiste* ("calamity meat"), are backed up by stories of the farmer who confronts the fairies when he discovers that they are responsible for the loss of his apparently dead cow. "We'll return your cow," they retort, "when you give back our old uncle whom you've salted and eaten!"

Any ill treatment meted out to a changeling may be visited in revenge on the abducted human, so a suspected changeling is supposed to be treated with cautious respect. Changelings' behavior is often intolerable, however, since they have the form of sickly babies who never stop crying, or adults who take to their beds, refuse to speak when spoken to, or otherwise conduct themselves in antisocial ways. A last resort is to threaten a changeling with fire. This is said to banish it for good and so force the return of the abducted human. Legend after legend recounts how what has seemed to be a baby in a cradle smartly takes to its heels and leaves the house when some adult, usually a visitor, builds up the fire and announces that the baby is to be placed on top.

The overwhelming message of the fairy legends is that the unexpected may be guarded against by careful observance of society's rules. These stories are important components of child-rearing practice, establishing the boundaries of normal, acceptable behavior, and spelling out the ways in which an individual who breaches them may forfeit his or her position. They recognize, however, that rules may be in conflict with each other, or with other imperatives in certain circumstances, and that accidents may happen. When accidents do happen, or when inexperience or inattention has led to a breaking of the rules, remedies are available.

Some remedies, prescribed by knowledgeable people known as "fairy men," "fairy women," or "fairy doctors," simply show how to avoid compounding the problem. They may use rest, measured and calibrated by ritual practice. Others involve herbal medicine, and an ethnobotany strikingly different in its organization from the Linnaean system, which superseded it in the nineteenth century. The tall purple foxglove, *Digitalis purpurea,* is perhaps the plant most heavily documented in Irish oral culture. It is a source of glycosides, which are at once a powerful cardiac medicine and a dangerous poison; called *lus mór* ("big plant") or *méaracán sí* ("fairy thimble"), it is credited with all manner of fairy associations. St. John's Wort, *Hypericum perforatum,* which has been widely adopted as a natural antidepressant in the developed world at the end of the twentieth century, is called, among other names in Irish, *luibh Eoin Bhaiste,* John the Baptist's herb. Geoffrey Grigson calls this one of the most famous of European white-magic plants. It is known in several languages as a devil chaser—*chasse-diable* in French—and traditionally is picked before sunrise on the morning of June 23, St. John's Eve.[10] It features in Irish oral tradition as a remedy against interference by the fairies—specifically when experienced as depression.[11] In 1998, a Channel 4 television series, *Sacred Weeds,* investigated the psychoactive properties of plants revered in certain cultures. One of them, the hallucinogenic and poisonous *Hyoscyamus niger,* called henbane in English because of the danger it poses to free-range poultry, has long been associated with witches in European tradition. Called in Irish *gafann,* it was used in carefully measured doses as a sedative and painkiller.[12]

Fairy-belief legend, with its constant theme of ambiguity and danger, could teach both the hazards and the benefits of important plants, drawing attention to them and making them recognizable. But not all remedies prescribed in oral culture are similarly "scientific": many depend on sympathetic magic, or association of ideas. Taken individually, the stories, and the remedies, can seem like nonsense. Taken as parts of a system, as a kind of taxonomy, or as components of a model of the symbolic universe, however, they represent an elegant economy of reasoning, imagery and memory.

Nineteenth-century antiquaries in Ireland noted the prevalence of "fairy doctors," to whom country people resorted for the relief of illness and injury in both humans and animals. Best known among them was perhaps Biddy Early of Feakle, "the Wise Woman of Clare," about whom Lady Gregory collected many stories after her death.[13] Biddy Early never visited her patients, so did not see them if they could not come to her, but she prescribed by means of a magic bottle and seemed to know details about them without being told. Many illnesses, as we have seen, were interpreted as fairy abduction. Mental retardation, failure to thrive, or the onset of infantile paralysis (polio) could appear as fairy work, and often Biddy Early's advice to those who sought her help was that nothing could be done.

In adults, the sudden paralysis caused by cerebral hemorrhage is still called "stroke" in English, recalling the Irish *poc sí,* "fairy stroke." The symptoms of tuberculosis corresponded to what was understood about fairy abduction, but so did lesser maladies, both mental and physical. Postnatal depression was called *an fiabhras aerach,* "airy [i.e., fairy] fever," though the term may have referred to puerperal fever, one symptom of which could be delirium. Descriptions of refusal of fairy food by human girls and women carry strong overtones of *anorexia nervosa.*[14] Sepsis, caused by splinters and other foreign bodies, was commonly known as "blast," and attributed to the fairies; it was noted that it happened more often to those who would not stop working long enough to attend to injuries. All this medical interpretation had a social dimension, with the fairies invoked as demanding behaviors whose short-term benefits might not be apparent. Unless Biddy Early's instructions were followed scrupulously, her prescriptions would not work. Like other fairy doctors, she was supposed to have gained her ability to cure through privileged acquaintance with the fairy world. Her moral authority was considerable—and it was diametrically opposed to that of the Catholic clergy, whom she is remembered as repeatedly outsmarting with dry wit and dignity.[15]

The first full and accurate census of population was taken in Ireland in 1841 and was repeated every ten years until 1911.[16] After the Famine, Sir William Wilde, the Dublin physician and later Oscar Wilde's father, was commissioned to interpret medical statistics gathered by the 1851 census. He was a noted antiquary and folklorist, who often bargained with his country patients for stories, instead of fowl or eggs, as payment for his services. After his death, his widow, "Speranza," published two volumes of the material he had collected.[17] Wilde's note on marasmus—emaciation and wasting in children—places scientific and vernacular taxonomies of illness side by side. It reflects his understanding of Irish fairy narratives in both languages and of how they were sometimes tragically implemented:

No. 53, Marasmus
   Tabes mesenterica, Anaemia, Atrophia, Tuberculosis mesenterica:
   Synonymes [*sic*]:
   Atrophy, Emaciation, Wasting away, Decline and Decay (infantile), general Cachectic and Tubercular diseases of early life, Infantile Consumption, Fairy Stricken, "Backgone," Struck, a

Blast; in Irish *Cnai* or *Cnaoidh,* wasting, with or without disease of the chest; *Cuirrethe* or *Millte,* fairy-stricken.[18]

In the Census Report for 1841 the name Marasmus was accepted as a generic term, under which to class all those various affections of infancy and early youth returned on the different Forms as "consumption (infantile), wasting, decay, decline, emaciation, general debility and loss of strength." This arrangement became necessary from the multitude of deaths returned as consumption and decline under 1 year of age and from 1 to 10. There can be little doubt that the great majority of cases of infantile death, returned under the above popular headings were caused by scrofulous tubercular diseases, chiefly of the abdominal cavity, many of *tabes mesenterica* and very many of *chronic peritonitis,* a disease of frequent and fatal occurrence to young children in this country. It is this affection which has given rise to the popular ideas respecting the "changeling" and in this country to the many superstitious notions entertained by the peasantry respecting their supposed "fairy stricken" children; so that year by year, up to the present day, we read accounts of deaths produced by cruel endeavours to cure children and young persons of such maladies, generally attempted by quacks and those termed "fairy men" and "fairy women."[19]

In a book on Irish folklore which Wilde published about the time he was analyzing the census returns, he mentioned a recent case: "About a year ago a man in the county of Kerry roasted his child to death, under the impression that it was a fairy. He was not brought to trial, as the Crown prosecutor mercifully looked upon him as insane."[20]

In 1828, Thomas Crofton Croker had noted a similar story, reported from the Tralee assizes in July 1826 by the *Morning Post:*

Ann Roche, an old woman of very advanced age, was indicted for the murder of Michael Leahy, a young child, by drowning him in the Flesk. This case . . . turned out to be a homicide committed under the delusion of the grossest superstition. The child, though four years old, could neither stand, walk, [n]or speak—*it was thought to be fairy struck* . . .

Upon cross-examination the witness said it was not done with intent to kill the child, but to cure it—*to put the fairy out of it.*

Verdict—not guilty.[21]

Several other accounts can be found in nineteenth-century newspapers and police reports of suspected child-changelings in Ireland being placed on red-hot shovels, drowned, or otherwise mistreated or killed. Only eleven years before Bridget Cleary's death, the *Daily Telegraph* of May 19, 1884, reported a case less than fifteen miles away from Ballyvadlea:

SUPERSTITION IN IRELAND

Ellen Cushion and Anastatia Rourke were arrested at Clonmel on Saturday charged with cruelly illtreating a child three years old, named Philip Dillon. The prisoners were taken before the mayor, when evidence was given showing that the neighbours fancied that the boy, who had not the use of his limbs, was a changeling left by the fairies in exchange for their original child. While the mother was absent the prisoners entered her house and placed the lad naked on a hot shovel under the impression that this would break the charm. The poor little thing was severely burned, and is in a precarious condition.[22]

Such incidents aroused horror and revulsion, but their perpetrators were usually treated leniently by the courts, which recognized the component of "superstition" in their actions. Here, as elsewhere, "superstition" meant a system of reasoning which was alien to those in power. Most of the accused were elderly women, and the children killed or injured were usually severely disabled. In County Kerry, on January 30, 1888, Joanna Doyle, aged forty-five and described as "a wild fierce Kerry peasant, scarcely able to speak English intelligibly," was admitted to Killarney Asylum, where a canvas camisole was used to restrain her from tearing her clothing. She had murdered her "imbecile" or "epileptic idiot" son, Patsy, with a hatchet, assisted by her husband and three older children. Her next son, Denis, aged twelve, was also described as an "imbecile." She insisted that Patsy, aged about thirteen, "was not my son, he was a devil, a bad fairy." Doyle was later transferred to Dundrum Mental Hospital in Dublin. Oscar T. Woods, Medical Superintendent at Killarney, reported that her eighteen-year-old daughter Mary had said of her dead brother, "I was not shocked when I heard my mother kill him, as I had heard people say he was a fairy, and I believed them."[23]

Fairy-belief legend provided a way of understanding congenital and other disabilities, or at least an imaginative framework that could accommodate them. Before the coming of state- or religious-sponsored social services, when a large part of the population lived at subsistence level, it also afforded a way for people driven to desperate remedies to rationalize their actions and live with the consequences.[24] But in most cases, accounts of fairies and of people who consorted with them are simply stories: fictions designed to entertain, or to instruct. They have a beginning, middle, and end, and, like many of the art forms that enrich people's lives, are structured in such a way as to leave their audiences pondering the messages they carry. Hundreds have been published; thousands more, from storytellers all over Ireland, are in the manuscripts of the Irish Folklore Collection. And these are only the stories that have been written down.

Michael Leahy, Patsy Doyle, and Bridget Cleary died; Philip Dillon was severely burned. Reports by officials and journalists have preserved their names in print along with the dates of their deaths or injuries. Their histories retain a rawness not found in the more ephemeral and timeless legends about "a young married woman in this parish," or "an orphan child." This is one of the most pointed differences between oral and written culture, or, in Walter Benjamin's terms, between story and information. His celebrated essay "The Storyteller" points to the differences between artfully constructed stories and mere information:

> The value of information does not survive the moment in which it was new. It lives only at that moment; it has to surrender to it completely and explain itself without losing any time. A story is different. It does not expend itself. It preserves and

concentrates its strength and is capable of releasing it even after a long time.[25]

Bridget Cleary was labeled a fairy changeling, and died of burns shortly afterward. The only possible reaction to an account of these events is revulsion and dismay, but when stories were told at firesides or on hillsides about women abducted by the fairies and replaced with changelings, the audience's response might sometimes be more nuanced.

Stories are told of women swept away by the fairies as they gave birth, midwives called to attend such women inside fairy hills, and women restored to their husbands after fairy abductions have been foiled. In one such, told in Irish in County Donegal and published with English translation, a shoemaker rides to town to fetch a midwife, leaving his wife in labor. He buys some nails (made of iron) for his work and returns with the midwife riding pillion:

It was a cloudy moonlit night and as they were going through a place called Ált an Tairbh he heard a sound as if a flock of birds was coming towards them in the air. It came directly in their way and as it was passing overhead he threw the paperful of nails up in the air. He was full of anger and spoke out from his heart:

"May the devil take you with him!"

No sooner were the words out of his mouth than he heard the sound of something falling at the horse's feet. He turned around and dismounted, and when he looked at the thing that had fallen, what did he find but a woman! He looked sharply at her and what did he find her to be but his own wife whom he had left lying at home. He took her up and put her on the horse with the midwife, who held her while he led the horse home by its head.

Well. As they were approaching the house there was a hullabaloo there that they were too late, that his wife had died since he left, and there was great crying and clamour. The man led the two women he had with him into the stable with the horse and asked them to stay until he returned. He himself went into the house as if nothing had happened, and went over to the bed where the supposed corpse was lying. Everyone was astonished that he was not crying nor [*sic*] the least distraught as men usually are when their wives die. He turned on his heel and out with him and in again in a moment with the pitch-fork from the byre. He went up to the bed and made a swipe at the thing that was lying there, but, well for her, when she saw him drawing at her she rose and went out of the window like a flash of lightning.

He went out then and brought his wife and the midwife. Everything went well then and in due time the child was born. He and his wife spent a long life after that at Gortalia and neither the wee folk nor the big people gave them any more trouble![26]

Order has been restored by the end of this story. Disruptions to social life are identified as coming from outside, and are forcefully repudiated. The protagonists live happily ever after, and the domestic violence the legend depicts has been contained, literally, within the fiction.

The many fairy legends which tell of women in childbirth being swept through the air are vividly metaphorical: narratives of passage—analogous to rites of passage. Stories like the one quoted above reflect the dangers and anxieties of childbirth, and the fact that women do sometimes die, or almost die. They also express the anxiety that can surround the whole question of human fertility, often compromised in post-Famine Ireland by late and selective marriage. Such stories express aggression against women in coded form: the husband's pitchfork attack on the changeling-corpse is justified by the terms of the narrative, but even the innocent wife is dropped from horseback in midair while in the last stages of pregnancy, and is then left in the stable.[27]

Fairy legends carry disciplinary messages for women as well as for children, warning them about behavior considered by a patriarchal society to be unacceptable. Undoubtedly, too, some of them have been used as euphemisms for domestic violence. Roddy Doyle's novel *The Woman Who Walked into Doors* takes its title from such a euphemism in modern life. A woman in nineteenth-century rural Ire-

land who had obviously been beaten might explain the marks of violence as having been inflicted by fairy abductors, while a violent
husband might account for his actions as loss of patience with a fairy
interloper. This is not to say that such explanations would normally
be accepted, or taken literally. Fairy legend charts the territory of no-
man's-land. It carries with it an air of the preposterous, the nod and
wink, that allows one thing to be said, while another is meant. It per-
mits face-saving lies to be told, and disturbing narratives to be safely
detoured into fiction if children are found to be listening, or if the
complex web of family relationships means that someone may take
offense, or threaten retaliation.

The most powerful narratives thrown up by the idiom of fairy belief have an emotional resonance that allows the oral tradition's verbal artists to refine and polish them continuously. One such is the
story of the woman taken by the fairies, who tells her husband,
brother, or lover that he may rescue her if he can pull her off her
horse when the fairies ride out together, usually at Halloween. With
genders reversed, it is the story of the Scottish ballad "Tam Lin," to
which Sir Walter Scott devoted many pages in *The Minstrelsy of the
Scottish Border,* first published in 1802 and revised and added to
throughout his life.[28] Emily Lyle has discussed eight Irish versions
of the legend and has referred to several others, describing it as
"among the commonest of the tales of the fairies." Many of these
stories, like the one above about the shoemaker, tell of women abducted while giving birth. Roughly half tell of successful rescues, the
others of disastrous failure. One version, where the wife apparently
dies in labor, reminds us that the marital calamities spoken of may be
physical as well as interpersonal:

> She said that if he was not a good soldier and didn't hold her,
> the walls of the house would be red in the morning with her
> blood. He did meet the horses and he pulled her off the third
> horse. Whatever devilment and tricks they started he let her go
> anyway. The next morning the walls of the house were covered
> with blood.[29]

There was nothing exotic or unusual in the suggestion that Bridget Cleary, ill in bed with bronchitis in her home in Ballyvadlea, County Tipperary in 1895, was a fairy changeling. Such language was common all over Ireland, and still is in places, although its weight and import may vary considerably. At its most innocuous, it is simply metaphor—a dismissive comment on someone's appearance: "he's like something the fairies left!" or general competence: "she's away with the fairies!"

The story of the white horse is different: it draws on a higher register of fairy narrative, a more elaborately wrought verbal art, and presupposes an intimate knowledge not only of fairy legend, but of the secret places of the local landscape. If Bridget Cleary did tell her husband that she would ride a white horse out of Kylenagranagh Fort on the Sunday night, she would have been trumping the card played by the men who had called her a fairy changeling. Many versions of the fairy fiction offered married women a fantasy of power and glamour: they showed the hapless husband gaping as his wife appeared, surrounded by all the trappings of nobility, only to disappear again forever. When local people around Ballyvadlea told inquirers that the missing woman had gone away with the fairies, however, and would come back on a white horse, they may have been almost anywhere on a scale between total belief and near-total disbelief in fairies. Their response may simply have been a way of saying, "Your questions are intrusive and embarrassing; we don't choose to answer them!"

The connotations of changeling-labeling are never positive, and a quick-tongued woman might well counter such a label with an alternative fairy narrative. Neighbors who might not assign a label themselves could nevertheless use one already assigned as euphemism or evasion. What was highly unusual, given that before her illness Bridget Cleary had been healthy, was that the label should be taken literally and used as a charter for action. Among the documented cases of changeling-burning in Ireland in the nineteenth century, Bridget Cleary's is the only one that involves an adult victim.

3

Reading, Sewing, Hens, and Houses

BRIDGET CLEARY was born in Ballyvadlea and died when she was twenty-six. According to a special correspondent of the *Cork Examiner* on March 29, 1895, she was "of middle height, perhaps, with brownish hair, blue eyes and regular features—a pretty woman." Attractive, according to other accounts also, and evidently a strong personality, she was well known around her home area, and not just among the laborers. One commentator notes that a gentleman "who had frequently seen her, before this dreadful business, on his way to hunt with the Tipperary hounds, tells me she was distinctly "good-looking."[1] Even the police knew Bridget Cleary. Constable Samuel Somers of Cloneen, one of the men who found her body, told the inquest that he had last seen her a month or six weeks before, and that she was a healthy woman.

Ballyvadlea, in the civil parish of Cloneen, barony of Middlethird, County Tipperary, is a rural townland of just over 272 acres, which had 9 houses at the census of 1891. Its population was 31, a little over a quarter of what it had been during, and immediately after, the Great Famine of 1845–49. Fuller records survive from the census of 1901. By then, six years after Bridget Cleary's death, and at least partly because of it, only 5 of the 9 houses were inhabited, and the population had halved again; the total, including 2 young children, was 7 males and 8 females, all Catholic.[2]

Bridget Cleary's father, Patrick Boland, and her mother, Bridget Keating, were both from Ballyvadlea. Born before the Great Famine, they belonged to the laboring class, the rural proletariat about whom until recently most historical works have been silent.[3]

Mary Carbery's classic, *The Farm by Lough Gur,* describes life on a two-hundred-acre farm in County Limerick, about fifty miles from Ballyvadlea, in the second half of the nineteenth century.[4] Unmarried maids and laborers lived with their employers, women usually in the house, men in an outbuilding. Married, they lived in rented cottages. The picture this account gives of their work is nostalgic and somewhat idealized, but we learn that men were employed in large numbers to plow, sow, and harvest, to make hay, maintain buildings and fences, and to tend the animals, including horses, which did the heaviest work. Women milked and churned butter by hand, tended hens and other poultry, made candles and clothing, and cooked food for humans and feed for animals, as well as doing laundry and other housework and caring for children.

For many of the laboring class, however, life was neither so productive nor so idyllic. They lived in squalor, without security of tenure, in tiny unsanitary cabins on plots of land that were severely inadequate to maintain their large families. Before the Famine, laborers had formed the largest section of Ireland's population; after it, their numbers were drastically reduced by starvation, disease, and emigration. For several decades after the Famine, however, even in prosperous County Tipperary, observers continued to be shocked by the conditions in which rural laborers lived. In a letter to the *Tipperary Leader* of November 22, 1882, Patrick O'Keeffe wrote that their cabins were "scarcely fit for savage men" and that they were "fed miserably and clad in rags." The Devonshire Commission's report on *The Agricultural Labourer,* published in 1893–94, noted that a significant proportion of laborers' incomes came from begging done by women.[5] In *The Farm by Lough Gur,* too, we read of people who came to the farmhouse door "to beg for food, old clothes, old linen for wounds or sores, 'bits' to make clothes for children and new babies, even for old sheets to make shrouds and a little money to pay for the coffin."[6]

In October 1856, Patrick Boland was twenty-seven. He and Bridget Keating were married by the parish priest of Drangan, Edmond O'Shaughnessy, possibly in the old chapel in Cloneen, but more probably in the fine new one that Fr. O'Shaughnessy had built just a few years before in Drangan. The contrast between its gothic spaciousness and the house in which the young couple were to begin life must have been striking. Their home was a tiny, mud-walled, thatched cabin, near the bridge at Ballyvadlea, typical of the housing of the rural poor.[7] It was on the opposite side of the main road from the very similar house where Patrick Boland's sister Mary Kennedy still lived in 1895, when her son Michael came looking for her with his wages after walking from Drangan. Seven years younger than her brother, Mary Boland married Richard Kennedy, also of Ballyvadlea, in January 1860, and the two couples' children grew up near neighbors as well as cousins. The Bolands' first child was a son, Michael, baptized in Drangan on August 3 of the year after their marriage. Edmond's baptism was recorded in 1860, and William's in 1863. Patrick Boland must have been forty when their daughter Bridget was born, in 1868 or 1869.[8]

When Fr. Edmond O'Shaughnessy died in 1869, the new chapel was not his only legacy to the Drangan parish. His will left his "lands, furniture, and nearly all he possessed" to the Sisters of Mercy, including Drangan House, the substantial dwelling at the east end of the village street, which he had built on arrival in the parish almost thirty years earlier. A group of Mercy sisters came from Tipperary town to found a new convent in the house, and later opened a school.[9] Bridget Cleary, who seems to have been the youngest in her family, was more likely to be indulged with education than an older child whose labor was needed. Needlework was a central part of the nineteenth-century curriculum for girls in primary school; the new convent school would also have taught her reading, writing, and arithmetic, as well as a considerable amount of Catholic doctrine, principles of hygiene, and "good," meaning middle-class, manners.[10]

Apart from a couple of passing references by her husband, Bridget Cleary's older brothers do not feature in the story of her death. We know that her mother had died some time previously; perhaps her brothers had died also, or had emigrated, or were simply living elsewhere. In any case, Patrick Boland made a poignant outburst in court, which clearly shows his daughter's importance in his life: "I had no one in the world to turn to but my daughter," he told Mr. Justice William O'Brien at the summer assizes in July 1895. "Her mother and myself gave her a good trade. She was only twenty-six years of age, and she was a fine milliner, and able to give us a bit of money, and when her mother died she was the only one I had in the world to look to. It was not me that should ever have put a finger to her." Patrick Boland's circumstances had improved out of all recognition since the time of his marriage, and it appears that his daughter was the key to his new prosperity.

As her father told the court, Bridget Cleary was a milliner; other sources call her a dressmaker. A dressmaker-milliner was a modern woman: much more likely to be literate than a "shirtmaker-seamstress," according to the census of 1901, and much less likely to be aged over forty-five.[11] In the 1870s, in *The Farm by Lough Gur,* the farmer's daughters and their mother spent long evening hours sewing household linens, underwear, and nightdresses by hand, for themselves and for the poor, while one of them read aloud, but their outer clothes would have been made by a dressmaker.

In 1895, Bridget Cleary had a sewing machine in her bedroom.[12] The American Isaac Singer had patented the foot treadle in 1851. He was the first manufacturer to spend more than a million dollars a year on advertising, and his product was soon to be found everywhere. The first Singer shop in Ireland was in Talbot Street, Dublin. By 1893, Jeremiah Carey was the agent in charge of the Singer Manufacturing Company's Sewing Machine Depot in Mitchell Street, Clonmel.[13]

The dressmaker learned her trade through apprenticeship, usually in the workroom of a retail draper's shop. A comprehensive essay in the *Woman's World,* the London paper edited by Oscar Wilde between 1887 and 1889, set out the various options available to beginners. It noted that "[t]he working dressmaker is generally drawn from the artisan, shopkeeping and 'clerking' classes; from those people, in fact, who think twelve to twenty shillings for a week's work a fair woman's wages."[14] These were London rates, of course, which a country dressmaker in Ireland could scarcely hope to command, but Bridget Boland went to Clonmel, eleven miles from her home, to learn her trade. Clonmel, the county town of South Tipperary, with a population of about 10,000 at the end of the nineteenth century, was an important municipal borough and railway junction. One hundred and sixty-seven gas lamps lit its streets. It had breweries, flour mills, tanneries, and two newspapers. It was the head of navigation for barges on the Suir, and an important export center. *Bassett's Book of County Tipperary,* published in 1889, listed seventeen drapers in the town, including merchant tailors, and noted approvingly: "The houses for the greater part are well built, and many of those devoted to business have quite a metropolitan appearance. In window-dressing and interior appointments the drapers and cabinet makers rival those in the same lines at Cork, Waterford and Limerick."[15] In London, a dressmaker's apprenticeship generally took two years, after which a young woman spent another year or more as an "improver," before she was considered to be a competent general dressmaker. A Clonmel apprenticeship may have been shorter, but Bridget Cleary's was a recognized and respected trade, and a fashionable one.

"[We] gave her a good trade," said Patrick Boland. Parents usually had to pay the tradespeople who took their children as apprentices, but even if they did not, they invested in their own future support by sacrificing the apprentice's labor in the short term. Bridget Cleary's possession of a sewing machine also represented a considerable investment. Machines were usually bought on installment, but they were expensive.[16]

The *Cork Examiner's* special reporter wrote on March 29 that "people speak of [Bridget Cleary] as being 'a bit queer' in her ways, and this they attribute to a certain superiority over the people with whom she came into contact . . . Her attire . . . is not that of every woman in the same social plane." Rather than the shawl or scarf with which Irish countrywomen covered their heads well into the twentieth century, Bridget Cleary, on special occasions at least, wore a black straw hat trimmed with navy-blue ribbon and a brown feather or two, with a large hat pin to hold it on her head. This hat was still hanging on a nail in her bedroom after her death.

The clothes Bridget Cleary wore on the evening she died give a vivid picture of this stylish young woman: a red petticoat, a striped petticoat, gray or green stays, a navy-blue flannel dress, a navy-blue cashmere jacket, a white knitted shawl, and black stockings and boots. She also wore "an ordinary calico chemise." Calico chemises were among the garments the girls of Lough Gur sewed for the poor in the 1870s, but the rest of Bridget Cleary's clothes suggest anything but poverty, and her ears must have been pierced, for she wore gold earrings. Michael Cleary, too, was well dressed, in his three-piece suit of light-gray tweed.

Bridget Cleary earned money by dressmaking. She also kept hens—source of the brown feathers in her hat, perhaps—and sold both eggs and fowl. Poultry keeping was a major occupation of women in rural Ireland, and often a significant source of family income. An official report for 1893–94 claimed that in Balieborough, County Cavan, women could make as much money in one day by selling eggs as their husbands could earn in a week by laboring, while in 1897 it was noted that "[poultry] is the chief source of income to many a poor woman who depends upon her egg money for many little purchases which could never be procured from the husband's hire." By 1900 the number of poultry in Ireland was about eighteen and a half million: more than three times that recorded fifty years earlier.[17]

Proper care of hens requires great attention to detail, and minute observation of the behavior of individual birds. Not surprisingly, in a society that allocated most work by gender, women were believed to be more adept at it than men, who usually scorned all involvement. Women's income from poultry was independent of male control, and their emotional investment in their hens could be correspondingly considerable. Many anecdotes are told about fights between women over entitlement to eggs, when hens wandered freely and laid wherever they pleased; more bitter stories are remembered of disputes between mothers-in-law and daughters-in-law who lived together. No more than one flock of hens could run in a farmyard, and control of the hens was the only way for a woman to have an income.

Less is said about the resentment men may have felt at the independence women gained through poultry keeping, but it is surely to be read in the derision they so often expressed for hens, even while eating eggs with enjoyment and benefiting from the income they earned.[18] However, arguments between men and women about hens often reflected an incompatibility between their concerns, or a competition for resources: farmers feared that cattle would not eat grass soiled with poultry droppings, and that the hens would be destructive to tillage.[19] On the windswept Great Blasket Island, County Kerry, where men built and maintained their own thatched houses, they cursed the hens that tore the thatch apart to lay their eggs on the low roofs, and blamed the women who owned them. A well-known legend says that hens were brought to Ireland by the Danes, who left them behind to cause damage: this is why they destroy thatched roofs, and will set houses on fire if given a chance.

In oral storytelling in Irish, the figure of *Cailleach na gCearc,* the Henwife, sums up some of the ambivalence felt about women who kept hens. Poor, marginalized, and dirty, the Henwife is nevertheless wise and well informed. Untouched by power struggles, she is independent of the romantic destiny that rules the lives of other female characters, and often comes to the aid of the struggling hero or heroine. In storytelling and in written reminiscences of rural life, we also find a recurring analogy between resistance to the keeping of hens and resistance to women's speech. That hens make too much noise, and that women talk too much, is a familiar theme in men's traditional storytelling. One account tells of a domestic dispute between a mother-in-law and daughter-in-law in County Mayo, when the son's reaction was to banish his mother from the house. Later he relented and allowed her to come back, but stipulated "*Ach ná bíodh aon chaint agat, agus ná bíodh aon chearc agat!*" [But no talking, and no hens!][20] Poultry keeping, like talkativeness, was a sign that a woman was not under a man's control.

Before Bridget Cleary died, she and her husband Michael were sharing a house with her father; they had no children and both were working and earning money. They had been married for seven and a half years, and it is unlikely that they were childless by choice, but their material circumstances had been improving steadily.

Killenaule, Michael Cleary's home town, had a population of about six hundred. It is only eight miles to the north of Ballyvadlea, but contact beween the two places was not significant. Killenaule lies in the Slieve Ardagh Hills, while Ballyvadlea looks south and west, towards Fethard and Clonmel.

Clonmel was where Michael Cleary and Bridget Boland met: he was working as a cooper, while she served her time as a dressmaker's apprentice. She moved back to her parents' home after her apprenticeship, and they married in August 1887, when he was twenty-seven and she eighteen. This was unusually young. Irish women of Bridget Cleary's generation usually married much later, if they married at all, and the average age was going up: from twenty-six years and some months for those born between 1821 and 1851, to twenty-seven and a half for women born in 1861. The average man of Michael Cleary's generation was just over thirty when he married.[21] At first, according to a journalist who investigated their background for the *Daily Express,* Michael Cleary continued to work in Clonmel. Bridget lived with her parents in the tiny mud-walled house near Ballyvadlea bridge, working as a dressmaker, and Michael came there on weekends. It was unusual for a married couple to live apart, but Bridget may have had to nurse her mother, who died sometime before 1895. As we shall see from an outburst Michael Cleary later made in court, the Clearys' arrangement caused gossip.[22]

Michael and Bridget Cleary's employment would have placed them far ahead of most rural working people in the last decades of the nineteenth century. The 1880s were particularly difficult for agricultural laborers, leading to more emigration than at any time since the period immediately after the Famine. The Labourers (Ireland) Act, introduced in 1883 and much amended in subsequent years, was an attempt to alleviate their living conditions and mitigate their sense of grievance. It provided for the construction of decent, well-built cottages on half-acre plots, to be rented to able-bodied laborers in places where their services were required, and to replace the filthy cabins in which so many of the poorer people lived. The Poor Law Guardians in the various unions were given responsibility for implementing the act, and precise specifications were drawn up. The scheme caused resentment among farmers and landowners, who were required to provide plots of land, but it was designed to offer them the inducement of making laborers available to work for them.[23]

That the Poor Law Guardians took their responsibilities in regard to the cottages seriously is shown in the copious minutes taken at their weekly meetings. On October 6, 1892, a report was read to the Cashel Poor Law Guardians from Thomas Ormond, Engineer, to the effect that the contractor for cottage No. 19 was not carrying out the work in accordance with specification: "[T]he footing course does not extend half the required distance, the fire place and chimney are after the old plan, the chimney shaft is half a brick too short, the slates are not of specified quality and are not bedded in mortar." On the following page we read, "Contractor has been before the Board and states he will take down and rebuild the works."[24]

Sometime after the Clearys' marriage, the Cashel Poor Law Guardians built one of these laborers' cottages in Ballyvadlea, about half a mile up the hill from the bridge, on the right hand side of the road. It faced south, commanding sweeping views of the Anner Valley, with Slievenamon, the famous mountain, beyond it. Like similar cottages being constructed all over Ireland in those years, it was of rectangular plan, with a high-pitched slated roof and a chimney in each gable.[25] Its door was slightly to the left of center, with a sliding-sash window on either side. Each window had three panes of glass in the upper sash and three below, and could be darkened from the inside by wooden shutters. There were two similar windows in the back of the house, a further small one high in the west gable, to one side of the chimney, and a slightly larger one in the center of the east gable. This was placed between the chimney shafts that led from two small bedrooms below it at the front and back of the house. It gave light to the loft above them, which was reached by a ladder from the kitchen.

The Catholic clergy had been particularly insistent that laborers' cottages should provide separate sleeping spaces for girls and boys, and surviving plans for cottages show "girls' room" and "boys' room" as well as "parents' room": no doubt the loft was intended for the boys.[26] The front door opened directly into the kitchen; the downstairs bedroom doors opened off the kitchen on the right, and the hearth for heating and cooking was on the gable wall opposite them. Outside at the back were one or two small outhouses, and the house was separated from the road by a low stone wall and a gate.

When we consider that in the census of 1901 houses were graded 1, 2, 3, and 4, and that a fourth-class house consisted of one room only, built of mud or other material considered impermanent, roofed with thatch, and often windowless, a new laborers' cottage, slated, high-ceilinged in the kitchen at least, well lit, and ventilated, with separate bedrooms, although it was classified as second class, represented something like luxury. The cottage in Ballyvadlea, however, had a disadvantage: it was built on a "rath," or as local people and nationalist newspapers called it, an old fort.

"Rath" (*ráth*), a common element in Irish place-names, was the term most commonly used by officials in the nineteenth century for the circular earthworks which archaeologists now call ringforts. Around Ballyvadlea they were known simply as "forts." Before the investigations of antiquaries and the depredations of agribusiness, they were left largely undisturbed, and it is estimated that there were as many as sixty thousand in the Irish landscape. Great numbers can still be seen from the air, contrasting with the rectilinear markings of modern field systems. In the areas where they occur, they are known variously as "rath," "rusheen," "fort," "forth," "cashel," or, in Irish, *ráth, lios, bruíon, sí,* and *cathair,* among other names. The majority appear to have been built as enclosures for dwellings in the second half of the first millennium.[27]

The large variety of local names given to these places, and the absence of a common colloquial name, alerts us to the importance of ringforts in people's imagination; names for "private" parts of the human body can be similarly awkward, offering a choice between scientific and intimate language, but leaving the more neutral middle ground empty. In both cases, the ambivalence of the language points to the emotional significance of what is being talked about. Ringforts are usually overgrown with vegetation. They are untouchable, sites of mystery and avoidance, and often of physical danger, since many of them contain underground passages. Archaeologists may explain what they are, or were, but oral tradition preserves its own ideas, which are too useful and interesting to be discarded, as Lady Gregory discov-

ered a few years before the events of this book, while exploring with
her husband in the west of Ireland:

> The old ring-shaped raths or forts are always fairy-haunted. I
> remember one day searching in vain for one we had been told
> of. We asked a countryman riding by if he knew of it, but he
> could not recognize it by any description till my husband said
> on chance, "A place the fairies come to."
>
> "Oh, the place where the fairies do be; I know that well
> enough," he said, and pointed out the way.[28]

In the narrative maps of oral storytelling, ringforts function as alternative reference points to places of human habitation and activity.
Telling stories about them allows an imaginative, fictional, or metaphorical dimension of experience to be accommodated along with
the practical, for they can serve as metaphors for areas of silence and
circumvention in the life of the society that tells stories about them.
All the ambivalence attached to them is contained in the common assertion that forts are where the fairies live.

The fairies are the invisible neighbors who must not be antago-
nized. Ordnance Survey maps show roads all over Ireland that
abruptly detour in a semicircle, and stories are told, and places
pointed out, where the progressive, linear optimism of nineteenth-
century engineering fell foul of fairy belief. Local workmen refused
to dig through forts, according to such legends, and strangers brought
in to replace them suffered mysterious injuries. After Bridget Cleary
disappeared, and sensational stories circulated, newspapers in Ireland
and Britain joined in a clamor of controversy about the meaning of
such accounts. Before her death, however, in common with almost
every other rural place in Ireland, and many urban districts too, Ballyvadlea allowed the fairies an existence in narrative, and even people
who took no part in telling or listening to such stories knew something of them.[29]

Even the most skillful storyteller could not expect to convince all
the people all the time. Some people in rural Ireland certainly believed some things about fairies some, or even most, of the time;

however, even a willing suspension of disbelief offered more skeptical listeners the aesthetic reward of hearing a story. And the stories were exciting, for the struggle against disbelief whetted the storytellers' skill, and made them craft narratives with structure, style, and elegance. Fairy legends told by Séan Ó Conaill of Cill Rialaigh, County Kerry; or Éamon a Búrc of County Galway; Irish-speaking contemporaries of Bridget Cleary; or by Jenny McGlynn, born in County Laois in 1939, show them taking evident delight in spinning out a tale, triumphing over the skepticism of their listeners.[30]

An ability to tell stories was (and is) a form of symbolic capital, which in Ireland in the nineteenth and twentieth centuries has been in complementary distribution with the monetary kind. Often it has stood in explicit opposition to material wealth, the most fervent tellers of stories about fairies being people whose worldly goods are modest, while their stories typically celebrate the virtues of cooperation and generosity, denigrating avarice and greed. Around Ballyvadlea and Kylenagranagh, Jack Dunne, cousin of Patrick Boland and Mary Kennedy, was known as someone who could tell stories about ghosts and fairies. According to the reporter from the conservative Dublin *Daily Express,* who visited the scene after Bridget Cleary's body was discovered, both Dunne and his wife were also "reported to be endowed with extraordinary powers of divination." Mary Battle, housekeeper to Yeats's uncle in County Sligo and the poet's mentor in Irish fairy lore, had a similar reputation. The value of such symbolic capital was dwindling, however. The building of a new laborers cottage in Ballyvadlea, on or beside a fort, typifies the contrast between the progressive attitudes that were becoming increasingly widespread as prosperity increased, and the worldview of the rural poor. Farmers who were reluctant to make agricultural land available for the building of cottages would sometimes compromise by offering a site that was otherwise worthless.[31] The presence of a ringfort may have made the Ballyvadlea site available, because undesirable for most purposes, but only a family that did not subscribe to the ideas propounded by Jack Dunne would have been willing to live there.

Bridget and Michael Cleary, with Bridget's parents, applied to the Cashel Poor Law Guardians for the tenancy of the new cottage in

Ballyvadlea, probably in the late 1880s, but they were not successful. The *Daily Express* journalist was told that it had been given instead to another laborer, but that problems soon arose:

> It is alleged that the fairies, who held high revel on moonlight nights on a rath quite close to the new cottage, were displeased with this tenant, and so annoyed him by unearthly cries and noises at night that he fled from the locality.

"This seems incredible," the journalist continues; "nevertheless it is believed by many of the peasantry."

This journalist may have been told a story in a code he did not fully understand: we read that the Clearys and the Bolands became tenants of the "haunted" house, and that the hauntings then ceased. It seems likely that someone among them was responsible—or was believed by neighbors to have been responsible—for the noises that drove their rivals away and left them in possession of the cottage. It is worth noting too that the Clearys were not strictly entitled to a cottage built under the Labourers (Ireland) Act. Cottages were funded by the taxpayers and designed to house able-bodied laborers and their families, which usually included numerous children, but Michael Cleary, a cooper, was not available for laboring work. Patrick Boland, already old at sixty-six, was the only agricultural laborer in the family, and he became the official tenant.

None of our sources say when the Clearys and Bridget's parents took possession of the cottage, but circumstantial evidence suggests that it happened in 1891. Theirs was the only new laborer's cottage in the townland, and on February 24 of that year a letter was read to the Cashel Poor Law Guardians from one of their number, William Meagher, of Tober, Fethard, requesting the board to give instructions for repairs to the cottage fences at Ballyvadlea. The board's resolution was that "the matter will be attended to as soon as the tenant pays up rent due." Arrears of rent were not unusual, but evictions often followed, and this may have been the moment of transfer, for William Simpson told the magistrates that he had known the Clearys as neighbors for four years, and Michael Cleary stated that he had worked in Clonmel until four years earlier.

If this is the case, then the family's circumstances had improved enormously just four years before Bridget Cleary's death, allowing her husband to live permanently with her and to set up in business as a cooper in Ballyvadlea. The *Cork Examiner* and the *Daily Express* tell us that the old cabin where the Bolands had lived became Michael's workshop, and that he had a lucrative trade. He made "butter firkins and other articles for a creamery at Fethard and for the farmers of the district," according to the *Daily Express* for March 30, 1895, while "in a shed at one side of his house" the *Cork Examiner* reporter saw

> . . . a small quantity of timber in the rough, and in the plot ad-
> joining at the other side a few bundles of prepared twigs and hoop
> timber for firkins, lying close to three little stacks of "scutched"
> corn, which was evidently about to be used for thatching a pigstye
> recently built next to the stable at the rere of the house.[32]

Either the Clearys kept a pig, or they were about to acquire one; pigs were selling very cheaply that spring.

The *Cork Examiner* reporter visited the house twice, and on both days found the Clearys' dog, Badger, waiting on the doorstep. The second time he went, William Simpson let him in with a key. He describes the young emergencyman as "an eminently practical man . . . intelligent and obliging." The dog was pining for Bridget Cleary. "There's not a woman comes up the road," Simpson said, "that he does not think 'tis her." The couple's cat, too, was prowling around. Simpson told the reporter that her name was Dotey, and that she used to climb on Bridget Cleary's shoulders.

The front door of the cottage had a half door, hinged to the same frame, which could be left closed while the front door was open, to keep out hens, animals, and blown debris while admitting light and air. Inside, the kitchen had an earthen floor, but contained a table, three *súgán* chairs with seats made of twisted hay rope, a form (a wooden bench), a little cupboard, and a kitchen dresser with "a lot of

common blue ware, and amongst other small articles, a prayer-book."
There was also a clock, "which was ticking away merrily." In a corner, the reporter found "two saws, one of the crosscut sort, which
were evidently used by Michael Cleary at his coopering work."

The reporter's attention was drawn to the fireplace where Bridget
Cleary had died: "The fireplace, in which so much ghastly interest is
centred, is sufficiently spacious for a small person to be slung across
it, but the fire grate is very small, about a foot long and not so broad."

The back bedroom held the rough wooden bed, covered with
straw, where Patrick Boland had slept up to the time of his arrest, and
where Michael Kennedy had woken up after his fainting fit. The
bedclothes were tumbled about. On the wooden floor were some
sacks of meal, and a box of eggs; several pictures hung on the walls.
Bridget and Michael Cleary's bedroom was almost filled by an iron
bedstead, with sheets, pillow, and woollen blankets, but it also had
room for "an old-fashioned wooden trunk, paper-covered, a sewing-
machine, and a box covered with coloured calico."

The RIC Divisional Commissioner had ordered photographs of
the scene, and on March 26 Constable Thomas McLoughlin traveled
from Kilkenny to take them. His photograph of the bedroom, now
in the National Archives in Dublin, shows the large box referred to
in the *Cork Examiner,* with the patterned cloth on top. The trunk is
under the bed. On the day she died, Bridget Cleary asked her cousin
Johanna Burke to pull it out, and handed her a canister with a large
sum of money to put away in it. Also in the room were several
items of the kind that characterized middle-class Catholicism in late
nineteenth-century Ireland: a crucifix, a rosary, a holy water font, a
medal suspended from a piece of broad red ribbon, and pictures of
religious subjects, "one of Our Lord and two of the Holy Family."
Two of the pictures in Patrick Boland's room were religious.

The reporter noted that the Clearys' bedroom floor was of wood,
but that it was "in a state of confusion with tossed bed-clothes and
the under-clothing removed from Mrs Cleary on Thursday night and
Friday night. Amidst this soiled heap was a new blue handkerchief
which William Simpson informed me was a present from the de-

ceased to her husband a few days before her illness." William Simpson obviously knew the Clearys very well indeed.

The house was comfortable and well appointed, and the Clearys were doing well. In fact they were doing significantly better than their relatives and neighbors, some of whom had large families to support, and several of whom were illiterate. Even Patrick Boland, who shared the couple's house, did not share their level of comfort, sleeping on straw in a room used to store eggs and sacks of meal.

Patrick Boland's sister, Mary Kennedy, still lived in her thatched "cabin" near Ballyvadlea bridge. She was by now fifty-nine, and a widow. Almost all the commentators who saw her in Clonmel courthouse described her as "an old woman" or a "poor old woman," although her hair was still brown. A sketch in the *Daily Graphic* shows her wearing a shawl or scarf that covers her head and is tied under her chin. Brown-eyed, with sallow skin, she was just over five feet in height, weighed only ninety-eight pounds, and could neither read nor write. Her evidence in court was described as rambling, incoherent, and sometimes inaudible, but she was a central figure in what happened in Ballyvadlea, and was the only woman among those tried for murder. Her four sons were accused along with her, but her daughter Johanna Burke was the chief witness for the Crown.

Mary Kennedy shared her house with her sons Patrick, James, and William, all farm laborers, and her eleven-year-old granddaughter, Katie Burke, Johanna's eldest child. It was not unusual in rural Ireland, until even quite recently, for the oldest grandchild to live with a widowed grandparent rather than with her parents. Katie Burke was described by several observers as a very pretty child, and remarkably intelligent. She probably shared Mary Kennedy's bed, helping to keep her warm in winter, ran errands, and generally helped out. Her school, in the convent of the Sisters of Mercy in Drangan, was nearer, in any case, to her grandmother's home than to her parents' in Rathkenny. Attendance at school had been compulsory for children between six and fourteen years since 1892.

Katie's mother, Johanna Kennedy, sometimes known as Hannah or "Han," seems to have been already pregnant with Katie when she married Michael Burke, a laborer, in August 1884. Her cousin, then Bridget Boland, was her bridesmaid. We do not know Johanna Burke's age, but she is unlikely to have been more than thirty-four at the time of Bridget Cleary's death, for her parents had not married until 1860. She carried an infant in her arms throughout the court proceedings—probably her namesake Johanna, just a few months old, who was baptized in January 1895. The Drangan Baptismal Register shows five other children born to Johanna Burke and her husband between 1888 and 1894, including two babies, a year apart, both called Bridget, which probably means that the first one died.

Patrick Kennedy was thirty-two, thin and wiry, with a straggly dark mustache. Prison records describe him as "spare but muscular." He was five feet seven and a half inches tall, and could neither read nor write. His brother Michael, also illiterate at twenty-seven, was tall, thin, and bearded, with the sort of fair skin that reddens easily: what official documents called "a fresh complexion." He was tubercular and subject to fits.

James Kennedy was twenty-two. Unlike his older brothers, and probably unlike his sister, he could read and write. Almost six feet tall, and strongly built, he wore a mustache like his brother Patrick, and took after his mother in coloring, with brown hair and eyes, and dark skin. William, the youngest brother, could also read and write, and was described by journalists as "a tall, good-looking and well-built young man." He was twenty-one. The difference in education and physique between the older and the younger brothers of the Kennedy family is striking, and may illustrate the rapidity of change in their society.

In 1895 it was still customary to refer to "the laborers" as a homogeneous class. When the story of Bridget Cleary's disappearance broke, unionist newspapers assumed, and wrote, that she was the wife of a laborer, but the laboring class was changing and diversifying, and some who had been born into it were moving upward. Literacy was the crucial qualification for advancement, and both Bridget and Michael Cleary could read and write. Both also practiced lucrative trades. The future that beckoned them, and which may have seemed available to the younger Kennedys, must have looked very different from the one awaiting Johanna and Michael Burke or Patrick and Michael Kennedy. Until crisis struck, the Clearys could take the well-lit streets of Clonmel or Fethard as their model of life, but for those who could not read or write, the countryside was still a dark and frightening place on winter nights. John Dunne, toothless and limping, with his stories of fairy forts and ghosts, still had authority there.

4

Bridget Cleary Falls Ill

WILLIAM GLADSTONE was over eighty when his Liberal government came to power for the fourth time in 1892. His third administration had collapsed in 1886 after only a few months, when the first Irish Home Rule Bill was defeated in the House of Commons by 341 votes to 311. John Morley, Chief Secretary for Ireland under the 1886 government, had helped his leader to draft that bill; now he was appointed to the post again.

Morley's name does not appear in most general histories of Ireland.[1] The governments he served were short-lived, and there is in any case a convention in Irish historiography that the last decade of the nineteenth century, especially after the death of Charles Stewart Parnell in 1891, was dominated by cultural, rather than political, issues. The effect of Gladstone's Land Act of 1881 had been to bring landlords gradually around to the idea of selling out to their tenants, while the Ashbourne Act of 1885 and Arthur Balfour's Land Act of 1891, with the setting up of the Congested Districts Board, had marked a new attitude to tenants on the part of the Conservative Party.

Morley was MP for Newcastle-upon-Tyne and a disciple of John Stuart Mill. An idealistic journalist, and editor of the *Fortnightly Review* from 1867 to 1882, he had a lifelong interest in Ireland; he had been granted the Freedom of the City of Dublin in 1888. Gladstone introduced a second Home Rule Bill in 1893, but it was defeated in the House of Lords by 419 votes to 41 in September, and in early March 1894, Gladstone retired. Morley was instrumental in the choice of a prominent Scottish Liberal, Archibald Philip Primrose, Lord Rosebery, as his successor.

The chief secretary's opposition to coercive legislation and his sympathy with the Irish tenants' cause won him the support of nationalists like the antilandlord MP John Dillon, but his attempts to introduce new land legislation were frustrated by the Opposition, whose supporters criticized him for overcaution, and ridiculed him as a pettifogging stickler for discipline in Dublin Castle. Morley's Evicted Tenants Bill passed the Commons in 1894, but was rejected by the Lords.[2] This was the background to his new Land Bill, which was designed to remedy defects in the 1881 act. At the time of Bridget Cleary's death, Irish farmers were eagerly awaiting its second reading in the House of Commons.

In January 1895, the RIC Divisional Commissioner, Western Region, wrote in his confidential report to Dublin Castle that "in spite of the bad season the general consensus of opinion as expressed by landagents is that rents have not been better paid for a long period of years."[3] A month later, Lady Gregory at Coole wrote to her friend Enid Layard: "the garden is like Italy, warm sunshine and many flowers out, wallflowers, grape hyacinths, violets and in the woods, primroses . . . Our people are paying rents and paying very well, and a policeman who came from Gort in the holidays to cut the boys' hair said he was glad of the distraction, as they have absolutely nothing to do about here now."[4]

"The boys" were the farm laborers employed on the Coole estate and "our people" were the tenants of farms owned by the Gregory family, paying their rents on time in anticipation of the new legislation. The South-Eastern Division, which included County Tipperary, was similarly calm. RIC Divisional Commissioner A. E. S. Heard, in Kilkenny, wrote early in 1895 that "great interest was taken by the farmers in the introduction of the new Land Bill by the Chief Secretary, and strong hopes were entertained that means would be contrived for reducing rents both judicial and non-judicial."[5]

As peace and confidence spread through the countryside in the 1890s, and crime figures fell, cultural and social initiatives came to the fore. The literary revival in English was well under way, and educated people's interest in folklore and in the Irish language was increasing steadily. On November 25, 1892, in Dublin, Douglas Hyde gave his lecture on "The Necessity for Deanglicizing Ireland," and in 1893 he became president of the newly founded Gaelic League. In 1894, Horace Plunkett founded the Irish Agricultural Organisation Society (IAOS); in the years that followed, it would promote the development of cooperative creameries and agricultural credit banks, and give the lead in modernizing poultry keeping and similar enterprises.[6]

The chief secretary's Land Bill was due to have its second reading in the House of Commons on April 2, 1895. Nationalist newspapers approved of the bill—the *Freeman's Journal* called it "a great land bill" after its first reading—but it attracted scathing editorial comment in the *Dublin Evening Mail* and *Daily Express,* both owned by the unionist J. P. Maunsell. The *Daily Express* published letters to the editor from members of the landowning aristocracy, commending the stand taken by the paper and deploring the new legislation. Edward Carson, at forty a rising star in the House of Commons and in the courts, was the darling of the *Express.* An Irish unionist, protégé of Arthur Balfour, and known as "Coercion Carson" for his prosecutions of Parnellites, he was closely identified with resistance to the bill and had replied for the Opposition on its first reading, but had "hinted obstruction instead of openly declaring war," according to the *Freeman's Journal.* He had just been engaged to defend the Marquess of Queensberry against a libel action brought by Oscar Wilde, and was among the speakers when "the resident Irish Unionists celebrated St. Patrick's Day under the happiest of auspices" in London in 1895.[7] Although Carson had not had much to say in the debate on the bill's first reading on March 4, he told a unionist meeting in Cambridge, the day Bridget Cleary's body was found, that "Mr Morley's Land Bill was a revolutionary monster, and would be strenuously Opposed."[8]

Even in 1895, despite the relative tranquillity of the countryside, occasional outbreaks of agrarian violence were reported in Ireland. Most newspaper accounts are brief, but police reports detail the protection afforded to tenants and "caretakers" of some evicted farms, as raiders fired shots through their windows, cut the tails and ears off their cattle, or mutilated other animals. From time to time, also, printed notices posted near Catholic chapels exhorted the community to boycott so-called "land-grabbers." Maunsell's newspapers made much of such incidents, pouring scorn on the idea that a population that perpetrated or tolerated them could be deemed fit for Home Rule.[9] When Bridget Cleary died, and when her death became known, the political climate was cool by comparison with the preceding seventeen years, but old debates had neither been resolved nor forgotten, and the temperature was rising.

Monday, March 4, 1895, was the day when Chief Secretary Morley moved the first reading of his Land Bill in the House of Commons. The weather in Ireland was dry and sunny, but very cold. It had snowed heavily on the previous day and the mountains were white. Bridget Cleary walked down the hill to Ballyvadlea bridge and up another hill to Kylenagranagh, a mile or two from her home. Her father's cousin Jack Dunne lived in a small house near the fairy fort with his wife Kate; they had no children. Bridget Cleary was delivering eggs, or perhaps attempting to collect payment for eggs, but neither of the Dunnes was at home.[10] She became chilled through, waiting on their doorstep, then walked home and tried to warm herself at the fire, but "the fire would not warm her, she was so cold," according to her cousin Johanna Burke.

The next day, Bridget Cleary complained of a violent headache. She had fits of shivering and was unable to leave her bed. Her illness continued for the rest of the week, and she stayed in bed while the weather grew milder, but much wetter. At some stage during the week, Jack Dunne and his wife came to visit her.

Dunne's interventions at all stages of this story were crucial. Several witnesses pointed to him as an instigator of Bridget Cleary's torture on the days that followed, but the subsequent record has tended to play down his role. Piecing together what the various sources say about him, however, we find an interesting figure: a man who might have commanded respect in an earlier generation or a more remote place, but who had become marginalized and isolated in an increasingly modern society.

At fifty-five, Jack Dunne, according to the *Cork Examiner,* "is an old man and is fairy-ridden. He has been chased up to his home by a man in black and a woman in white . . . He is learned apparently in incantations, charms and spells, and he can tell ghost stories and fairy tales—is the veritable *shanachie* of ancient Ireland." "Shanachie" is the Irish *seanchaí,* a storyteller, particularly one who specializes in oral history; the word had entered English through the Irish literary revival.

The driver of a horse-drawn cab had told this reporter stories about "one of the men who are in gaol." The man is not identified, but only Dunne fits the description. He had complained of a pain in his back, which he said was caused when the fairies lifted him out of his bed, carried him out to the yard, and left him lying on the ground. He said he heard fairies outside his house every night, and that sometimes they played hurling matches there.

Jack Dunne lived near a fort, and he walked with a limp, for a fracture had left his right leg shorter than his left. A knowledge of fairy tradition gave a storyteller a certain prestige, but it could also buy privacy, or at least immunity from teasing. Eccentric, deviant, or reclusive individuals—or people with mental or physical disabilities—were often said to be "in the fairies," or to have spent time "away" among them; people who acquired unexplained wealth were similarly suspect, while women said to have been taken by the fairies, even if they were later returned, were often infertile afterwards. These people's association with fairies might be simply a convenient metaphor, or it might be taken literally, but in either case it drew on a vast oral literature whose imagery and concepts were densely inscribed on the landscape—with fairy forts as major reference points—and the individuals concerned were treated with caution, if not always with respect.[11]

We can gain some idea of the cultural loss suffered by people like Jack Dunne by comparing them with their contemporaries in *Gaeltacht,* or Irish-speaking districts. The great cultural shifts that followed the Famine in Ireland were felt less in the densely populated areas of mostly poor land, chiefly along the Atlantic coast and on islands, where Irish was still the language of daily life. The influence of priests and police was less in *Gaeltacht* areas than in other parts of the country; there were no large farms; towns were small and far apart, and the restless young looked toward America, rather than to Irish towns and cities, for prospects of advancement. Singing and storytelling were still major outlets for cultural expression, as well as important vehicles of education, so that when the collectors of the Irish Folklore Commission began work in 1935, they found a rich harvest.

Just as musicians in Ireland were often blind, storytellers were frequently lame. In rural society, certain occupations and preoccupations attracted (and sheltered) people with special needs. Tadhg Ó Buachalla, the famous "Tailor Buckley" from Gougane Barra, County Cork, and Éamon Liam a Búrc were both tailors. Both compensated for physical limitations with virtuoso storytelling, which brought visitors from considerable distances to listen to them.[12] At nine years of age, Tadhg Ó Buachalla lost the use of his right leg overnight, probably through polio, and at thirteen began a five-year apprenticeship as a tailor. Éamon a Búrc was fourteen when his family emigrated to Minnesota; seventeen when he lost a leg, jumping from a train in St. Paul. He returned to the west of Ireland, learned tailoring, and went on to become the finest storyteller of his generation.

The stories told by these two men, unlike Jack Dunne's, have been extensively documented, for both spoke Irish and lived long enough to be recognized and celebrated by collectors of folklore. Throughout both their repertoires runs a theme of resistance to the dominant culture, along with a skepticism that belies the credulity often ascribed to those who talk of fairies. Both storytellers also maintained a lively, if unconventional, interest in current international news.

Men like these, along with some women, such as Peig Sayers of Great Blasket Island, County Kerry, or Sorcha Mhic Ghrianna (Sorcha Chonaill), of Rinn na Feirste, County Donegal, were the artists and intellectuals of a tradition that was not amenable to the rules of the logical and literate nineteenth and twentieth centuries.[13] Theirs was an oral culture, its knowledge stored in human memory, in retrievable form, in stories of human action. They used vivid imagery and repetition to make facts, techniques, and ideas memorable, and employed riddles, paradox, and humor to teach the mental discipline at which they themselves excelled. Their stories often hinge on what has come to be known as "lateral thinking," the solving of problems by indirect, or apparently illogical means. The question of whether these storytellers "really believed" in the fairies they told stories about is less important than the use they made of them as scaffolding for the construction and maintenance of a whole worldview.[14]

Tadhg Ó Buachalla and Éamon a Búrc both lived in areas where they had appreciative, informed audiences, and where the dichotomy between dominant and vernacular culture found ready expression in switches between the two languages in daily use. However, Jack Dunne may also have experienced his world bilingually. In his native barony of Middlethird in 1851, when he was eleven years old, one solitary old man, aged over eighty, spoke Irish only, but a further 7,237 people—over 20 percent of the population—spoke both Irish and English. Less prosperous parts of County Tipperary had far more Irish speakers (almost two-thirds of the population in Iffa and Offa West, for instance), but between 1851 and the end of the century numbers declined dramatically, a fact often attributed to the influence of the National Schools.

There was a National School in Cloneen as early as 1846 but judging by his level of literacy, Jack Dunne cannot have attended it for any appreciable length of time.[15] Many of those who grew up around Drangan and Ballyvadlea in the second half of the nineteenth century would have heard Irish spoken, but small clues survive that, unlike almost all the people around him, Jack Dunne as an adult may have spoken it himself. This could easily have been the case if, for instance, he had grown up in a household of elderly people.[16]

The *Cork Examiner* reported, by hearsay, that Jack Dunne was "learned . . . in incantations, charms and spells," calling him "the veritable *shanachie* of ancient Ireland," but more suggestive is the appearance of his name in the 1901 census. The census return shows a

John Dunne, aged sixty, farm servant, speaking Irish and English, in the home of James Skehan, thirty-five, farmer, in Ballyhomuck, County Tipperary. Ballyhomuck is the townland between Bally-vadlea and Cloneen, adjacent to Kylenagranagh, and Skehan was the name of the farmer on whose land the fairy fort lay. Jack Dunne served a three-year prison sentence for his part in Bridget Cleary's killing, but local tradition around Ballyvadlea says that he then re-turned to the area and worked as a laborer.[17] His prison record shows that his wife was reported to have died during his imprisonment. As a childless widower, he would have had no option but to seek work on a farm where he would also be given accommodation.

The "incantations, charms and spells" referred to by the *Cork Ex-aminer* might well have been traditional formulae in Irish. Charms are still found as rhymes in children's folklore, and some adults use them in certain situations. Nineteenth-century antiquaries collected great quantities of them, along with traditional prayers, particularly in ar-eas of Europe not affected by the Protestant Reformation. As might be expected, they are more common in Irish than in English. Some charms are very ancient, and have been traced to the archaic Indo-European tradition, but most consist of scraps of narrative on Chris-tian themes originally circulated in medieval times, faithfully recited word-for-word even when garbled and incomprehensible, and usu-ally whispered, or spoken very fast.[18] They were used to prevent and cure toothache and headache, to stop bleeding, and to treat sprains and other ailments, and most required the performance of certain ac-tions. Many of them may have had the simple effect of calming the patient, human or animal, and certainly they could do no harm; nev-ertheless, their use, and the ritual that surrounded them, also served to dramatize social relations.[19] Like stories, charms were a form of symbolic capital, which could enhance the prestige of poor, elderly, or otherwise vulnerable people who knew them. Most were closely guarded secrets.

From the point of view of the centralized authorities, both secu-lar and religious, charms were anathema. For administrators, and for the medical establishment, charms—and folk medicine gener-ally—smacked of what the British colonizer everywhere called "mumbo-jumbo." For the Catholic Church, on the other hand, charms represented an appropriation of part of its own stock-in-trade and a subversion of its authority. Unlike prayers, which appeal to the deity to produce various effects, charms are purported to work directly, without divine intervention, though this is rarely claimed explicitly.[20]

If Jack Dunne did speak Irish, this would give further credence to his supposed acquaintance with fairies, for the fairies were associated with everything that was being swept away by modernity. Compare Lady Gregory's description of "Mrs Sheridan," who used to claim that the fairies had been in the habit of taking her from her home. "What language had they?" Lady Gregory asked, to which Mrs Sheridan replied, "Irish of course—what else would they talk?"[21]

After several days in bed with illness, which may have been pneumonia, Bridget Cleary did not look like her usual neatly turned-out self. Jack Dunne's eyesight was poor, and in any case he was probably not used to seeing her in bed, but he made a dramatic pronouncement. "That is not Bridgie Boland!" he said when he saw her. His words could have been interpreted simply as a social judgement, a manner of speaking, as though he had said, "She's not herself today," but, as the *Cork Examiner*'s reporter wrote later, "his remark set all the fairy machinery in motion."

Neighbors or relatives who disliked Bridget Cleary, or who were envious of her, as some must have been, might easily have expressed their concern about her sudden loss of health as speculation about fairies, especially given her recent prosperity and her childlessness. Jack Dunne, however, made a further, more explicit, remark, reported by the *Daily Express* and by the Tory newspapers in Ireland and England, but not by the *Nationalist,* the *Freeman's Journal,* or the *Cork Examiner,* perhaps for fear of ridicule: he said that the woman in the bed was a fairy and, enigmatically, that one of her legs was longer than the other.

In the currency of popular belief-legend, humans who spend time "away with the fairies" come back to their everyday lives marked with some physical sign. In a story told by Éamon a Búrc in

1937, net maker Seoirse Lap, whose home is beside a fairy fort, returns from an extended stay with the fairies to find that, although he has outwitted them, one of his legs is now six inches shorter than the other.[22] Measurement with a thread or ribbon features both in stories of fairy interference and in folk cures: perhaps Jack Dunne, whose own right leg was shorter than his left, measured Bridget Cleary as she lay in bed. Michael Cleary, however, appears to have got hold of this idea in a less traditional form. When he and Dunne were searching for Bridget Cleary around Kylenagranagh on the morning after her disappearance, Cleary apparently told Dunne, "She was not my wife. She was too fine to be my wife; she was two inches taller than my wife!" "Fine" seems to be equivalent to the Irish word *breá,* here meaning "well built," or "tall."

By Saturday, March 9, Bridget Cleary felt worse. She believed, Johanna Burke said, that she had caught a fresh cold. Whatever Jack Dunne may have said about fairies, Bridget, her husband, and her father were determined to consult a university-trained medical doctor. It rained heavily that morning, but Patrick Boland walked the four miles to Fethard to ask Dr. William Crean to call.

Fethard's population in 1891 was roughly the same as a hundred years later—about 1,600. Since 1880, the town had had a direct rail link, via Thurles, with Dublin, 103 miles away. Cork was even closer, and fifteen horse-drawn cabs were available for hire in the town for those who wished to travel into the surrounding villages and countryside, as reporters from the *Cork Examiner* and the Dublin *Daily Express* would do at the end of March. The streets were lit by twenty-seven oil lamps, and Fethard had a pumped water supply, post and telegraph offices, a military barracks, an RIC barracks, sawmills, two creameries, two hotels, and a dispensary.

Medical relief was available to the "*destitute poor person*" in Ireland under the provisions of the Medical Charities Act of 1851, through a network of 723 dispensaries set up under the various Poor Law Unions.[23] The Irish Poor Law had evolved into an embryo national health system around the time of the Famine, so that by the end of the nineteenth century Ireland had perhaps one of the most widely available public health services in Europe. Dr. William Crean had been medical officer for the Fethard Dispensary District since 1885. His salary, £120 a year with £20 expenses, was paid by the Cashel Poor Law Guardians. Dr. William Heffernan was employed in a similar position in Killenaule.[24] Dispensary doctors were elected by the Poor Law Guardians, who were themselves elected by the local taxpayers, so they were often political appointees, but they were obliged to attend any sick person in their district who could produce a dispensary ticket: black for dispensary attendance, red for house calls.

Patrick Boland must have gone to one of the guardians who lived locally—probably Edmond Cummins of Brook Hill, on the way to Fethard—for a red ticket. He then went to the dispensary, presented the ticket and asked Dr. Crean to visit his daughter. He returned to Ballyvadlea and waited, but the doctor did not come. The next day, Sunday, March 10, was wet and dull. By Monday morning the rain had stopped, but by two in the afternoon there was no sign of Dr. Crean, and Bridget Cleary was still ill. Descriptions of her symptoms suggest that she may have had a fever. This time her husband walked to Fethard.

Ten years later, in prison in Maryborough, Queen's County (now Portlaoise, County Laois), Michael Cleary wrote his own account of these days:

> Petitionar wishes to stait that the Medical Doctor of the district was noticed [given notice] to attend the deceased 6 days previous to her death, Patrick Boland father to deceased noticed Doctor Crehan with a Red ticked to . . . attend deceased ameadetly at 10 o'clock in the morning the Doctor did not come that day or the day after so Petitionar went at 2 oclock the next day and had to return without him leaving Word to have him follow if he could be found as quick as possible.[25]

It was by now a week since Bridget Cleary had caught a chill outside Jack Dunne's house, and her condition was causing concern.

In the oral culture of rural Ireland, as we have seen, fairy legend was so much invoked in cases of illness that when Bridget Cleary told her cousin Johanna that her illness had started when she "took like a trembling coming by Kylenagranagh," this was easily interpreted as a reference to the fairy fort. Even as the dispensary doctor was being summoned, the "fairy machinery" was working.

Dr. William Crean did not visit Bridget Cleary following her husband's Monday walk to the dispensary; nor did he come on Tuesday. On Wednesday morning, March 13, Cleary again walked to Fethard to fetch him, while a messenger went to Drangan to ask one of the priests to come. Fr. Con Ryan told the magistrates in Clonmel, "I did not see who called, but I heard it was Simpson's servant."

That William Simpson, a Protestant, should send his maid or workman to fetch a priest for Bridget Cleary underlines the close connection between the two households. It also incidentally illustrates the disparity between them, for of course the Clearys had no servant. As an emergencyman, Simpson ran a farm, and so employed people, if laborers and maidservants could be found who were willing to work for him. The Clearys, by contrast, were artisans, and their relatives were laborers. The class difference between farmers, who rented land, and the laborers who worked for them was enormous, but the Simpsons could hardly afford to be snobbish. For the Clearys, such a friendship must have represented a move up in the world, even if it was one that would not endear them to their farmer neighbors. A hundred years later, when most Irish farmers have long owned their land, the distrust their ancestors felt for emergencymen and for the laborers who worked for them is still remembered around Ballyvadlea.[26]

Michael Cleary left home at five o'clock on the Wednesday morning, almost two hours before sunrise, leaving his wife and her father in the house. Here is what he wrote ten years later:

[T]he 3 morning Petitionar started at 5 oclock in the morning it being neerly 4 miles to Fethard from Petitionars house on his way Petitionar reported the conduct of the doctor to Mr Edmond Cummins of Brook Hill near Fethard Petitionar got a written order from Mr Cumins he being P[oor] L[aw] G[uardian] for the district he told me to give him that and if you cannot see him come back to me ameadeatly and he would telegraph to Clonmel for a Doctor if it cost £20 you will have a Doctor in 2 hours at your house. he was not there when Petitionar went to his house the servant told me he went with a man the name of OBrienne about a half hour ago and left word that he would attend my wife before he would come back.

Cleary's persistence paid off; before he left Fethard that day, Dr. Crean had visited his wife. At the inquest for Bridget Cleary's death on March 23, the doctor was asked if he had recently been called to see her. "I was, on the eleventh of March," he replied, "but I was not able to go to see her until the morning of the thirteenth." He made no mention of Patrick Boland's red ticket on the previous Friday. "I found her suffering, Sir," he told Coroner John J. Shee, of Clonmel, "simply from nervous excitement and slight bronchitis." He had asked his patient, he said, what had caused her nervous excitement, but could not elicit any explanation. He prescribed medicine, but did not know whether or not she had obtained it.

At the hearing of charges against the prisoners in Clonmel almost two weeks later, the resident magistrate, Colonel Richard Evanson, asked Dr. Crean, "Can you tell the magistrates that Bridget Cleary was a healthy subject?"

"She was perfectly healthy. She had a body of good physique and well nourished. The only thing I can say is that she was awfully nervous."

"Can you tell what you mean by being awfully nervous?"

"She had been attending me for the last eight or nine years, and I always found her a nervous, irritable sort of woman."

Dr. Crean did not say for what reason Bridget Cleary had been attending him. A century later, local people maintain that she was suffering from tuberculosis, and even that she was attending a TB clinic in Clonmel.[27] This would certainly account for some of the treatment she received in the days before her death, but contemporary accounts generally insist that her health was good: "I never knew her to be delicate in mind or body," William Simpson said, and other witnesses agreed with him. The postmortem examination simply found her lungs "slightly congested."

Left alone with his sick daughter that morning, Patrick Boland went down the hill to where his sister Mary Kennedy lived, and asked her to visit Bridget Cleary. Mary Kennedy told the Clonmel magistrates on April 5 what happened:

> It was Bridget Cleary's father came down for me on Wednesday, and said, "Go up to Bridget; she wants you, Mary."
>
> I said, "What is on her?"
>
> "Oh, she's very bad," says he, "with a pain in her head." So I went up then, and went into the room, and asked her what way was she. She said she was very bad, with a pain in her head and in her temples. I said it would be nothing, with the help of God.
>
> "I don't know," she says, "I'm very bad. He's making a fairy of me now, and an emergency."
>
> I said, "Don't mind him."
>
> "Oh," she said, "he thought to burn me about three months ago, but if I had my mother I would not be this way."
>
> I said, "Don't mind, and it will be nothing by and by."
>
> "I have some washing, if I had the hands to wash them," she said.
>
> "I will go up for Hanney and she will wash," I said. I then went up for Hanney, who came with me.

"Hanney" was Mary Kennedy's daughter, Johanna Burke, who lived with her husband and most of her children in Rathkenny, a mile to the west of the Clearys' house.

Bridget Cleary's conversation with her aunt, relayed to the court in the vivid words of someone who does not write, corroborates the doctor's evidence of her "nervous excitement." She was clearly not just ill, but distressed too, and there was obviously some difficulty between her and her husband. "He's making a fairy of me" seems to mean that Michael had distanced himself from her, whether simply by panicking at her condition, as he certainly seems to have done, or by expressly joining with Jack Dunne and others who had labeled her a fairy.

To "make a fairy of someone" is to isolate and repudiate him or her. "He thought to burn me about three months ago" tells us that this was not the first crisis of its kind. Bridget Cleary "would not be this way" if she had her mother, she says, and she has asked her aunt, her nearest woman relative, to visit.

Some commentators have interpreted Bridget Cleary's reported words, "he thought to burn me about three months ago," as meaning that Michael Cleary had long planned to kill his wife, and that the story of fairy intervention was nothing more than a ploy. Others have seen him as incorrigibly superstitious, convinced from the outset that his wife was with the fairies. However, his behavior, including his complaint to Edmond Cummins, and even the passionate tone of his petitions more than ten years later, suggest that the truth is less clear-cut. The matter-of-fact way Mary Kennedy conveyed this information suggests that the burning in question was relatively minor. It is possible that Michael Cleary had attempted to burn his wife, to punish her for some real or imagined offense, and that it was she who fitted his action into a paradigm of fairy belief by saying, "He's making a fairy of me." Bridget Cleary, well versed in fairy lore, would have found in its stories a language through which to resist her husband's negative assessment of her. A wife who could persuade a violent husband that she was a fairy changeling might even be able to convince him that he was damaging his chances of getting his "real" wife back.

Bridget Cleary's mother was certainly dead, and there are repeated hints in the court record and in modern Tipperary folklore that she, like Jack Dunne, had been credited with knowledge of fairies and herbs. It may be that the dynamics of the Clearys' household had changed with her death. The young couple would have been thrown more together, and Bridget Cleary may have taken on some of her mother's role, as possessor of esoteric knowledge, in a way that made her husband nervous. Without another woman in the house, in any case, responsibility for nursing her must fall either to her elderly and ineffectual father, or to Michael Cleary: "Petitionar attended to the wants of his wife during her sickness boath night and day untill he was in a manner just as bad as deceased."

Michael Cleary cannot have slept much, or eaten much, between March 4 and 14; when he was arrested on March 21, he weighed 154 pounds. The *Daily Graphic* sketch, made as he stood in the dock in Clonmel courthouse, shows him looking haggard and drawn. Just over three months later, on his transfer from Clonmel to Mountjoy Prison in Dublin, his weight was 167½ pounds, and it remained stable at around 176 pounds for a further six years. His prison medical history describes him as "stout & strong," so he must have been significantly underweight about the time of his wife's death, as might be expected when he was under severe stress.[28]

When Bridget Cleary said that her husband was making a fairy of her, Mary Kennedy simply told her not to mind him. This woman, described by all commentators as old, illiterate, and frail, apparently a perfect candidate for an uncritical belief in fairies, crisply dismisses them when they are invoked against someone she knows well. She also evidently allies herself with her niece against that niece's husband. Her testimony shows her as dealing with the practical problems caused by Bridget Cleary's illness. She fetched her daughter Johanna to wash Bridget's sheets, which would have been heavy to rinse and wring by hand, and apparently more than she herself could manage; she reassured the sick woman and, she told the court, returned to the house later that evening and prepared a chicken for her. Chicken was, of course, a luxury food: Mary Kennedy would have had to catch and kill one of her niece's fowls, and pluck and clean it before cooking it over the open fire.

Johanna Burke came with her mother to the Clearys' house at about the time the doctor left: "I saw Dr. Crean coming from her house," she told the magistrates; "[Bridget Cleary] asked why he did not come when he was sent for." This understandable anxiety may explain why the doctor described his patient as "irritable."

Meanwhile in Fethard, Michael Cleary was angry—"vexed" is his word—as he waited for the doctor. Dr. Crean finally returned, having seen Bridget Cleary, but was visibly annoyed that her husband had reported him to one of the Poor Law Guardians. Cleary refers to himself in the third person as "Petitionar," but then veers back to the first person when he writes that the doctor shouted at him:

> It being a Despencery Petitionar no [knew] he should come back soon when he came back his wife was with him and he was drunk he shouted at me that he attend my wife for he no Petitionar was very vext to him for the way he was traited [treated] with regard to his wife. he told petitionar that his wife was very weak and nervous he proscribed medson and ordered wine which Petitionar brought home with him and he told Petitionar to tell Edmond Cumins that he was afther attending his wife and also to return the Wrighting that he got from him Petitionar did as he was desired returned the Writing to Edmond Cummins and went home.

Michael Cleary had left home at five in the morning, but did not get back there for almost eleven hours. He had been away all day on what he represents in his petition as a fairly straightforward mission, although a frustrating one. Evidence given in court, however, by Jack Dunne and by Johanna Burke, who were both in the house when he returned, reveals that Michael Cleary brought home something more than doctor's medicine and wine, for he told them he had got herbs from a woman in Fethard.

Fr. Con Ryan was also at the house when Cleary returned. The curate told the magistrates that Bridget Cleary was in bed when he visited her at about half past three on Wednesday afternoon, March 13. He too reported that she appeared to be in a very nervous state and "possibly hysterical." (His use of language reminds us of hysteria's etymology and history: until the twentieth century the idea persisted that it was an illness, and peculiar to women; as early as the fourth century B.C., Hippocrates had identified symptoms of madness in women as originating from excess blood that accumulated in the womb.)[29] Fr. Ryan thought he might be witnessing the beginning of mental derangement, but he stayed with Bridget Cleary for only about twenty minutes. His rule of celibacy forbade him to have any more dealings than necessary with women, and lying in her small, low-ceilinged bedroom, his parishioner did not converse with him "except as a priest." He did not consider her dangerously ill, he said, but thought her sickness might become dangerous later on, and possibly develop into brain fever or something of that kind, so that he decided to administer the last rites of the church.

Michael Cleary spoke to him:

> when Petitionar reached home he found that his wife was afther being prepaired for death by a Priest the nam of Father Ryan Petitionar had a convrsation [sic] with the Priest and he told me that he prepared my wife for death that she was very weak, and he also asked was the Doctor drunk and Petitionar tolt him that he was he also examened the medson and did not aprove of it but said that the doctor was never sober.

Neither at the inquest nor at the magistrates' inquiry, nor even at the murder trial which followed in July, was any mention made of Dr. Crean's drinking, so far as the record shows, and the newspapers make no reference to it. Indeed the *Cork Examiner* refers to Dr. Crean as "a highly esteemed medical man who has occupied the chairmanship of the Fethard Town Commission Board for the past eight years uninterruptedly." Michael Cleary, however, by his own account, had brought a complaint about the doctor to Edmond Cummins, and the Cashel Poor Law Guardians had no option but to discuss the matter when further correspondence came before them. Their minutes for the weeks and months that followed show that Michael Cleary's accusation was not unfounded, but also testifies to the guardians' pained reluctance to record damaging information about a man of their own class, their appointee and perhaps their friend.[30] In 1910, a Royal Commission on the Poor Laws and Relief of Distress published a memorandum by the medical commissioner of the Local Government Board, which detailed the weaknesses of the dispensary system. "In many instances," the writer remarked, "the standard of sobriety is below what it ought to be."[31]

At their meeting on May 2, 1895, only six weeks after Bridget Cleary's death, the Cashel Guardians considered a resolution passed by the Fethard Dispensary Management Committee on April 15. It had received a letter, dated April 9, from the Local Government Board, apparently ordering Dr. Crean's dismissal on the grounds that he had been drunk when visited by an inspector. It resolved as follows:

> That we respectfully and earnestly ask the Local Government Board to rescind the document received by our Hon. Secretary re. Dr Creane [sic], as on the day of Dr Browne's visit Dr Creane was after [had done] a heavy morning's work and that same morning performed a serious operation and had not even breakfasted at noon when the Inspector arrived. We are all aware that Dr Creane has not been very strong lately consequently a small portion of stimulants would cause him to be irritable and excitable . . .

The Cashel Guardians endorsed the Dispensary Committee's resolution and suggested "that a caution from the LGB will meet the case."

The Local Government Board, set up in 1872, controlled health services in Ireland until after independence, when its functions were taken over by the Department of Local Government and Public Health. On the subject of Dr. Crean, it was not to be swayed, and on May 10, Fethard Dispensary Committee resolved that an advertisement be inserted in the newspaper for a duly qualified medical officer for the district. Dr. Crean was deemed to have resigned on May 2.

Four months later, when Michael Cleary, Jack Dunne, Patrick Boland, and the four Kennedy brothers were in jail, the Poor Law Guardians considered a motion from the Fethard Dispensary Committee, dated September 2, "to grant a pension to Dr William Creane [sic], late Medical Officer of Fethard Dispensary District, who has been incapacitated by ill health from discharging his duties and who has had accordingly to resign office." Medical certificates were attached: one, from Dr. C. Moloney, Mullinahone, stating that Dr. Crean was "suffering from general debility and [was] unfit for active duty," the other, signed by Dr. William Heffernan of Killenaule, claiming that he had been "for some time suffering from debility, chronic bronchitis and muscular rheumatism and unable to discharge his duties."

Again, the Cashel Guardians endorsed the Dispensary Committee's position, and voted Dr. Crean an annual pension of £45, subject to the Local Government Board's approval. But the board did not approve. On October 5, the Guardians received a letter to the effect that the Local Government Board was "unable to consent to any retiring allowance being made to Dr Crean." It is not known what became of the doctor following this disgrace. The 1901 census does not show anyone called Crean as head of a household in Fethard.

Fr. Con Ryan left the house in Ballyvadlea after he had spoken to Michael Cleary on the Wednesday afternoon. Cleary arrived indoors, bringing the wine, medicine, and herbs from Fethard, and found Mary Kennedy there with Johanna Burke, who had come to do the washing. Jack Dunne arrived shortly afterwards. He gave evidence about what happened. "He is an old man, but spoke intelligently," said the *Irish Times:*

> [Dunne] said that he went up to Michael Cleary's on Wednesday, and asked him what way was his wife. Cleary said that she was only very middling, and that the priest and doctor was with her. He (Dunne) went up to see her in the bed, and said to Cleary that she was not too bad.
>
> Cleary said, "I have something here which I'll give her, and 'twill make her better."
>
> "What are they?" said he (Dunne).
>
> Cleary replied, "They are herbs I got from a woman in Fethard."
>
> He (Dunne) saw the herbs given to her. He remained for about an hour, and then went home.

Dunne claims that he simply went home after watching Michael Cleary administer the herbs. Johanna Burke too told the court that she saw Cleary give something to his wife, but that she did not at first know what it was. "He told me it was herbs he gave her, that he got from a woman in Fethard," she said. However, her testimony at the July assizes shows Jack Dunne in a more active role:

Cleary then said to Dunne, "I have something here that will make her all right."

Dunne said, "It is not today you have a right [you ought] to get anything for her; it is not in Fethard you had a right to be for a doctor. Three days ago you had a right to be beyond with Ganey, for the doctor had nothing to do with her. It is not your wife is there. You will have enough to do to bring her back. This is the eighth day, and you had a right to have gone to Ganey on the fifth day."

He added that herbs should be given to her on the fifth day.

Hearing this evidence, Mr. Justice William O'Brien warned the jury at the July assizes that Johanna Burke might have been influenced to testify against Dunne by family feeling for Michael Cleary, her cousin's husband. He does not seem to have taken into account that she was, if anything, more closely related to Dunne, who was her mother's first cousin.

Jack Dunne's words as quoted amount to a clear diagnosis according to the terms of fairy belief: the real Bridget Cleary has been taken away, and must be rescued and brought back; the woman in the bed is not Bridget, but something put in her place by the fairies: a changeling. Instead of suggesting, therefore, that Bridget Cleary has spent time with the fairies in the past and so is somehow "different," Dunne seems to be saying that her condition is acute, not chronic, and that something must be done without delay.

Cross-examined in court by John Boursiquot Falconer, counsel for Michael Cleary, Johanna Burke again quoted Jack Dunne:

"Did he mention the name of the herb? Did he say it was 'lus-more'?" [Irish *lus mór,* foxglove, *Digitalis purpurea*]

"No, he said it was the seventh brother of the seventh sister or the seventh sister of the seventh brother, or something like that; he said that was the last herb that could be given to her, and he said it would either kill or cure; he had herbs in his hand, and he gave instructions to Michael Cleary to boil them and make the sign of the cross and go round the house making pishrogues. Cleary asked Dunne was he doing it right and Dunne said he was. Then Cleary went round the house using pishrogues and charms. Dunne whispered to Cleary so that I should not hear what the charm was."

"Pishrogue" is from the Irish *pisreog*. The word is usually glossed "charm," "spell," or, in the plural, "superstition," and can be heavily pejorative. The *Daily Express* says that what Michael Cleary got from the woman in Fethard was called "the seven cure," but that it failed to work. The seventh daughter of a seventh daughter, or the seventh son of a seventh son was (and in many places in Ireland still is) widely reputed to have special powers of healing. Apparently, too, it was common to count the days of an illness.[32]

Jack Dunne himself had some knowledge of herbs, but insisted that Denis Ganey of Kyleatlea, and not Dr. Crean of Fethard, should have been consulted about Bridget Cleary's illness. Ganey was the herb doctor or fairy doctor, the ninth person arrested when Bridget Cleary went missing. He did not visit Bridget Cleary, but he did prescribe an herbal remedy. He was popular, the *Cork Examiner* tells us, for ailments of animals and humans, including "blast," the name given to a range of sudden ailments, which were explained as attacks by the fairies. He never prescribed twice for the same case.

Lady Gregory, fascinated by herb doctors, once quoted an informant she called "Old Heffernan" in terms that remind us that Denis Ganey, like Jack Dunne, walked with a limp:

The best herb doctor ever I knew was Conolly up at Ballyturn. He knew every herb that grew in the earth. It was said he was away with the faeries one time, and when I knew him he had the two thumbs turned in, and it was said that was the sign they left on him.

Two years after Bridget Cleary's death, Lady Gregory went across the mountains from her home at Coole into County Clare in search of stories about the most famous herb doctor of all, Biddy Early. At that time a widow of forty-five, Augusta Gregory drove her pony, Shamrock, with the old-fashioned phaeton that had been a wedding present seventeen years before. She crossed "two unbridged rivers," found the healer's house, and spoke to several people. "Mr Mc-Cabe's" account of his dealings with Biddy Early sums up much of the authority and charisma of the fairy doctor:

> Biddy Early? Not far from this she lived, above at Feakle. I got cured by her myself one time. Look at this thumb—I got it hurted one time, and I went out into the field after and was ploughing all the day, I was that greedy for work. And when I went in I had to lie on the bed with the pain of it, and it swelled and the arm with it, to the size of a horse's thigh. I stopped two or three days in the bed with the pain of it, and then my wife went to see Biddy Early and told her about it and she came home and the next day it burst, and you never seen anything like all the stuff that came away from it. A good bit after I went to her myself, where it wasn't quite healed, and she said, "You'd have lost it altogether if your wife hadn't been so quick to come." She brought me into a small room, and said holy words and sprinkled holy water and told me to believe. The priests were against her, but they were wrong. How could that be evil doing that was all charity and kindness and healing?[33]

Charity and kindness and healing are here explicitly opposed to the social evil of working so hard as to neglect other needs.

The measures taken by fairy doctors were often described, as in Johanna Burke's evidence, as "pishogues" or "pish[e]rogues," (*piseog* or *pisreog*). The word will occur again before Bridget Cleary finally meets her death. For the moment, however, we leave her in bed in the cottage in Ballyvadlea on the Wednesday night, distressed, unhappy, and feverish. She may have eaten some of the chicken her aunt had cooked, but "her face was very red, and she was sweating," Johanna Burke told the July assizes in Clonmel. "Her husband gave her claret wine to drink," she added.

5

"Take It, You Witch!"

THE CLEARYS' COTTAGE in Ballyvadlea, with the hill of Tullowcossaun behind it, looks south across the Anner Valley, toward Slievenamon. Below the mountain, the river flows east-west, left to right, before turning south to join Fethard's Clashawley and flow into the Suir below Clonmel. Thursday morning, March 14, was overcast, but much warmer than the day before. Standing at his front door, Michael Cleary would have seen the prow of the mountain to his right, with the valley opening up beyond it toward prosperous, modern Clonmel, eleven miles away. To the left was the way back up the valley, toward Kyleatlea, where Denis Ganey, the fairy doctor, lived, on the northern slope of Slievenamon.

"Three days ago you had a right to be beyond with Ganey," Jack Dunne is reported to have told Cleary on Wednesday night. He meant that Cleary ought to have consulted the fairy doctor by the fifth day of his wife's illness. By Wednesday, Michael Cleary and his father-in-law, with help from Mary Kennedy and Johanna Burke, had nursed the feverish Bridget for over a week, watching her condition deteriorate. Between them they had made three attempts to fetch Dr. Crean from Fethard, but even when he had finally arrived they had had little satisfaction. He did not take her condition particularly seriously; Michael Cleary was not present for the consultation, and, when he did meet Crean, both were angry and the doctor, apparently, had been drinking. Fr. Con Ryan had come from Drangan to visit Bridget Cleary too, but had brought no reassurance. Indeed, by administering the last rites he had appeared to give his parishioner up for dead.

Meanwhile, Jack Dunne continued to talk of fairies. Michael Cleary's faith in Dr. Crean's medicine had evidently been seriously undermined by Wednesday afternoon, when he had consulted an herb woman in Fethard. That evening, he had dosed his wife with the herb woman's prescription, although he does not mention this in his own account of what happened:

> Petitionar,s [*sic*] wife got sick and was attended by the Doctor of the District, but his treatment did not benefit her she became dispondent and emaciated, she was also attended by the Clergy, and no hopes was, entertained of her recovery. Friends came to the house to see her, a Man naimed Dunne a first cousin to the deceased,s Father came to see her and had a conversation with her Father and the other relations who was present gave it as his opinion that it was from no ordinary illness she suffered he said it was a case of witchcraft they listened to him and after a time gave credit to his story.

So wrote Michael Cleary on November 8, 1902, in Maryborough Prison. He was adamant that it was Dunne who had insisted that he consult Denis Ganey:

> It was believed in the locality that Dunne had knowledge in the use of Herbs, And told petitionar he would rid his wife of the enchament if the treatment which he perscribed was carried out, so Dunne and the other Friends and petitionar,s Fatherin-law insisted on petitionar to go to a quack or fairy Doctor 3 miles from Petitionar,s house to get the Herbs from him he said it would not do to have any other person get them but the womans husbant. Petitionar at the time was foolish enough to do anything he would be told do especially when it was for his wifes welfare. So he brought the Herbs to Dunne and they were perscribed by him as was proved at court.

In another petition addressed to the Lord Lieutenant three years later, on June 28, 1905, Cleary reiterated the story, adding the detail that he set out for Kyleatlea at first light on Thursday morning:

When the Priest left the house [on Wednesday]. Patrick Bolan and Mrs Kennedy Mrs Burke and John Dunne wre[sic] in the house and told Petitionar that if he did not do what they would tell him his wife would dye in a day or two Dunne told Petitionar that it was not a case for the Doctor atall. Next morning at 6 oclock Petitionar went to a quack docto [sic] the name of Geainy about 4 miles from Petitionars house he done as they had told him and brought the Herbs that he got from the quack doctor . . .

Before he left Ballyvadlea on March 14, Michael Cleary called at Mary Kennedy's house and asked her to go up to visit his wife. He also asked a neighbor to fetch Jack Dunne, and sent a messenger to Drangan, to request the priest to call to the house again. Fr. Ryan told the magistrates that "On [Thursday] morning at about 7 o'clock he was called to see her, but he told the messenger that having administered the last rites of the Church on the previous occasion there was no need to see her so soon again."

According to Jack Dunne's testimony, "a girl of the name of Mary Smith" came to his house with a message that Michael Cleary wanted him; "that he could not depend on the lot that was about him." Dunne walked the mile or so from Kylenagranagh to Ballyvadlea, and was at the Clearys' house there when Michael arrived home from Kyleatlea. Again, in giving evidence, Dunne minimized his own role:

I was not there very long till he came. "I have something now," says he, "that will cure her."

"What have you?" said I.

"I have herbs that there is nine cures in; it will be very hard to make her take this. You must assist me with her, and she will be cured then."

We gave it to her then, so I sat down to the fire then for a few minutes.

Johanna Burke may also have been in the house at this stage. She went to Cloneen between four and five o'clock, "for bread for my children" she told the magistrates, but came back to the Clearys' house as darkness fell, about seven. She left again at some point, and returned later with her daughter, Katie. Mary Kennedy, Johanna Burke's mother, was also there more than once during the day.

Michael Cleary was showing signs of strain by Thursday evening. He had been up and out early both that day and the day before, and had lost a lot of sleep during the previous week. He had had an altercation with the dispensary doctor; the priest had declined his appeal to visit his wife a second time; she was still sick, and now, to crown it all, the message came that his father had died in Killenaule. As we have seen, the wake was being held in Killenaule, but Cleary made no move to go to it.

At some time during the afternoon or evening, William Ahearne came to the house. He was from Kylenagranagh: a neighbor of Jack Dunne's. Aged sixteen, and described as "delicate," he had been sent by his mother to ask after Bridget Cleary's health, and he may have been present when Cleary and Dunne administered the herbs for the first time. When night fell, Ahearne suggested to Dunne that they might walk home together. Dunne agreed, but Michael Cleary objected: "Cleary told me I would not go yet, as he wanted me for another start [another while]; this was about 8 or 9 at night."[1]

Some time after nine o'clock, Mary Kennedy's sons Patrick and James arrived at the house, followed shortly afterwards by their younger brother William, who asked if they were going to the wake. They said they were, but Michael Cleary told them they could not go yet. He told James Kennedy that "his wife was better, that he was after giving her herbs he had got from Ganey, over the mountain, and they done her good; he said he suffered so much about his wife he would suffer more." William Kennedy saw him by the fire with a saucepan, "with some green things and new milk." Cleary told him that "he had some herbs he wanted to give his wife, and that he should give them before they went."

Michael Kennedy, the fourth brother, who had walked from Drangan and followed his mother to the house, arrived about now. He too asked if his brothers were going to the wake, but they told him they could not go yet, and he saw Michael Cleary lock the door. According to Dunne again:

> "I think then," said [Cleary] after a start, "it is time to give her this." He had it in a pint which he held against his breast; the four of us caught her and I had her by the neck; it was very hard on her to take it; Cleary told me that after taking that she should be brought to the fire; so we brought her to the fire; we raised her over it, but did not burn her; I thought it belonged to the cure; he told me it belonged to the cure.

By this time, there were nine people in the house along with the sick Bridget Cleary: her husband Michael; her father Patrick Boland; her aunt Mary Kennedy; her four cousins, Patrick, Michael, James, and William Kennedy; Jack Dunne; and William Ahearne.

William and Minnie Simpson, the emergencyman and his wife, left their home to visit Bridget Cleary sometime before ten o'clock. About thirty yards from the cottage, they met Johanna Burke, also on her way there, with eleven-year-old Katie. Johanna Burke told them that herbs were being given to Bridget Cleary, which her husband had got "from Ganey over the mountain." She herself was bringing a fresh supply of "new milk" to the house.

The first milk given by a cow after calving is also known as "beestings" or "beastlings," *nús* in Irish. It has a strong smell and flavor, and is especially rich in nutrients and antibodies. It was said to be particularly attractive to the fairies, who could be prevented from stealing the cow if the beestings were poured in a fairy fort, or at the roots of a fairy thorn—a lone thorn tree said to belong to the "good people"—or if it were simply allowed to spill on the ground. After calving, the cow should be milked into a bucket containing a coin or other piece of metal. The cure prescribed by Denis Ganey—or by Jack Dunne, perhaps—seems to have required that certain herbs be boiled in this new milk and given to Bridget Cleary.[2]

When the Simpsons and the Burkes, mother and daughter, arrived at the house, they found the door locked; the men inside were forcing Bridget Cleary to drink the herbal mixture. They heard loud shouting from the front bedroom, whose window was directly in front of them. "Take that, you rap!" a man's voice said, but the wooden shutters were closed inside the glass and they could see nothing. They knocked on the door, but Michael Cleary shouted from inside that no one could come in yet, so they waited for some five minutes. Standing outside, they heard words that sounded like "Take it, you old bitch, or I'll kill you!" or perhaps "Take it, you witch!"

Eventually, Michael Cleary opened the door, and the four went in. William Simpson heard someone shouting "Away she go! Away she go!" He could not say who had said it, but understood that the door had been opened to let the fairy or fairies out. Michael Cleary told Simpson that the house was full of fairies.

Patrick Boland was in the kitchen, where the large oil lamp was burning, but almost everyone else was in the bedroom. Bridget Cleary was lying in bed, wearing a striped flannel nightdress over a calico chemise, and Jack Dunne, who was not tall, but weighed 176 pounds, was sitting on the bed beside her, gripping both her ears to hold her head down. Thirty-two-year-old Patrick Kennedy was on the far side of the bed, also sitting or lying on it, pinning down his cousin's right arm, while his brother James held her left arm. The youngest of the Kennedys, twenty-one-year-old William, lay across Bridget Cleary's legs to prevent her moving them. Michael Cleary stood beside the bed, holding a small saucepan—what Jack Dunne called a "pint"—and a spoon. Young William Ahearne was in the bedroom too, holding a candle, while Mary Kennedy hovered anxiously near the door.

Bridget Cleary struggled and protested as her husband tried to force the "medicine" down her throat. William Simpson heard her "scream a little," and said she appeared to be in pain. She told the men to leave her alone. She said the medicine was bitter, and clamped her mouth shut to resist taking it.

When Michael Cleary was being tried for his wife's murder the following July, this was how the *Irish Times* reported Johanna Burke's description of the scene:

Cleary was giving her medicine—some herbs on a spoon. Bridget Cleary was trying not to take it. She said it was too bitter. When Cleary put the milk into the mouth he put his hand on her mouth to prevent the medicine coming up. He said if it went on the ground that she could not be brought back from the fairies. Cleary asked her was she Bridget Cleary or Bridget Boland, wife of Michael Cleary, in the name of God. He asked her more than once. She answered three times before he was satisfied.

William Simpson, who remained by the kitchen fire, heard these questions put repeatedly, and said that the sick woman answered a few times. Finally, Michael Cleary succeeded in forcing some of the herbal mixture down his wife's throat.

This was the third dose. Already, before the arrival of the Simpsons with Johanna Burke and Katie, Bridget Cleary had been forced to swallow the mixture twice. William Simpson and his wife both noticed a slight burn mark on her forehead. They were told that a hot poker had been brandished in her face on the first occasion to make her take the mixture. Johanna Burke seems to have been present when this happened, for at the July assizes she recalled that Jack Dunne had heated the poker in the kitchen fire and brought it to the bed.

Iron and fire are both well-known weapons against the fairies. Another is human urine, often mixed with hen's droppings, and mentioned frequently, though usually briefly, in published collections of Irish folklore and in the archives of the Irish Folklore Collection. The men who waited at Kylenagranagh Fort after Bridget Cleary's death, to see her ride out on horseback, carried black-handled knives, but some versions of the legend that underlies their action specify that urine and chicken dung must be thrown at the woman to rescue her.[3] Some newspapers quoted witnesses as saying that "wine and water" were thrown on Bridget Cleary as she lay in bed, but others mention "a noxious fluid," and some specify urine. Urine is certainly what was meant. William Simpson said that Mary Kennedy brought water to the bedroom when Cleary called for it, but here is her own testimony as reported in the *Cork Examiner:*

He had an old black pint by the side of the bed. "Mary," says he, "reach me that pint."

"What do you want of it; is it to drown her?" I was reaching him the pint and he snapped it out of my hand. He threw it then on her face and drowned [drenched] her.

According to William Simpson, Bridget Cleary was drenched like this three or four times while he was in the house. After she had swallowed the herbs for the third time, a man on either side of the bed lifted her and shook her back and forth:

[H]er legs were still on the bed, and the men holding her arms on both sides and her head, they lifted her body and wound it backwards and forwards.[4]

As this was done, all together shouted, "Away with you; come home, Bridget Boland, in the name of God!" The men slapped her hands, or clapped them together. Bridget Cleary "screamed terribly."

Throughout this manhandling, and her violent force-feeding with herbs and new milk, the men who were gathered around the sick woman's bed continued to ask her, "Are you Bridget Boland, wife of Michael Cleary, in the name of God?" She must not have answered loudly or strongly enough, because both Johanna Burke and William Simpson testified that Jack Dunne said, "Make down a good fire and we will make her answer."

The fire was burning slowly in the kitchen grate. No fuel was added, but the men who had been immobilizing and then "winding" Bridget Cleary in her bed lifted her and carried her to the fireplace: Jack Dunne still had hold of her head, but now James Kennedy, who had been on the near side of the bed all along, took her feet. Michael Cleary followed with the spoon and saucepan, and her father moved to hold her body clear of the bars of the grate. Bridget Cleary was conscious, and apparently well aware of what was going on: Minnie Simpson and her husband heard her tell the men "not to make a herring of her," and to "give her a chance." She almost seems to have been joking with them. William Simpson recalled:

I remember the position she was in; I can see it all before me now; her head was to the left of the grate, and her right hip rested on it; her legs were partly projecting out.

He also said that when she was placed upon the grate "she gave no evidence of being in pain. She did not scream."

Simpson heard people say that if the questions were not answered by midnight, the "real" Bridget Cleary would be lost forever. It was now after half past eleven. At the fireplace, Patrick Boland let go of his daughter's body long enough to ask her again, "Are you the daughter of Patrick Boland, wife of Michael Cleary? Answer in the name of God."

"I am, Dada," Bridget Cleary replied, according to Simpson's evidence. Her husband then asked a similar question, and again she answered, "I am the daughter of Pat Boland, in the name of God!" She was kept at the fireplace for about ten minutes in all. The men then carried her back to her bed.

Midnight passed, and the atmosphere in the house changed. Bridget Cleary was still severely distressed: her eyes were rolling around. Minnie Simpson said that she was "raving—talking as if she did not know what she was saying," while William Simpson heard her say something about "leaving the house and going home." Johanna Burke described her cousin as "wild and deranged," but the men were noticeably more relaxed. "They were satisfied that they had their own," according to William Simpson—meaning that the woman before them was Bridget Cleary, and not a changeling. "They were all delighted at it," he said, as they assured each other that the treatment had worked.

If the object of the exercise had been to break the will of a woman who was not conforming to social expectations, then it certainly seemed to have worked: back in bed, Bridget Cleary must have been a pathetic sight, her nightdress and chemise streaked with soot and soaked in urine. The men now held back, while the women moved to help her. William Simpson heard Mary Kennedy and Johanna Burke say they must put some dry clothing on her. Torture gave way to domesticity as Johanna Burke produced a fresh nightdress, which she aired in front of the fire, and Minnie Simpson helped Mary Kennedy to remove Bridget Cleary's soiled clothing and put the clean garment on her.

When the sick woman's clothes had been changed, the men gathered around her bed again, but less threateningly this time. Michael Cleary pointed to them one by one, asking his wife if she recognized them, and she did. "The people then began to console her," Minnie Simpson said, "saying that she would be all right now." But William Simpson recalled that Bridget Cleary asked him "what had the police there, and why was the kitchen filled with smoke?" "I said they came to see her; she asked me who were they, and I said the sergeant from Cloneen and Constable Morgan. She made some remark about them that they were nice men or something to that effect." Colonel Evanson, the resident magistrate in Clonmel, was puzzled by this evidence. "If they were not really there," he asked Simpson, "what was your object in telling her that they were?"

"To satisfy her mind," Simpson replied.

According to Jack Dunne's testimony, the men who carried Bridget Cleary to the kitchen fire and held her over it "did not burn her." This evidence was corroborated by several people who were present: witness after witness said that the fire was low, and that holding Bridget Cleary over it did her no physical harm. Johanna Burke said she had built the fire up with green whitethorn stumps, which would not burn quickly unless they were dry, and that she had not done so with any intention of burning her cousin; she simply wanted to make tea. Minnie Simpson noticed that the lower part of the fire was lighting but the upper part was not: "I don't think it would be enough to boil a kettle," she said. Katie Burke saw all that went on: "Michael Cleary and John Dunne brought her down to the fire to frighten her. They left her there only a few minutes. There was hardly any fire." A small burn mark was found on the sick woman's flannel nightdress, which was produced in court, and William Simpson caused a sensation when he mentioned having smelt it scorching. William Kennedy had rubbed it between his fingers at the fireplace, presumably to extinguish a spark, but there was no other evidence of burning on Thursday night.

The testimony of these witnesses horrified the readers of news-papers published in Clonmel, Cork, Dublin, London, and Manches-ter, who read of it on March 25, 26, 27, and 28, days after Bridget Cleary's grotesquely burned body was discovered in its rough grave. The newspaper accounts conveyed the terror Bridget Cleary must have felt. The picture they painted was one of cruelty, but also of a chilling deliberation on the part of the men who had carried out the treatment, and an incomprehensible callousness in those who had watched. Knowing that the unfortunate woman had died of burns, people who read these reports—and the journalists who wrote them—could only interpret her being held over the grate as part of this lethal burning: a sadistic, systematic torture by fire. An editorial in the *Dublin Evening Mail* of March 25 set the tone:

> [The] History of Witchcraft contains nothing more horrible than the cruelties practised on Bridget Cleary by a number of persons acting under the impression that the screaming thing they were searing with red-hot irons and holding over a fire, and otherwise ill-treating, was not a human being and a woman whom they well knew, but a demon who had taken possession of her form. Eleven persons are in custody for this crime, and among them is her husband, Michael Cleary, and a medicine-man named Ganey, who concocted, it is said, the herbs which the unfortunate woman was brutally compelled to swallow. A long series of cruelties culminated on the 14th instant in atroc-ities which proved fatal, and which were witnessed by a crowd of "neighbours," not one of whom interfered, by hand or word, on behalf of the victim of superstition.

As we know, however, Bridget Cleary did not die until the night of Friday, March 15. On the Thursday evening, she was cruelly man-handled, but "searing [a screaming thing] with red-hot irons" does seem to exaggerate the drama of what went on, and it is hard to imagine that anyone could have predicted what was yet to happen.

All the witnesses agreed about what the men had done, and ac-knowledged that no one had attempted to stop them, but they differed significantly about who had been in charge. Jack Dunne presented himself as merely following Michael Cleary's instructions, while most of the others alleged that Dunne was the ringleader, but any or all of them may have decided to make him, or indeed Cleary, the scapegoat at different times. All by their presence were implicated in what may have started as a defensible, if horribly cruel, ordeal, but turned out to be a killing, and each was surely anxious to deflect blame from himself or herself.

With hindsight, we know that the story was by no means over, but for those who were present it seems to have come to a satisfactory conclusion about midnight on Thursday. Bridget Cleary had been severely maltreated, and some of the language used shows that her husband's temper at least was running high, but a ritual healing process had been three times completed, and a kind of catharsis achieved. Many procedures of orthodox medicine at the end of the nineteenth century would have required the patient to be held down by force; the herbal mixture may have had some effect in treating Bridget Cleary's respiratory condition, and even the grim ritual of holding her over the fire could have had its origin in a traditional therapy for fever. Certainly, however, Michael Cleary had been engaged in a psychological struggle, although it is difficult to say with whom. He may have thought his wife, ill as she was, was his adversary, but he may just as well have felt that Jack Dunne, or Johanna Burke, or even William Simpson was his tormentor.

Michael Cleary had no relatives close by, as far as the record shows; in fact his father had just died, two hours' walk away. For over a week his wife's relatives had been in and out of his home, shaking their heads and making dark insinuations about her condition. A suggestion that she was away with the fairies was a serious reflection on him and on their marriage, which was, we remember, childless. It was an unusual marriage, too, in that for a number of years Cleary had continued to work in Clonmel, visiting his wife only at weekends. In an outburst before the magistrates in Clonmel, he denied that Bridget's cousin Johanna Burke had been a friend to him or his wife, and described how she and her father, Richard Kennedy, had angered him during that time:

> I worked here in the town of Clonmel four years ago and her father, who is dead now and herself could do nothing to me but run away with my character behind my back to my wife. Her father used to say, "Oh it is seldom he will come home to her now; he has plenty of women where he is, and seldom will do to see her."

But Michael Cleary was not the only one whose fidelity was in question. Rumors were in circulation, and are still remembered around Ballyvadlea, that Bridget Cleary had a lover. Newspapers reported her husband as saying that "she used to be meeting an egg-man on the low road," but local farmer Patrick Power, who grew up when an older generation still remembered these events, was told that she was "involved" with the emergencyman William Simpson. When local shopkeepers refused to serve Simpson, it is said, Bridget Cleary did his shopping, but people were convinced that there was more to the relationship than that. Both William Simpson and Bridget Cleary were in their twenties; both emerge from the various sources that recall them as ambitious, clever, sexually attractive, and arrogant; it may be that both were also dissatisfied with their marriages. Simpson's wife was ten years older than he was and, in a society that valued sons, had borne only two daughters, while Bridget Cleary was married to a man nine years her senior, and their marriage was childless. For the pretty young dressmaker, the emergencyman with his neatly trimmed mustache and the wing collar he wore on formal occasions, may have been more attractive than her cooper husband.

A story told to Edmund Lenihan in County Clare about the famous healer, Biddy Early, offers another clue as to the meaning of the night's activities. Biddy Early, it seems, was not popular with women, who resented the amount of time their husbands spent drinking whiskey with her:

> Their husbands went an' drank, an' came home drunk. An'
> they made out that the women followed her an' burned her,
> rose up her clothes an' burned her on the rump when she got
> married the fourth time. They make out that, that the women
> were disgusted with her.

Perhaps burning on the buttocks was a punishment for sexual mis-
conduct?[5]

Certainly Michael Cleary's behavior at his wife's bedside on that
Thursday evening had something in it of frantic display. People were
talking about Bridget Cleary; she was an attractive and strong-
minded woman, who enjoyed a higher level of personal and economic independence than most of her peers. Those who were
jealous of her would have gained a certain satisfaction from seeing
her chastened by illness, while stories about her abduction by fairies
could have been a euphemistic way of noting her extramarital activities. Michael Cleary's success as a cooper, and his economic prosperity, would be of very little use to him if he could not convince his
neighbors and his wife's relatives that he was man enough to keep her
and even to control her.

The house grew quiet after Bridget Cleary was settled in her bed
around midnight; tea was made at last, and Jack Dunne drank some.
Michael Kennedy woke up in Patrick Boland's bedroom and joined
his brothers and the other neighbors in the kitchen, where he sat on
the table for a while, all the chairs being taken. The visitors stayed
until about one o'clock, when the four Kennedy brothers set off for
the wake in Killenaule. Michael Cleary still refused to go, but told
them to tell his mother that he "had his wife back from the fairies."
Jack Dunne and young William Ahearne were the next to leave, at
about two in the morning, but the Simpsons remained, as did Mary
Kennedy, Johanna Burke, and Katie Burke. They sat talking until first
light, about six, "speaking to Mrs Cleary and taking her drinks as she
called . . . endeavouring to put her to sleep," as William Simpson testified. "She was nervous and not sensible," Johanna Burke remembered, and did not sleep at all.

Simpson and his wife went home before the sun rose. Mary Kennedy set out to return to her house at Ballyvadlea bridge, taking the exhausted Katie with her, and Michael Cleary set off for Drangan to call on Fr. Ryan yet again. As William Simpson said, "They thought there were some evil spirits in the house, and they wanted to have Mass said to banish them."

6

"Bridgie Is Burned!"

AT ABOUT SEVEN O'CLOCK on Friday morning, March 15, Michael Cleary arrived on foot at Fr. Con Ryan's house in Drangan. The priest had given Bridget Cleary the last rites of the church two days before, but he had refused to come a second time when summoned on Thursday morning. Now the sick woman's husband asked him again to come to Ballyvadlea.

"He told me she had had a very bad night, and he asked me to go to the house to say Mass," the priest told Colonel Evanson, the resident magistrate, on April 1.

"Did you go?"

"Yes. I followed him riding on horseback, and arrived about eight fifteen. My horse was taken to the house of Mr Shea of Garrangyle, in the neighborhood." Farmers, unlike laborers and artisans, kept horses. New laborers' cottages, though equipped with pigsties and privies, did not have stables. Neither did priests normally make social, rather than pastoral, visits to such houses. Garrangyle, or Garrankyle, is the townland directly to the southwest of Ballyvadlea. The census returns for 1901 do not show any Sheas living there, but a Thomas Shea, farmer, aged seventy-one, is listed as sharing a second-class house in Ballyvadlea with his wife Anne, seventy-three, and their unmarried thirty-year-old daughter Bridget. All were Catholic and could read and write; their household also included twenty-eight-year-old Edmond Connors, an unmarried servant.

Fr. Ryan said mass in Bridget Cleary's bedroom, and gave her

Holy Communion. He told Colonel Evanson and the other magistrates that although she appeared "more nervous and excited" on Friday morning than when he had seen her on Wednesday, "notwithstanding her wild and excited looks, Mrs Cleary's conversations were coherent and intelligent." In all, he spent less than an hour at the house. Before he had finished, he said, "Miss Shea" arrived to ask him to go down to breakfast. This was probably Bridget Shea, then aged twenty-four, come to offer the priest the hospitality of her family's house, which, though built of mud and roofed with thatch, was a substantial dwelling with five rooms and seven outbuildings.[1]

As the priest left the cottage, he asked Michael Cleary if he was giving his wife the medicine the doctor had ordered. Cleary replied that he had no faith in the doctor's medicine. "I said what a pity it was," Fr. Ryan recalled, "to give the trouble to a doctor of calling him in and not to use his medicine. I told him that I thought the medicine was good. I tasted it and smelled it, and said that he ought to give it to her. Cleary then said, 'People may have some remedy of their own that might do more good than doctor's medicine,' or something to that effect."

Michael Cleary claimed in his prison petition quoted in Chapter 4 that the priest did not approve of the medicine Dr. Crean had prescribed, and that he spoke of him as "always drunk." Fr. Ryan's own testimony here appears to contradict Cleary's, but the middle class may have been closing ranks to protect the dispensary doctor's reputation, as the Poor Law Guardians certainly attempted to do in the months that followed. Middle-class solidarity would explain Fr. Ryan's account to the court of his Friday visit to the house, and his claim that he advised Michael Cleary to give his wife the medicine as prescribed. He might nevertheless have spoken of Dr. Crean's drunkenness to Michael Cleary on the Wednesday, as Cleary maintains. It is clear in any case that between Wednesday and Friday, Michael Cleary lost whatever faith he might have had in the power of dispensary medicine to cure his wife. After her body was discovered, the *Cork Examiner* reporter found a mineral-water bottle in a corner of the empty cottage.

It was stained with a thick, yellowish liquid; medicine prescribed by the Fairy-doctor, but never used—so William Simpson told me. The directions on the printed label were—"Four teaspoonfuls to be taken in a little of water three times a day."

But of course this must have been the medicine prescribed by Dr. Crean, not by Denis Ganey. Fairy doctors did not use printed labels, and Ganey's medicine—herbs boiled in new milk—had, as we have seen, been used on Thursday, the day before Bridget Cleary died, while the "seven cure," obtained in Fethard, had been administered on Wednesday.

While Fr. Ryan was saying mass in the Clearys' bedroom on Friday morning, Johanna Burke was in the kitchen; she seems to have stayed at the house after the others had left in the early hours, and to have remained with her cousin while Michael Cleary went to Drangan to fetch the priest. In March 1895, she was the mother of an eight-week-old infant daughter, whom, as we have seen, she carried in her arms throughout the magistrates' inquiry. The surviving records make no mention of a baby at this point, but we must imagine that the baby, who was called Johanna after her mother, was with her in the Clearys' house. Fr. Ryan mentioned seeing Michael Cleary, Patrick Boland (who must have already returned from Killenaule), and a neighbor called Miss or Mrs. Nagle at the house too.

Like Fr. Ryan, Johanna Burke told the magistrates that the sick woman "looked nervous."

"Did she get up at all during Mass?"

"No, she was not sensible. I know she did not swallow the Holy Communion. I saw her take it out. That is why I say she had not the whole of her sense."

A Clonmel solicitor, Richard J. Crean of Abbey Street, a nephew of the Fethard dispensary doctor appeared for Michael Cleary and Denis Ganey at the magistrates' inquiry. He cross-examined Fr. Con Ryan about his administering Holy Communion. The priest replied that there was no person in the room at the time except the boy who served mass, Bridget Cleary, and himself.

"Would it be true if a witness swore that Bridget Cleary took the Holy Communion out of her mouth and did not swallow it?"

"I would not like to swear it is untrue, but I don't think it is true," Fr. Ryan replied. He went on to say that he had never heard anything against Michael Cleary's character. District Inspector Wansbrough intervened then, to point out that the bedroom door had been open during mass. The priest would have had his back to his tiny congregation, so would not have been in a position to observe who was there, or what they did; however, those in the kitchen could have kept an eye on what was going on in the bedroom. "If any Catholic saw Bridget Cleary remove the Blessed Sacrament from her mouth," Fr. Ryan reminded the magistrates, "he would be strictly bound to tell me at once, so as to enable me to save the Sacred Species from profanation."

At the summer assizes in July 1895, Mr. Justice William O'Brien, one of only seven Catholic judges on the Irish bench, questioned Johanna Burke further about her evidence concerning the Holy Communion: "Did you see anything which led you to believe she had not swallowed the sacred particle?"

> No, but she said to me, "Father Ryan put something in my mouth to save me," and she put her finger in her mouth, and said, "Look, Han," taking some little thing out of her mouth and rubbing it in the blanket. I afterwards asked Mike Cleary did Father Ryan give Bridget Communion, and he told me Father Ryan called him outside and asked him was the Mass for Bridget's purpose. He said "Yes," and Father Ryan said, "If so, I will give her Communion."

This was circumstantial evidence that Bridget Cleary had removed the communion host from her mouth with her fingers—something strictly forbidden by Catholic teaching—but it may also have indicated a much greater sacrilege, and one that smacked of magic ritual.

Johanna Burke's evidence was central to the case taken by the Crown against Michael Cleary and several others, including her own mother and four brothers. It must be read with caution, however, for it is often confusing, and sometimes seems deliberately so. Johanna Burke was only a few years older than Bridget Cleary, but led a very different life, and had every reason to be jealous of her cousin, as indeed Michael Cleary's outbursts in court suggest she was. Her "information," sworn before William Walker Tennant of Ballinard Castle immediately after her cousin disappeared, contained at least one blatant lie, for she said that Bridget Cleary had pushed past her out of the house on the Friday night and had not been seen since. Then, when the body was found, Johanna Burke was herself arrested. It is likely that the police used the day or so during which she was in custody to spell out the consequences for her and for her children if she were found guilty, as well as the protection and other inducements they could offer her if she were to testify, for they needed a witness. Johanna Burke soon turned Queen's evidence and bought immunity for herself, at the expense of her family and neighbors.

Inconsistencies in the evidence Johanna Burke gave in court may have been due to fear, but, even while Bridget was still alive on the Thursday and Friday, Johanna Burke seems to have behaved disingenuously. Considerable confusion and disagreement surrounded the question of whether or not she had been paid for the milk she had brought to the house. Her suggestion that Bridget Cleary had "rubbed something in the blanket" after receiving Holy Communion recalls some of that discussion. In her evidence she spoke of the sick woman having taken a shilling from her on the Friday, which she had just been given by Michael Cleary, and putting it under the blankets before handing it back. Michael Cleary accused his wife that evening of rubbing the shilling to her thigh—a suggestion Bridget Cleary angrily rebutted, saying "there were no pishogues about her!"

Although the connection is almost never made explicit, *piseog* is a diminutive form of the Irish word for the vulva, *pis* or *pit*. *Piseog* can also have the very specific meaning of malevolent sympathetic magic, when something organic is hidden and left to rot on another's land. The belief was widely held, and still prevails in places, that that person's well-being would decay as a result. As with voodoo dolls, it is not difficult to understand the devastating psychological effect the practice would have, while of course it could also have served to spread infection and disease among animals and people.

The *piseog's* semantic connection with the hidden, taboo places of the female body is underlined in this description, based on anthropological fieldwork carried out in the late twentieth century in north County Cork, no great distance from southeast Tipperary:

> The practice consists of making a *piseog,* which is frequently a nest of hay or straw in which is placed a piece of rotting meat or rotten eggs or a used sanitary towel. This is then hidden on the land of the person one wishes to use it against. The logic of the belief is that as the *piseog* decays so will the good luck of the farmer. When these *piseogs* are discovered—and it may be that, in some cases, they are meant to be discovered—certain procedures are recommended for disposing of them. The following is typical. Firstly, holy water is sprinkled on the *piseog* before it is touched, then it is lifted with a makeshift shovel, the shovel and the *piseog* are then burned in the ditch or in the corner of a field. It is believed that a burning *piseog* gives off brilliantly coloured flames and a dreadful stench. Finally a prayer is said for the perpetrators and holy water sprinkled liberally over the area. In some cases of very bad or persistent *piseogery* St Benedict is invoked for protection. Often medals of St Benedict will be blessed by the priest or by missioners and hung in the house and outbuildings of the farm or buried in the fields. In severe attacks the priest might be called in to say Mass and bless the farm and buildings and animals for protection. In this area of Co. Cork it is believed that families practising *piseogery* die out after one or two generations.[2]

The purification ritual, used here in combination with the trappings of Catholicism, supplies a context for the fear Bridget Cleary's behavior and illness inspired, and for the summoning of Fr. Ryan to say mass in her room. We remember that those who were said to consort with the fairies were usually marginal, transitional, or eccentric, and that they were often unable to have children, so that their families too died out. The huge oral repertoire of Irish fairy narrative constantly reinforces the idea that it is a mistake to sacrifice long-term stability for short-term gain, or to place individual interests above those of the community. People who would allow envy to dominate them to the extent of hiding rotting matter on a neighbor's land were dangerous to everyone, but so were those who were selfish, or impatient, or overly materialistic, or who acted, for whatever reason, without consideration for past and future generations. The description given above suggests too that women's sexuality, when not controlled within the orderly progressions of marriage and pregnancy, was seen as horrifically powerful.

Fr. Con Ryan's predecessor, Fr. John Power, is said to be the priest remembered in the following anecdote about Bridget Cleary, which was told to historian Thomas McGrath on two separate occasions in 1979. It underlines the independence and haughtiness for which Bridget Cleary is remembered, but also recalls a well-known scenario in oral tradition, which features a confrontation, often involving a horse, between a priest and a woman reputed to have special powers.[3]

> The story goes that Mrs Cleary was straining potatoes in her yard when the local priest chanced to ride by. Mrs Cleary's dog attacked the priest's horse and he asked her to call off the dog, but she made no attempt to do so and the priest kicked the dog out of his way. Mrs Cleary reacted by throwing boiling water from the potatoes at him. When this happened the priest told her to beware that she would die a violent death—a death by fire.[4]

The priest was the minister of a religion whose doctrines were dictated by Rome, but he was also credited with powerful magic and moral authority. Stories of the fairies often end with their banishment by a priest, and a mass said in the house had something about it of the power of exorcism. It was a decisive way of reestablishing normality, a ritual of purification. In terms of social dynamics, it also represented a substantial and highly visible symbolic investment in conformity, for people would not dream of asking a priest to say mass, especially in a private home, without making him a handsome gift of money. Cynics commented on the quasi-commercial nature of these transactions, and on the preference some priests showed for those who could best support them financially, with the tag, "High money, high mass; low money, low mass; no money, no mass!"[5] Rates for masses were well known, and were beyond the means of the poor, but the Clearys were not poor, and by summoning the priest a second time to their house, they let their neighbors know this.

William Simpson, Protestant neighbor, friend, and rumored to be the lover of Bridget Cleary, visited her again late on Friday morning, after the priest had left. She was in bed. She seemed weaker, he said, and he found her appearance changed. She was drinking milk, Johanna Burke was with her, and her husband Michael was outside with Jack Dunne. Simpson asked the sick woman whether she recognized him. She said she did, and he pointed to his dog, which she also recognized. That was the last time he saw her alive.

Simpson had left, but Michael Cleary, Jack Dunne, and Johanna Burke were still at the house when another neighbor, Thomas Smyth, arrived. He was a farmer, but evidently in a small way, for by the time of the 1901 census he was still living in a one-room, windowless, thatched house in Ballyvadlea, which he shared with his twenty-three-year-old daughter Bridget. Smyth, aged fifty-four in 1895, was ploughing in a field near the Clearys' house when he heard of Bridget Cleary's illness and took a break from his work to visit her. He had known her since she was a baby. "Her face was pale and washy," as she lay in bed, he said. "I asked her how she was, and I couldn't understand the reply."

It is worth noting here that a plowman called from his plow was sometimes believed to have special powers. Writing in the *Monthly Journal of Medical Science* in May 1849 about traditional midwifery in Ireland, Sir William Wilde wrote:

In some localities it was not in former times uncommon, when the labour was very tedious, to get two or three stout men to shake the unhappy patient backwards and forwards in her bed with great violence; and for some reason, which I am unable to account for, a ploughman was more frequently chosen for such purposes than any other person; but, to prove efficacious, he should be taken direct from the plough.

The same account notes that "in cases of want of uterine action . . . the husband's urine was regarded as highly efficacious."[6] Bridget Cleary was not in labor, but on the previous night urine had been thrown on her, and several stout men had gathered around her bed to shake her. It may well be that whoever told Thomas Smyth of her illness had something of this kind in mind, for the dangers of childbirth were often talked about in terms of fairy interference, and death in childbirth could be presented as fairy abduction. A traditional Bolivian practice, noted by Jo Murphy-Lawless, suggests why Irish women might have been shaken during difficult labor:

> In a slow labour . . . when the slowness is linked to a malpresentation, a birth technology called a *manteo* is used. The woman is placed on a blanket which is then held securely at its four corners by her husband and three others and she is gently rolled back and forth in the blanket, a movement which frees the baby in the pelvis and so enables it to turn spontaneously or be turned by a *partera* [midwife] to a more advantageous position for birth.[7]

Thomas Smyth stayed only about ten minutes in the Clearys' house, but he asked whether the sick woman was eating, and was told that she was. He "saw stirabout preparing on the fire" for her, and told the court that "she was longing for a bit."

Johanna Burke was probably in charge of the stirabout. At some stage, too, she did more laundry. Unionist newspapers—the *Irish Times* and *Clonmel Chronicle,* for instance—say that she "washed some shirts," while the *Freeman's Journal* and other nationalist papers say "sheets." The difference is not important, but serves to underline the separate sources used by journalists of the two main political affiliations at the time.

At about one or two o'clock on that Friday afternoon, so Johanna Burke testified before the magistrates,

> I saw a small, flat coffee-canister with Cleary and he told me it contained £20; he was standing at his wife's bed side at the time, and he handed her the box; she took the lid off and I saw the notes in it; she tied the twine round it and gave it to me to put in the box under the bed; she said to her husband, "Mike, mind that; you won't know the difference until you are without it"; she told me to pull out the box from under the bed, which I did; she told me to put it in the bottom of the box and push it back.

Bridget Cleary addressed her husband as "Mike," and later evidence shows that he called her "Bridgie." The box Johanna Burke mentioned was probably the "old-fashioned wooden trunk, paper-covered," which the *Cork Examiner* reporter saw in the house two weeks later, and which appears, pushed under the bed, in one of the RIC photographs. The coffee canister full of banknotes is not mentioned again, however.

Twenty pounds was an enormous sum for a woman of Bridget Cleary's or Johanna Burke's background in 1895. It represented two months' salary for a dispensary doctor, ten months' wages for a laborer, up to a quarter of the cost of building a laborers' cottage, or four boat tickets to America. Michael Cleary had probably taken out the canister with the couple's savings to pay the priest for saying mass in the house. Now he was returning the money to its hiding place. Even in illness, his wife seems to have been the stronger character. Thrifty and resourceful, with her hens and her sewing machine, her smart clothes and her feathered hat, she was clearly the manager of their household budget. And early on Friday afternoon, her strength seems to have been returning; she was no longer feverish, and had had something to eat. Her instructions to her husband and her cousin about the money-filled coffee canister contrast sharply with the rambling and incoherent talk that her visitors had noticed on the previous night and earlier that day. But at some point during the afternoon, according to Johanna Burke, "Mrs Cleary asked her husband if I was paid for the milk. I said yes, and showed her the shilling, which she took and put under the blankets and gave it back again in a minute."

This shilling, which was to be the subject of disastrous disagreement between Bridget and Michael Cleary, was much more than the market value of whatever milk Johanna Burke had brought to the house over the previous few days. Coincidentally, as the events in Ballyvadlea were being investigated, a Royal Commission on Agriculture in London was hearing detailed reports of the activities of the fledgling Irish Agricultural Organisation Society and the going rates for farm produce. The new cooperative dairies could make a pound of butter from two and a half gallons (twenty pints) of milk, as opposed to an average of three gallons (twenty-four pints) for home dairies—but the price of a pound of butter had fallen from 11½d (just under a shilling) in 1893 to just over 10d in 1894. Irish bacon pigs were meanwhile selling for as little as 3½d to 4d a pound.

However, Johanna Burke had brought not just ordinary milk, but new milk, or beestings, to the Clearys' house, and a shilling was a silver coin. This was no ordinary transaction then, but an exchange and allocation of symbolic power. If Bridget Cleary was believed to have rubbed the shilling on her thigh, or indeed on her vulva, before handing it over to her cousin, this could have been interpreted as an attempt to withhold or divert the "luck" that should accompany the payment. Such an action need not have had a sinister intent: it could have been almost automatic, as when some Catholics make the sign of the cross on their bodies with objects that are invested with emotional or symbolic importance. Unlike the sign of the cross, however, this action would have smacked of unorthodox practice—*piseogery*—and it would therefore not be forgotten.

Late on the Friday afternoon, Johanna Burke left the Clearys' house to return to her own home in Rathkenny for more milk, apparently at Bridget Cleary's request. Outside the house, she met her mother, Mary Kennedy, and her daughter Katie walking up the hill with a

woman neighbor, Johanna Meara. The child later gave an account
before the magistrates of this part of the day:

> I went there the next evening. I went with Johanna Meara, and
> I met my grandmother; she went up along with me; I don't
> know what time it was, but it was daylight; my mother was com-
> ing out of Cleary's going home, and I went up with her to her
> house; we went back then to Cleary's and went in.

Sunset that Friday evening was at twenty-eight minutes past six.
Mary Kennedy testified that she and Johanna Meara had entered the
house together, and sat down beside the sick woman's bed:

> Mrs Burke was gone for milk and the child with her. Johanna
> Meara came in and I and she sat at the bedside with Bridget
> Cleary, and when Johanna Burke came with the milk, herself
> and the child, she left the bottle of milk on the window, and
> Bridget Cleary said, "Will you give me a sup of it?"
>   Michael Cleary was sitting down and he said he would not,
> that she could take a drink of water.
>   I said "What nourishment is a sup of water for the poor
> creature?" So he took the bottle of milk off the window and
> brought it away and did not give her e'er a tint of it.
>   "No matter, Bridgie," said I. "Hanny will give you a sup bye
> and bye."
>   So she said no more, but she said to Hanny, "If I had Tom
> Smyth and David Hogan, they'd settle what's between me and
> Mick."

Thomas Smyth was the farmer who had interrupted his plow-
ing to visit Bridget Cleary earlier in the day. David Hogan appears in
the 1901 census as another farmer, forty years old, unmarried, and
able to read and write, who lived in Garrangyle with his widowed
mother and two sisters. Both he and Smyth were Catholic. Tension
by now surrounded the question of milk in the Cleary household,
and relations between Bridget and Michael were obviously strained.

As with the previous encounter she described, when she was first called to visit Bridget Cleary on the Wednesday, Mary Kennedy did not confront her niece's husband openly; instead, she attempted to reduce tension and reassure the sick woman. Again, her evidence, consistently described by journalists as "rambling" or "incoherent," has a narrative vividness matched only by Jack Dunne's. It is no coincidence that these two, with Patrick Boland, were the least modern of all the people involved in these events; they lived still in a world where meaning was expressed through oral narrative, not through the abstractions that writing fosters.[8]

Michael Cleary would not allow his wife to drink the milk her cousin had brought. Commentators on the case, both at the time and since, have glossed over this fact, taking it as simply another example of the churlish and irrational behavior that led to Bridget Cleary's gruesome death. When we consider the severe psychological strain Michael Cleary had suffered for many days and nights, however, the suspicion with which he certainly viewed Johanna Burke, and especially the question of the shilling, it seems likely that he had some particular fear about his wife drinking this milk.

Bridget Cleary, however, seems by now to have been more frustrated than frightened by her husband's behavior. She asked her cousin to fetch Thomas Smyth and David Hogan, two men who would perhaps be able to make him see sense.

At about eight o'clock on the Friday evening, Johanna Burke walked to Smyth's house with her daughter Katie, and told him that Bridget Cleary had asked for him. They did not wait for him to accompany them, but went on to call for David Hogan. At about half past eight all four arrived back together at the Clearys' house. Johanna Meara and Mary Kennedy were still there, and another neighbor, Patrick Leahy, had arrived. Bridget Cleary's elderly father was also in the house at this stage. He had been up all the previous night, however, and had walked to and from Michael Cleary's father's wake in Killenaule, so he may have been in bed in his own room.

Cleary ushered Smyth and Hogan into the front bedroom, where Bridget Cleary was lying propped up on pillows. "Here's Tom Smyth and David Hogan, now," he said.

While the two men stood there, Michael Cleary produced a flask, which he said contained holy water, and asked his wife to drink it "in the name of the Father, Son, and Holy Ghost." Then—after she had taken the holy water—he gave her a drink of milk. The sick woman was agitated again, and probably angry. Smyth testified that, although he did not observe any marks on her body, "she appeared to be in a very excited state and did not appear to be right in her mind." Physically, though, she was much better. When Smyth and Hogan left the bedroom, Michael Cleary followed them to where they were sitting at the kitchen fire and told them that "as she had the company, his wife was going to dress herself and get up."

Cleary himself handed his wife her clothes, and Johanna Burke and Mary Kennedy helped her to dress:

> He gave her two petticoats and she put them on her. He gave her a navy-blue skirt and a navy-blue jacket and a white knitted shawl. He got her shoes and stockings for her then.
>
> I said [this is Mary Kennedy's testimony], "Bridgie are you able to put them on yourself?"
>
> "Yes," said she, coming out of the bed and standing up against it and putting them on herself.

Johanna Burke had a sharper eye for colors and fabrics than her mother. She told the magistrates that when her cousin had got up that evening, she had put on "a red petticoat, a striped petticoat, a navy-blue flannel dress, grey (or green) stays, a navy-blue cashmere jacket, black stockings and boots," and that she also wore an ordinary calico chemise.

Johanna Burke further said that while the sick woman was dressing, she suddenly called out, "The peelers are at the window. They are coming; let ye mind me now!" whereupon Michael Cleary "took up the chamber[pot] and threw the contents of it over her head and breast; he also threw some on the window where she said the peelers were." The witness may, however, have confused the events of Friday with those of Thursday night, for she quotes the sick woman as using almost exactly the same words on Thursday, and none of the others present in the house on Friday make any mention of this incident.

When Bridget Cleary dressed with the other women's help, it was the first time she had done so since the beginning of her illness, eleven days before. Asked by the magistrates why her cousin had dressed herself, Johanna Burke replied that it was "to give her courage when she would go among the people." Bridget Cleary also wore a pair of gold earrings. She had started to present her usual image again to her neighbors—as a stylish and successful young woman.

Michael Cleary brought his wife from the bedroom to the kitchen fireplace where the visitors were seated. According to Mary Kennedy:

> He put her sitting on a form and she caught the form and pushed it up [closer to the fire]. Tom Smyth asked her how was she, and she said she was middling, that he was making a fairy of her now, and an emergency [accusing her of being a fairy changeling].
>
> "Don't mind him, Bridgie," said I to her. "Don't be that way."
>
> "I sent Han," said she, "for milk, and he wouldn't give me a drop of it, and I never asked for milk," said she, "without buying it."
>
> So I told her to hold her tongue, and not to be minding him, that it would be nothing, that she could drink it bye and bye. She said no more then.

Of all aspects of human life and commerce touched by traditional belief, narrative, and practice, none maintained its connection with magic and the supernatural longer than did the production of milk and butter. The new cooperative and privately owned creameries in 1895 were introducing scientific methods of maintaining dairy hygiene, regulating the temperature and measuring the butterfat content of milk, but the vernacular system's methods of safeguarding the dairy and attempting to control the alchemy of butter making were articulated through stories and through ritual practice. We have already noted some of the customs associated with calving, and with the cow's first milk. Churning, too, was surrounded by precautions, some of which were practical, while others had what was clearly a mnemonic or marking function. A red ribbon or a sprig of mountain ash tied to a cow's tail, or to the wooden dash the dairywoman plunged up and down in the churn to agitate the cream, would remind her to take care, while reassuring, or warning, others about her vigilance; it would also prompt the telling of cautionary stories to children or others who might ask why it was there.

Long after it became normal to pour scorn on ideas about fairy abduction, it was commonly believed that certain women could acquire magic power to steal the butter "profit" from their neighbors' milk. May Eve—the opposite point on the calendar to Halloween—was the temporal focus of anxiety about milk and butter, and the occasion when most precautions were taken. Women strewed primroses on their doorsteps, or tied red threads, rags, or ribbons to their cows' tails, but most important was that nothing whatever—tools, tackle, or farm produce, and most emphatically not milk, milk products, fire, or even a spark to light a pipe—should be allowed to leave the premises. Stories are told of a hare seen sucking milk from cows at night: when a man with a gun shoots the hare and injures it, he follows it to a house, where he finds an old woman sitting by the fire, her leg bleeding. To succeed in shooting one of these milk-stealing witches, the hunter must use a silver bullet—usually made from a silver sixpence.[9]

This is the background against which Bridget Cleary indignantly insisted that she had never asked for milk without paying for it. It was still more than six weeks before May Eve, but the cows were calving, and a new year's milking was beginning. Bridget Cleary did not herself keep a cow, but she lived in an area where much of the land was used for dairying. Any suggestion that she had failed to fulfill her obligations regarding milk would be tantamount to an accusation of profoundly antisocial behavior. A recurring theme of the oral traditions surrounding milk is the (often symbolically phallic) violence employed in the discovery of the suspected witch, defined as a neighbor who is a secret enemy.[10] When a hot poker was plunged into the milk churn, "it was believed [that] the charm setter who had stolen the butter was afflicted with the agony of a red hot iron thrust into her vitals and had to undo the charm."[11]

At the magistrates' inquiry held after the finding of Bridget Cleary's body, and again at the summer assizes in Clonmel the following July, Johanna Burke was questioned closely about the conversation that had taken place at the Clearys' kitchen fire between her cousin Bridget and her cousin's husband Michael. This is how she responded to Colonel Evanson's questions on March 26 about the words that had been spoken:

"What did she say?"

"She was talking of several things, and made a remark about a shilling I had got."

"When she spoke first she was sensible?"

"He made some remark that she had rubbed the shilling to her leg, and she appeared to get vexed about it; she said 'If I gave the shilling to Hanna I did not rub it to my leg. I used no "pishogues." I gave more shillings to Hanna than you know anything about.'"

Johanna Burke presents herself as simply listening to this conversation, but Thomas Smyth recalled that there had been a dispute about a bottle of milk and a shilling, and that Johanna Burke had taken part in it. Asked by District Inspector Wansbrough whether there was anything said about "pishogues," Smyth replied:

I believe there was. She said that she never got a bottle of milk or anything but she paid for it. She asked Johanna Burke, "Did I give you a shilling?" and Johanna Burke said not. Bridget Cleary repeated the question and Johanna Burke denied it a second time. Bridget Cleary then said, "Thanks be to God; there's no use in me saying anything now," and "There's no pishogues in me," or something like that.

Technically, Johanna Burke may have meant that Michael, and not Bridget, Cleary had paid her for the milk, but suspicion about the sick woman was clearly building, and in light of the suggestions made on the previous night that she was a fairy changeling, Johanna Burke's denial reads like a brutal repudiation of her cousin. Her ambivalence about this woman who was just a few years younger than she was, but who had immeasurably more independence, seems to have been expressed in a willingness to take care of Bridget Cleary physically while withholding from her the kind of psychological support that her mother, Mary Kennedy, was giving freely.

While Thomas Smyth and David Hogan were still in the house, Bridget Cleary said something to the effect that "They left me by myself on the road at Skehan's yard." The ringfort of Kylenagranagh was on land farmed by a man named Skehan. Nobody appears to have responded to the sick woman's assertion, although it did attract the court's attention later.

At about eleven that night, Johanna Burke's brothers, Patrick, James, and William, arrived back from Michael Cleary's father's wake and joined their mother, their sister, and their young niece at the Clearys'. Entering the house, Patrick Kennedy saw his cousin at the fire in her navy jacket and skirt and her white woollen shawl. He walked over to where she was sitting, shook her hand and said, "Bridgie, I am very glad to see you up." The others also greeted her, and all three sat down, two of them on the table, the third in the corner on a low stool.

The house was becoming crowded. Patrick Boland was now in the kitchen along with his daughter, her husband, his own sister, Mary Kennedy, four of her children and one granddaughter, and several neighbors. Smyth and Hogan left a little before midnight, together with another neighbor called Tom Anglin, who had been in the house for part of the evening. Patrick Leahy had also been there earlier, along with his brother, and the woman called Johanna Meara. When the men had gone, the table was free. Johanna Burke made tea and cut bread by the light of the oil lamp. She laid out a glass pot of jam along with the Clearys' thick blue cups.

Burke said in evidence that at some stage before she made the tea, she heard a continuation of the argument about *piseogs* and fairies between Bridget and Michael Cleary. No other witness reported hearing this, but several conversations were probably going on at once, and most of those present were very tired. Bridget had "appeared to get vexed" at her husband's suggestion that she had rubbed the shilling on her leg. Now she said, "Your mother was going with the fairies. That's why you say I am going there now."

"Did she tell you she was?" he asked.

"She did; she said she gave [spent] two days with them," was the reply.

This would have been a devastating allegation for Michael Cleary to hear. It neatly turned the tables on whatever strategy he may have been employing: either to isolate his wife and bring her back into line, or to reestablish the normality of their position as a married couple in their neighbors' eyes. All his efforts with the priest's visit, and the bottle of holy water from which he had made his wife drink in Thomas Smyth's presence, would be worth nothing if he himself was tainted by association with a mother who had spent time with the fairies. Michael Cleary was a blow-in: a person from another community whose status among his wife's neighbors could not be guaranteed, and he and Bridget were childless. Saying that his mother had been away with the fairies was to cast doubt on everything about his background, from his mother's virtue, to her sanity, to his own fertility. News of his father's death had come just the previous evening, and Michael Cleary had not slept for several days. His wife's illness was officially over, but the tension between the couple remained acute as they sat by the fire in their enviably "modern" house during the last hour of Bridget Cleary's life.

When the tea was ready, Bridget Cleary moved the few feet from the form by the fire to a chair at the table. All three of the low *súgán* chairs in the kitchen had been occupied by the visiting men when she had first entered the room, but none of them would have been expected to offer her his seat. She now sat at the table with her husband and Johanna Burke, both of whom tried to persuade her to eat and drink. Michael Cleary had his arm around his wife's neck "as though he was fond of her," Johanna Burke said.

Patrick Kennedy took a cup of tea, as did his uncle, Patrick Boland, but his brother James, tired after his night at the wake followed by the long walk from Killenaule, went to lie down on Patrick Boland's bed. Patrick Kennedy joined him there when he had drunk his tea. Mary Kennedy was tired too; she went and stretched out on the Clearys' bed, but Katie saw all that went on:

> When the tea was ready my mother filled out some for Bridget Cleary; she then filled a cup for Pat; Bridget Cleary sat down by Michael Cleary's side, and he wanted her to eat three bits [of bread and jam] before she would take the tea; she ate two bits, and she wouldn't eat the third; he said that if she would not eat the third bit down she'd go; he knocked her down as she would not eat it; he put his hand on her mouth; then he got a red stump, and told her he would put it down her mouth if she didn't eat the bit.

Patrick Boland corroborated the child's account:

> We were taking a cup of tea, and he asked her to eat a bit of bread along with him, and she said she would. He gave her a small little bit, and she ate two bits; she would not eat a third, and he caught her then and knocked her; he thought to put it in her mouth in spite of her.

Once again, Johanna Burke's evidence is the most detailed:

> I made tea, and offered Bridget Cleary a cup of it. Her husband got three bits of bread and jam, and said she should eat them before she should take a sup. He asked her three times, "Are you Bridget Cleary, my wife, in the name of God?" She answered twice, and ate two pieces of bread and jam. When she did not answer the third time, he forced her to eat the third bit, saying, "If you won't take it, down you will go." He flung her on the ground, put his knee on her chest, one hand on her throat, and forced the bit of bread and jam down her throat, saying, "Swallow it. Is it down? Is it down?"

District Inspector Wansbrough asked Johanna Burke if she herself had said anything when she saw her cousin thrown to the ground and held there so menacingly by her husband.

I said "Mike, let her alone, don't you see it is Bridget that is in it," meaning that it was Bridget, his wife, and not the fairy, for he suspected that it was a fairy and not his wife that was there. Michael Cleary then stripped his wife's clothes off, except her chemise, and got a lighting stick out of the fire. She was lying on the floor, and he held it near her mouth.

There is a certain prudery in the evidence given throughout this case. Witness after witness is at pains to tell the court that Bridget Cleary's body was clothed at all times. It is as though nothing improper was thought to have occurred throughout all the violent abuse and man-handling she suffered, as long as the men who participated did not catch sight of, or lay hands on, her naked body. Even in telling how Bridget Cleary was made to drink the herbs boiled in new milk on Thursday, William Simpson stressed that young William Kennedy *had lain across* the bottom of the bed to prevent her moving: he had not put his hands on her legs.

For all this insistence, however, the violence meted out to Bridget Cleary before her death has an unmistakably sexual character. On Thursday, when he used a metal spoon, and again on Friday, when his weapon was a burning stump of wood, Michael Cleary's actions amounted to a kind of oral rape. On both occasions Bridget Cleary was pinned down and prevented from struggling free, while a substance was forced into her body. At the inquest held after her death, Dr. William Crean and Dr. William Heffernan reported that they had found evidence of injury to her mouth:

[T]here was an abrasion on the inner side of the lip at the right side of the mouth, and the tongue on that side was slightly lacerated. On opening the neck we found the tissues slightly discoloured, which might be caused by some person holding the neck, but there were no great marks of violence.

The violence used in holding Bridget Cleary down was certainly not sufficient to kill her, but its scale and ferocity would have been enough to terrify her, and to show her and anyone watching just who was master.

Photographs of the Clearys' house, Ballyvadlea, taken by Constable Thomas McLoughlin, RIC, March 26, 1895.

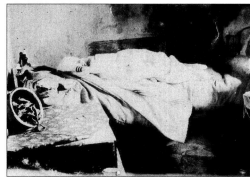

(*above*) The house, seen from the public road; (*right*) Bridget and Michael Cleary's bedroom; (*below*) the kitchen, showing the fireplace where Bridget Cleary died.

District Inspector Alfred
Joseph Wansbrough,
Royal Irish Constabulary.

The corner of a field where Bridget Cleary's body was found buried.

Front-page illustration from the *Daily Graphic*, April 10, 1895, showing the prisoners in Clonmel being conducted from the prison to the courthouse under heavy RIC escort.

the result be that men below the average strength, or above a certain age, would find it more and more difficult to obtain employment? It would, he thought, be well worth while if the trades councils would consider whether any steps could be taken to deal with that point.

THE WITCH-BURNING CASE.

The prisoners who are now being charged at Clonmel Court-house with the wilful murder of Mrs. Bridget Cleary, at Ballyvadlea, near Clonmel, on March 14th last, are: Michael Cleary, husband; Patrick Boland, father; William, Patrick, Michael, and James Kennedy, cousins; Mary Kennedy, aunt; and Patrick Dunne, William Ahearn, and Denis Ganey, the latter of whom is known as the "fairy doctor." Ganey is charged as an accessory before the fact. The circumstances of this remarkable case, which have been already reported in the *Daily Graphic*, will be remembered. The Rev. Father Ryan, whose portrait we include among our sketches, is one of the witnesses, and the Father of the flock to which the Clearys belong. Mary Kennedy is the aunt of the victim, and is one of the prisoners charged with her death. William Simpson is the witness who was present with his wife during the burning of the woman, and who has described in detail the treatment to which she was subjected. To-day the trial will be resumed.

change, but with a dull tone, which was maintained throughout the day. Consols improved 1-16 for the day. Bank stock is 1 lower.

FOREIGN STOCKS LOWER.

With the exception of Greek Rentes, which improved ½, the changes in this market are downwards. Spanish is 1 lower. Argentine are ¾ down.

The gold premium is ·50 lower at 254 per cent.

The Chilian rate is 1-16 lower at 16 11-16d.; and the Brazilian Exchange also 1-16 down at 9⅝d.—the bonds are ½ to 1 lower. Ecuador close 1 higher.

HOME RAILS RELAPSE.

Home Railway stocks were weak, and mark a decline in most cases, the heaviest fall being 1 in South Eastern ordinary. North Eastern, however, is ⅜ higher. The traffic returns, which compare with Easter week, show the following decreases:—Midland, £3,636; North Eastern, £11,118; Lancashire and Yorkshire, £7,519; Great Southern and Western, £1,074; Cheshire Lines, £669; North Western, £1,572; Caledonian, £6,740; North British, £6,466; Great Northern, £2,843; Great Western, £17,990; Chatham and Dover, £2,764; Great North of Scotland, £51; Tilbury and Southend, £066; and South Western, £9,307. Increases are reported as follow:—District, £546; North Staffordshire, £176; Hull and Barnsley, £312; and Sheffield, £2,315.

AMERICANS WEAKER.

This market opened dull, and there was no recovery throughout the day.

The bondholders of the Northern Pacific and Mon-

At the forty-eighth annual meeting of the British Empire Mutual Life Assurance Company, held on the 2nd inst., it was reported that during last year 970 policies were issued for the assurance of £525,650. The premium income amounted to £497,445. The rate of interest yielded by the total funds was £4 5s. per cent. after deducting income-tax. Claims were paid under 363 policies for £121,286, including reversionary bonus; this amount being less by £12,831 than in the preceding year. The assurance fund was increased by £50,818, and amounted at the end of the year to £1,728,880, while the reserve funds rose from £31,103 to £41,023.

The list of applications for shares in T. R. Roberts, Limited, will open on Thursday, the 4th April, and close at 4 p.m. the same day for town and the following morning for the country

London Metal Exchange closing prices:—

COPPER.—G.M.B.'s, 39 5/16-7/16 cash, 39 11/16-13/16 three months.

TIN.—Fine foreign, 64-½ cash, 64⅝-¾ three months. Australian, 64½-65 cash.

LEAD.—English, 10⅛-¼; foreign, 10 1/16.

SPELTER.—Foreign, 13⅝-¾.

SUGAR.—Beet is quiet; April sold at 9s. 3d. plus ½, and June at 9s. 6d. Nothing reported in cane. Home and foreign refines slow, unchanged. German granulated ready sold and buyers at 10s. 9d. Fowler's syrup selling at 12s. 6d.

COFFEE.—The auctions went off flatly, but 5,980 packages offered were mostly sold, prices being irregular, and about 1s. lower. 3,130 bags Costa Rica sold, fine ordinary brownish to low middling, at 88s. 6d. to 93s., middling to very good blue 94s. to 99s., fine and bold 100s. to 103s. 6d. 1,250 bags East India sold, chiefly Coorg, small 92s. to 93s. 6d., medium 96s. to 98s. 6d., bold 105s. to 108s. 6d.

TEA.—Market still flat, but 3,110 packages Indian at auction sold without further change in value. China Congou has again declined, common selling down to 3¼.

COMPANY MEETINGS.

Agnes Blocks, 2; Alamillos, 1.45; Bank of Australasia, 1; Buenos Ayres and Belgrano Tramways, 3; Buenos Ayres Great Southern Railway, 12; Commercial Gas, 12; Durban-Roodeport Gold Mining, 2.30; East London Waterworks, 12; Fortuna, 1.30; Linares Lead Mining, 1; Panawal Tea, 3.

THE Prince of Wales's yacht Britannia left Cannes for Cowes yesterday morning.

IT is officially announced that Colonel A. C. Talbot, Deputy Secretary of the Foreign Department of the Indian Secretariat, will accompany the Ameer's son on his visit to England.

WESTERN AUSTRALIAN REVENUE RETURNS.—The Agent-General for Western Australia has received a telegram from the Colonial Treasurer, dated Perth (W.A.), April 3rd, giving the following returns:—The revenue received in the colony during the twelve months ended March 31st, 1895, amounted to £1,019,947. This, when compared with £610,917 received during the similar period of the previous year, shows an increase of over £409,000. The receipts for the quarter ended March 31st, 1895, amounted to £335,865, against £179,597 received during the March quarter of 1894, the increase in this case being over £156,260.

Father Ryan. Mary Kennedy, the female prisoner. William Simpson, one of the witnesses.

The Prisoners in the dock.

Sketches made in Clonmel Courthouse, from *Daily Graphic*, April 4, 1895: (*above*) Fr. Con Ryan, Mary Kennedy, William Simpson; (*below*) the prisoners in the dock (numbered from left): Michael Cleary, Michael Kennedy, William Ahearne, Jack Dunne, James Kennedy, William Kennedy, Patrick Kennedy, Denis Ganey, Patrick Boland.

Opposite page: Mug shots taken on admission to prison in 1895: (*top*) Michael Cleary; (*bottom*) Patrick Kennedy.

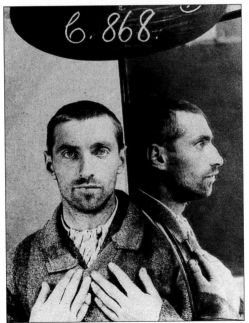

THE TIPPERARY WIFE BURNING.

Statements by the Prisoners.

All Returned for Trial on the Capital Charge.

On Friday the further hearing of the charge of murdering Bridget Cleary against Michael Cleary (husband), Pat Boland (father), William, Michael, and James Kennedy (cousins), Mary Kennedy (aunt), and John Dunne, and William Aherne was resumed before the magistrates at Clonmel. Medical evidence having been given as to the horrible condition of the injuries sustained by the deceased as the consequence of the burning she was subjected to, the herb doctor, Ganey, who was not affected by any of the evidence adduced, was discharged. The principal prisoner, the husband, made a statement contradicting Mrs Burke as to his throwing paraffin on the victim, denying that it was his wife he put on the fire, and accusing her relatives of causing dissension and unhappiness in their conjugal relations. The aged father of the deceased stated that he had been advised by Father Ryan to tell the truth, and he went on to make a statement closely agreeing with that of Mrs Burke, except as to the paraffin, and stating that the husband placed his wife on the fire and burnt her, while he the father had to retreat from the stench. Mary Kennedy also made a somewhat similar statement. On Saturday, on the resumption of the case, these statements were read over to the prisoners, the statement of each of the three having been made in the absence of the other prisoners. When the statement of Pat Boland had been read,

Michael Cleary said—There is not one word of truth in that, and if I will not get justice here I will get it in heaven. They are all one lot. They are after doing their best, and her father is the worst to do the like of that on me. If I am going to get justice—I don't care whether I do or not—I will get it in another place. I did not do it; but they did it, and burned her.

Mary Kennedy's statement was then continued. She was allowed to come into the witness box, while the other prisoners remained in the dock. The statement now dealt with the second night's occurrences—those of the 15th March. She described the visits of Thomas Smyth and David Hogan to the house on the morning of the 15th, when Thomas Smyth asked deceased how she was. She replied to him, "He is making a fairy of me." Three of the boys came at eleven and they said, "Bridgie, I am very glad to see you up." Cleary and Johanna Bourke were at the table for a long time, till about one o'clock in the night. She (prisoner) went and stretched at the side of the bed herself, and she was not a long time asleep when she heard a roar, and someone saying "Mother, mother, Bridgie is burnt." She ran to the door and said "What ails ye," and she ran down and said to Cleary "What are you doing to the creature; is it roasting her you are." Cleary gave her (prisoner) a shoulder and pitched her aside, Johanna Bourke ran to her and pulled her back into the room. She (prisoner) looked out again in a little time. "If you come out any more," said Cleary, "I'll roast you down as well as her." She (prisoner) stayed sitting on the chair opposite the door and saw Bridget Cleary in a blaze with lamp oil. When she turned and looked out Cleary caught Bridget Cleary on the head and threw her on the floor like he would throw an old churn; then he got an old blanket and an old sheet and put Mrs Cleary in it. One of her feet was up to the grate, and Cleary gave her a crack of the shoe of his foot, and the shock of it went all over her clothes, and she (prisoner) nearly died with the fright. So Cleary rolled his wife up in the bag and in the sheet and he left her on the middle of the floor and went to the door and opened it and locked it against her when she was opening the door again. "Oh, God help me," said she (Mary Kennedy), "He'll stick us all with his knife." Cleary had a black-handled knife. He pulled the knife out of his pocket, came to the room door, and said, "Are you there, Patsey Kennedy." He got no answer. "Well, said Cleary, "I'll call your name three times, and drive the knife to the handle through you." "Oh, Patsey," said she (prisoner), "answer him at all events or he'll stick you." So

from the Board of Works for buildings and other improvements. With his own hands he built the greater portion of a residence and valuable out-offices. He paid over £2,000 of the purchase money, but bad years and failing health brought unfortunate Quinn into arrears. He got married to a young girl about ten years ago, with whom he got a considerable fortune, which helped him to clear off a further portion of the debt; but continual disappointments and the successive bad seasons left him unable to satisfy the Church Commissioners and his other creditors, with the result that last summer he was evicted from the home which he had built for himself, and the property which he expected to leave to his wife and family.

Although there had been reports that the shopkeeper was about to take the place the people did not generally credit the rumours, as they thought a man who had lived by the farmers would be the last to take advantage of the distress of one of them, and drive a helpless, and, as he thought, a friendless, poor man with his wife and child on the world. Certainly this is a case where all parties will unite in demanding justice from one who can be made to feel the just indignation of the tenant-farmers of the locality.

Boycotting Prosecution at Drogheda.

On Monday at Drogheda Petty Sessions a case was heard in which a respectable well-to-do farmer named William Woods, residing on his farm at Strinagh, Collon, preferred a charge of boycotting against a man named James Mathews, one of the evicted tenants on the Massereene estate. Mr Wood and his people have lived for generations past at Strinagh, and were always held in esteem by the surrounding farmers and people. The complaint was brought on summons at the suit of District-Inspector Browne, R I C, and was as follows:—"That defendant, on the 13th March, in the County of the Town of Drogheda, with a view to compel William Woods to abstain from doing an act which he (William Woods) had a legal right to do—namely, to receive payment for certain cattle of the said Wm Woods, sold by him on said date in said town of Drogheda, aforesaid, and wrongfully and without legal authority persistently followed the said Wm Woods about from place to place." In a second summons the defendant was charged with preventing the sale of the cattle. The courthouse was very much thronged.

Mr William Woods, the complainant, was sworn and examined by Mr Moynagh, Crown Solicitor. His direct evidence was to the effect that on the 13th March last, being the fair day of Drogheda he brought three calves for sale. He was standing beside his cattle in the fair for some short time when a man came up, and after a little bargaining bought them. He observed the defendant Mathews, who was standing close by put his hand on the arm of the man who bought the cattle and say to him that he (Woods) had reared the cattle on the Massereene evicted tenants' land. The man went away then and never returned. Matthews continued following him (Woods) through the fair. Another man came up afterwards, and after some bargaining bought the cattle, and directed him (Woods) to leave them in a certain place, which he did, but the man never called for them, and the cattle were afterwards driven home unsold. He (Woods) observed Mathews talking to the man.

The magistrates, by a majority of one, decided on sending the case forward for trial to the ensuing quarter sessions, and admitting the defendant to bail in the meantime.

Tenants' Rights on the Norwich Union Estate

On Sunday the Norwich Union Company's tenants and their sympathisers met at Davidstown to discuss their position. Up to the hour of meeting no reply had been received to the last letter sent by the tenants to the Company, but as the proceedings were about to commence the tenants received an offer by telegraph from their solicitor, Mr Healy, who had an interview with the directors on Saturday. Mr Jeremiah Morrissey, Ballygillostown, was moved to the chair, and amongst those present were Messrs Mark Codd, Garr, and John T Keating, Moneyhone, hon secs to the tenants; Thomas Mullett, Wm Hussey, Pat Doyle, John Rooney, P Neill, John Synnett, P L G; James Parker, John Hassy, Peter Kinsella, Thomas Lacy, Martin Mulligan, J Murphy, M Leary, J N Murphy, John Dempsey, John Kehoe, Garrett Murphy, P Furlong, P Daly, P Donnelly, Thomas Mullett (Toberona), J Sinnott, L Fortune, Jas Murphy, Thomas Larkin, Thomas Rooney, J Dunbar, Jas Morragh, John Gordon, John Franklin, Maurice Murphy, John Cowman, Miles Slevin, Jas Jordan, J Mullett, P Condon, James Murphy (Ballygillestown), James Keating, &c.

Mr John Keating announced that the Company informed Mr Thomas Healy, M P, that the Company "would sell at seventeen years through the

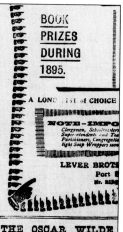

THE OSCAR WILDE SCANDAL.

Oscar Wilde has very much reason we opine to regret the action he took against the Marquis of Queensberry. Strange that while he took the action in defence of his character the proceedings in court have only resulted in damaging his character, and instead of having the Marquis of Queensberry punished he is now in jail himself on the worse and most loathsome charge that can be preferred against a human being. This sequel to the trial was to be expected when on Thursday his counsel practically threw up his brief and admitted that they could not sustain the action against Queensberry.

Wilde Arrested.

Mr Oscar Wilde was arrested between six and seven o'clock on Friday evening and conveyed to Bow-street police station, where he arrived at ten minutes past eight. The arrest was made by Inspector Richards at half-past six o'clock at the Cadogan Hotel, Sloane-street, Chelsea, where Mr Wilde, it appears, drove after leaving Holborn Viaduct Hotel. Mr Wilde's visit to the hotel was of a casual character, he being accompanied by two gentlemen. Throughout the day the accused had been closely followed by two officers, and when Inspector Richards entered the hotel and asked for Mr Wilde it was stated that he was not staying there. This was virtually correct. But when the inspector insisted that he was in the establishment, and explained the circumstances, he was conducted to a room in the establishment where Mr Wilde was engaged with his two friends. The inspector informed him that he was a police officer, and that he would arrest him, a warrant being out for his arrest. Mr Wilde made no reply. Mr Wilde, in custody of two officers, was conducted to a cab, which conveyed the party to Scotland Yard, where Inspector Brockwell was waiting with a warrant for Mr Wilde's arrest. The formality of reading the warrant to the accused and the administration of the statutory caution having been gone through, Mr Wilde hazarded no remark. The trio, Mr Wilde, Inspector Richards, and Inspector Brockwell, then drove to Bow-street, where they arrived at ten minutes past eight o'clock in a four-wheeled cab. The accused was first to alight from the vehicle, and walked direct into the station, followed by the detectives. He was attired in a long black frock coat, dark trousers, and silk hat. He was at once placed in the prisoners' dock in the charge room, and while the charge was being taken he stood with his hands in his pockets. Inspector Digby, who took the charge, read it to the prisoner, and warned him that anything he might say could be used in evidence against him. Mr Wilde maintained his reticence and indifferent air. Having been searched he was removed to the cells. Shortly after Mr Wilde's arrival at Bow-street a Mr Rosse, a friend of the prisoner's, drove up to the station with a small Gladstone bag containing a change of clothes and other necessaries for the prisoner, but after a short interview with the inspector on duty, Mr

Page from *United Ireland*, April 13, 1895, showing coverage of the Cleary case and of Oscar Wilde's arrest.

To His *Excellency* Writt C 43/05 H. M. Prison
Maryboro
'28.6.05

the Lord Lieutenant of Ireland: 9109

7 JUL 1905

The Petition of* *Michael Cleary*

8 JUL 1905

Humbly Sheweth *That your Petitioner*

Was tried at the Clonmel asizes on the 4th of July
1895 for the Manslaughter of his Wife and was sentenced
to 20 years P. S Petitionar wish to stait that Patrick Boland
Father to the deceased was present, and also his
Sister Mrs Kennedy and her 4 Sons, and daughter
Mrs Burk, and a man the name of John Dunne
a first cousin to Patrick Boland and a relation of
the Kennedys by being married to their aunt
and they were all equally guilty, of the crime that was
Committed, and those of the above named that was
convicted of the crime their sentences varied from 5
years to 6 Months. Which was very small taking in
to account the long sentence Petitionar got. Petitionar
do not bring under observation the above names through
any hatred or mallice but mearly bring to your
Gracious Excellencys mind the position in which
Petitionar was placed. the deceased got suddenly sick
on the 4th of March 1895 with a reaging pain in the head
which continued till the morning of 7th which was the morng
of her death; Petitionar attended to the wants of his
his wife during her sickness booth night and day
untill he was in a manner just as bad as deceased

* Only one Prisoner may Memorial on this paper.

Opening of a petition written by Michael Cleary to the Lord Lieutenant of Ireland in 1905, appealing for part of his sentence to be remitted.

Michael Cleary on his release from prison, 1910.

In terms of fairy narrative, we do well to remember here that the whole Irish tradition of fairies is preoccupied with boundaries, including those of the human body. Visits to the fairy realm may be presented as illicit penetrations of the earth's orifices, when curiosity and lack of caution make human characters, who are usually young and male, explore caves, rock clefts, or other hidden openings that unexpectedly appear on the familiar landscape. Young women taken by the fairies bear on their bodies the marks of their adventures: some are unable to speak until the fairies' *biorán suain,* a kind of tranquillizer dart or "slumber-pin," is discovered and removed; others are immobilized by painful swellings, caused by invasion of their flesh by some foreign body, and cured only when the offending matter is expelled.[12]

Chief among the ways in which young people are counseled to protect themselves is to refuse any food offered them by strangers. Stories of fairy interference tell of abductions foiled when the protagonist steadfastly refuses to eat; storytellers explain that once fairy food has been eaten, oblivion follows, and, like the "stolen child" of Yeats's poem, the victims must stay forever with their captors. In fairy legend we find a vernacular textbook of belonging: a way of teaching about the many boundaries that social life imposes, about the peril of transgressing them, and the necessity of revising them.

The emotional implications and repercussions of such transgressions and revisions are catered for through the subtlety of stories. The grief of bereaved or deserted parents, relatives, and friends is given expression, as is the fear experienced by the young person who first decides to do without the safety net of rules. More important, perhaps, ambivalence is given a stage on which to perform. The changeling said to be substituted for an abducted human behaves antisocially, but also mirrors the behavior of the absent one. Refusal to eat is therefore both a highly appropriate behavior when under threat from strangers, and a symptomatic expression of serious alienation when at home. Michael Cleary's crazed insistence that his wife swallow three pieces of bread and jam before she was allowed to drink anything would have had its origin in a sense that her refusal to eat what he gave her had sinister implications for the body politic within which they lived. It was not so very different in its significance from the force-feeding of suffragists and other prisoners by state authorities in later years.[13]

Bridget Cleary, weak from bronchitis, was lying on the earthen floor in her own kitchen, where her husband's sudden blow had knocked her. Beside her, a fire was burning in the grate, where the kettle had just boiled. "Oh Han, Han!" she called, but her cousin did not intervene as Michael Cleary tore off his wife's shawl, her skirt and petticoats, her jacket and stays, and left her lying on the floor in her chemise. He may have used violence against her before: most witnesses said they got on well together, but Johanna Burke did testify that she had witnessed disagreements between them. He was kneeling above her now, brandishing the red-hot piece of wood from the fire in her face, and his knee was on her chest as he threatened to shove the burning wood down her throat.

"Give me a chance!" was all Johanna Burke heard Bridget Cleary say. She interpreted it, she said, as meaning that her cousin wanted to be allowed to drink something before she would swallow the bread. Johanna Burke told the court that she heard Bridget Cleary's head striking the floor, and then heard her scream. The kitchen must have been pandemonium. Michael Cleary is said to have normally been a silent man, but he was clearly beside himself, looming over his wife's body, shouting and gesticulating with the red-hot stick. It can only have taken seconds for her calico chemise to catch fire.

It was sometime after one in the morning when flames leapt up from where Bridget Cleary was lying. Mary Kennedy testified that she had not been long asleep in the bedroom when she heard a roar, and her son William saying "Mother, Mother, Bridgie is burned!" She ran to the bedroom door, saying, "What ails ye?"

Bridget Cleary lay on the hearth, her clothing still on fire, as Michael Cleary said, "Hannah, I believe she is dead." Johanna Burke saw her cousin's head hanging down—which may mean that Michael had lifted her body off the floor—and her eyes closed. She too believed that Bridget Cleary was dead—or so she said at the summer assizes, although her evidence before the magistrates in the spring was more ambiguous. She then saw Michael Cleary pick up the lamp from the table and throw paraffin oil over his wife. Cleary later denied that he had thrown oil on her, but the evidence of witnesses and of the post-mortem examination seem irrefutable. Perhaps his horror was so great when he believed her dead that he no longer thought of her as a person: this does seem to have been the moment when he became convinced that she really was a changeling left by the fairies. The lamp oil was to hand. Throwing it on the flames was a reckless, panicky act; Cleary himself and the others in the house might easily have died had the furnishings caught fire—the door was locked, after all—but to a man out of control it could have seemed almost a hygienic impulse, a necessarily violent way of driving out a sickening pollution from the heart of his household.

Patrick and James Kennedy, who were dozing on the bed in Patrick Boland's room, heard their brother William roar that "Bridgie" was burned. Patrick heard his mother and sister tell Michael Cleary, "Don't burn her!" Mary Kennedy ran to the fireplace and said, "What are you doing with the creature? Is it roasting her you are?" Emerging from the back bedroom just then, James Kennedy saw Cleary give his mother a push with his shoulder, and knock her back against the table so that she fell on her side. Johanna Burke ran to her and pulled her back into the front bedroom.

"My mother and brothers and myself wanted to leave the house when he flung her on the floor," Johanna Burke told the magistrates,

but Michael Cleary held the key of the door in his pocket, and said the door would not be opened until he got his wife back. My brothers and I threatened to break down the door and call the Peelers, but he said that no one would leave the house till he got his wife back. When he held the stick near her mouth he wanted her to answer her name three times. He said he would burn her if she did not answer. She answered him, but the answer did not satisfy him, and he got an oil lamp and threw it over her. In a few minutes I saw her in a blaze.

"For the love of God," James Kennedy said to Michael Cleary, according to his own testimony, "don't burn your wife!"

"She's not my wife," Cleary replied. "She's an old deceiver sent in place of my wife. She's after deceiving me for the last seven or eight days, and deceived the priest today too, but she won't deceive anyone any more. As I beginned it with her, I will finish it with her!" Patrick Kennedy also heard him say, "You'll soon see her go up the chimney."

According to James Kennedy, "We asked him to give us the key, and let us home; we went to the door, but he would not give the key to my mother; he drew a knife from his pocket, saying he would have our lives if we would attempt to leave the house until he would get his wife back; so we turned back and went into the [front bed]room then."

The youngest of the Kennedys, William, fainted when Cleary threatened to "run the knife through him" if he attempted to leave the house. His mother and brothers dragged him into the bedroom and laid him on the bed, and Mary Kennedy threw holy water over him. She looked out again into the kitchen, but Michael Cleary told her, "If you come out any more, I'll roast you down as well as her." She sat down on a chair near the door and saw Bridget Cleary "in a blaze with lamp oil."

According to their own testimony, everyone present remonstrated with Michael Cleary, but none of them attempted physically to stop him. They could not, they said, for Bridget Cleary had "blazed up all in a minute," and the flames reached right across the kitchen to the door of the bedroom where they were huddling in terror.

Michael Cleary seems to have been alone in the kitchen with his wife's body. His original impulse in knocking her to the floor and forcing the bread down her throat appears to have been born of frustration and rage, but his subsequent actions were more deliberate. One of the magistrates, Thomas Cambridge Grubb, the Quaker sawmill owner from Clonmel, asked Johanna Burke to describe more precisely how Cleary had thrown the oil on his wife. "He threw it several times on her," she replied. "When it blazed up he bent back and then threw some more on. He threw it on her about three times." She added that she had seen him take an oilcan from between the table and the dresser.

When Michael Cleary first believed his wife was dead—either because she had struck her head or because her clothing and skin had caught fire—the shock must have been enormous. However angry he was, or whatever the public later thought, it does not appear that he had had any intention, or even felt himself capable, of murdering his wife. Seeing her unconscious—apparently dead—on the floor, however, he reentered the drama of the previous evening. This was *not* his wife, but a substitute foisted on him by the fairies, and it must be got rid of. His actions in throwing lamp oil on her body again and again as it burned were obviously an attempt to destroy it completely: a sickening task, but one that he might have had to perform before with dead farm animals.[14]

In July 1895, Johanna Burke remembered that while his wife's body was burning, Cleary accused her relatives: "You are a dirty set. You would rather have her with the fairies in Kylenagranagh than have her here with me." She continued:

Patrick Boland, Bridget Cleary's father said, "If I can do anything to save my child I will." Cleary said he would bury her with her mother, and that he would go to Kylenagranagh Fort on the following Sunday night. There he would see her riding on a white horse, and he said he would bring a knife to cut the straps with, and rescue her from the fairies.

This was the story that would travel through the countryside the next day, when Michael Cleary would claim that Bridget herself had told him that she would be in Kylenagranagh.

After about twenty minutes in the bedroom, Mary Kennedy opened the door:

When I looked out again he caught her by the head and threw her on the floor like he would throw an old turnip, and he got an old bag and an old sheet and put her in it. One of her feet was up that way (lifting her hand)—God bless the mark—and he gave it a knock with the shoe of his foot. The shock went all over the house, and I nearly died with it. So he rolled her up in the bag and the old sheet, and left her on the middle of the floor.

While Bridget Cleary's body was burning on the hearth, according to Johanna Burke, "the house was full of smoke and smell":

> I had to go up to the room. I could not stand. When I looked down to the kitchen I saw the remains of Bridget Cleary on the floor, lying on a sheet. She was lying on her face, and her legs turned upwards, as if they had contracted in the burning. ["Up" and "down" refer to the movements away from and towards the fireplace. The "room" (bedroom) was on the ground floor.]

At the petty sessions, Colonel Evanson questioned her further about this testimony: "You speak of remains—was she dead at this time?"

"She was, and burned."

Michael Cleary left the house, locking the door from the outside, and leaving his father-in-law and all the Kennedys, including Johanna and Katie Burke, in the house with his wife's charred body.

The Kennedys, the Burkes, and Patrick Boland knelt down and said the Rosary. They waited for about an hour, still behind the bedroom door, until they heard Michael Cleary come back.

"Oh, God help us!" Mary Kennedy said, "he'll stick us all with the black-handled knife he has."

Cleary came with the knife in his hand to the bedroom door and spoke through it: "Are you there, Patsy Kennedy?"

Patrick, eldest of the Kennedy brothers, made no reply.

"I'll call your name three times, and if you don't come to me and answer me, I'll drive the knife to the handle in through you," Cleary said.

"Oh, Patsy," said his mother, "answer him, *a chroí* [dear heart], or he'll stick you!"

Patrick Kennedy answered at last.

"Come on out here now," Cleary told him. "I have the hole nearly made. As I couldn't drive the devil out through the chimney, I'll drive him out through the door."

Someone in the bedroom opened the door, and Patrick Kennedy went into the kitchen. Johanna Burke described Michael Cleary as "very excited": "She's burned now," he said, "and God knows I would never do it but for Jack Dunne. I would never have forced my wife into the fire but for Jack. It was he who told me my wife was a fairy."

Patrick Kennedy at first refused to go with Cleary to bury his wife:

He said if I did not come he would do away with me. I said I would if he would go to the churchyard, to consecrated ground, to bury her along with her mother. He said he had a place ready for her, and he stuck her into an old bag and an old sheet. He asked me would I come with him, and I said I would then, be-fore I'd be killed. I went after him, and he took a spade and shovel from under the furze bush. He threw her partly on her side and pressed her down with his foot. I have no more to say. I am not steady this good start [while]. I am crushed after it, to see my poor cousin burned; I am under the care of Doctor Crean for six years; this is as true as God is above me.

Patrick Kennedy was sentenced to a five-year prison term for his part in the killing of Bridget Cleary, chiefly because he had assisted "in the secret removal and burial of the body." He and Michael Cleary carried the dead woman's charred remains about a quarter of a mile uphill from the house, to the shallow grave where the RIC search party found it a week later: a marshy hole, "about three feet in length and two in breadth and depth." They covered the body with soil, and threw some branches over the leveled earth. As the *Cork Examiner* reporter remarked on March 30, 1895: "That must have been a horrible interment at two o'clock on the morning of the 16th of March."

Cleary and Kennedy got back to the cottage at about 5:00 A.M. and Cleary unlocked the front door. "Now ye can't inform where I did put her," he told Mary Kennedy.

"He took the knife out of his pocket," she told the magistrates:

"I'll make ye now," said he, "take your oath, or I'll drive the knife through ye."
    "Oh you need not mind," says I, "drive any knife through us."
    "I am not," says he, "in dread of anyone but of Hanna."

"Oh you need not be in dread of Han at all," says I, "because neither Han nor us will discover [inform] on you, for as sure as wherever you put her, God will show to the people where you put her." I and the two boys [James and William] came down [out of the bedroom] then, and Mike Cleary kept scraping the juice of the poor creature off his clothes.

At Cleary's insistence, Johanna Burke and Patrick Boland knelt down and swore not to tell what had happened. Cleary talked about emigrating to America, about going to Cloneen and pretending to be mad, and about doing away with himself. Mary Kennedy, according to her own testimony, tried to persuade her son Patrick to give himself up:

"Patsy," says I, "go down to the Police barrack and tell them what you have done."

"Oh no, Mother," says he, "because the people would be calling me a prosecutor."

"Well, don't mind them," says I. "God will prosecute him." I said no more. I finished at that, until Mike Cleary came down to me. "Mike," said I, "if you were scraping your clothes and if you cut them off you, God will never let the stains of your wife out of your clothes."

"Oh, Mary," said Cleary, "she wasn't my wife, and we'll go tonight," says he, "to Kylenagranagh Fort, and we'll cut the ropes," says he, "and we'll bring her home."

A few hours later, on Saturday morning, Johanna Burke saw Michael Cleary scraping the cuffs of his gray tweed trousers, and washing them in water:

There were stains on his clothes like grease, and he said, "Oh God! Hannah, there is the substance of poor Bridget's body." He gathered the ashes and the remains of the fire on which his wife had been burned into a bucket, and buried them in the manure heap in the yard.

Later the same morning, Michael Cleary and Jack Dunne walked to Drangan, where Michael Kennedy met them, and went with them to the chapel.

Over the next days, rumors spread, policemen searched, and Michael Cleary spent three nights on Kylenagranagh Hill, apparently in the belief that his wife would appear on horseback from the fairy fort. William Simpson and Johanna Burke swore "informations" before William Walker Tennant, and on Wednesday, March 20, arrest warrants were issued. The next day, Johanna Burke witnessed another grisly detail:

> On the day Cleary was arrested I was passing his house, and I saw him poking the ashes he had buried. He called me and said, "Hannah, I have got one of poor Bridget's ear-rings." He showed me the ring, and told me not to be coming near the house, as it would draw suspicion on him.

This was the gold earring Bridget Cleary had worn in her right ear: the other one was still on her body.

7

"Amongst Hottentots . . .":
The Inquest and Inquiry

WHEN BRIDGET CLEARY'S BODY was found on Friday, March 22, 1895, newspapers were informed by telegram, and the coroner for the district was alerted. This was John J. Shee, JP, of Abbey View, Clonmel, and on March 23 he traveled to Ballyvadlea to conduct the inquest. It took place in a vacant house owned by a farmer called John Anglin, of Tullowcossaun, and formerly occupied by Fr. Con Ryan's predecessor as curate in Drangan.[1] The body had been guarded overnight by police and was lying on a table in an outbuilding. Policemen were everywhere around as reporters waited for the verdict. The day was windy, but not cold, and local tradition remembers that small boys climbed onto the windowsills to look in—until they were dislodged by a constable's boot.

Coroner Shee addressed the jury: "[He] said that if what he had heard about the case was true, it was one of the most fearful things which had happened in this country for years. Amongst Hottentots one would not expect to hear of such an occurrence."

"Hottentots" were much spoken of in 1895. The name is Dutch, and refers to the Nama, or *Khoikhoi* people, originally hunter-gatherers displaced by Dutch settlers throughout a large area of southern Africa; their descendants live chiefly in western South Africa and in Namibia. To northern Europeans at the end of the nineteenth century, their name was synonymous with "savage." Measurements taken in Paris from the skeleton of an African woman known as the "Hottentot Venus" had been used in the pursuit of the new discipline of "criminal anthropology" by a succession of French scientists, one of whom pronounced, "I have never seen a human head more like an ape than that of this woman."[2] European states were carving the continent of Africa into colonies and justifying their interventions by appeals to Charles Darwin's *The Origin of Species* (1859) and *The Descent of Man* (1871). "Hottentots," whose language includes nonvocal clicks as speech sounds, were assigned a place at the bottom of the human "evolutionary tree," whose topmost branches, not surprisingly, were occupied by Europeans of Teutonic origin.[3]

It was telling that the coroner, a Catholic, should mention "Hottentots" in the context of Bridget Cleary's death.[4] The name had been an inflammatory one in Ireland since the time of Gladstone's first Home Rule Bill in 1886. Robert Cecil, third Marquess of Salisbury, succeeded Gladstone as Prime Minister after that bill was defeated. During the debates, he had argued that Irish people lacked the necessary maturity for Home Rule, and enraged the Parnellites by observing, "You would not confide free representative institutions to the Hottentots, for instance."[5] Coroner Shee's remark was to be the first in a long series of analogies drawn—or repudiated—between the Irish people and various African civilizations in the weeks that followed. For the moment, however, Bridget Cleary's violent death had to be investigated.

The coroner told the jury that he would spare them the distress of inquiring into the full circumstances of the case: "[H]is idea was that they would fulfil the cause of justice, so far as their inquiry was concerned, by ascertaining the cause of death." It was exactly a week since Bridget Cleary's disappearance had become known. Reports had spread rapidly by word of mouth and in print; the two Clonmel newspapers that had broken the story on Wednesday were standing by, awaiting the latest developments, and in Dublin and Cork the nationalist press had begun to take notice. The *Freeman's Journal* for March 23 carried an article headed "The Mysterious Disappearance of a Woman; The Body Discovered; Nine Persons Arrested and Remanded," in which it supplied the information, not found in unionist papers, that William Simmons (*recte* Simpson), the most important witness so far, was "caretaker of an evicted farm." The *Cork Examiner* announced: "Disappearance of a Woman; Extraordinary Developments; Numerous Arrests."

Much speculation surrounded the role of Denis Ganey, and the effect of the herbs he was understood to have prescribed. He was one of those arrested, and the inquest would have to ascertain what part, if any, his herbs had played in Bridget Cleary's death.

By Saturday, eleven people were in custody, for William Kennedy, youngest of the brothers, had now been arrested, as had his sister, Johanna Burke, following the discovery of the body on Friday evening. Michael Cleary, the dead woman's husband; her father, Patrick Boland; Jack Dunne from Kylenagranagh; his sixteen-year-old neighbor William Ahearne; Denis Ganey the herb doctor; and the four Kennedy brothers were all in Clonmel Prison. Johanna Burke and her mother Mary Kennedy were in Limerick Female Prison, although Burke would be released within days. Coroner Shee was unwilling, as he put it, to hold an inquiry behind the backs of these people, into a crime with which they were charged. He proposed therefore simply to hear evidence of identification and the results of the postmortem examination, and to leave all further inquiry to the magistrates in Clonmel.

The jury was led to the outbuilding where the body lay, to view it formally. Journalists described what they saw:

> It was wrapped in the sheet in which it was when discovered, and presented a most ghastly appearance. The back and lower part of the body were severely burned, the bones and intestines protruding. The head and face were apparently uninjured. The features were those of a young woman and were much distorted, indicating the terrible sufferings which the poor creature endured.

Constable Samuel Somers, of Cloneen, one of the three officers who had found the body, gave evidence of identification. He had last seen Bridget Cleary a month or six weeks earlier, when, he said, she was a healthy woman. Two of the local dispensary doctors, William

Crean from Fethard and William Heffernan from Killenaule, carried out a postmortem examination. Dr. William Kickham Heffernan, aged forty-five, was one of the colleagues who would certify in September that Dr. Crean was suffering from "debility, chronic bronchitis and muscular rheumatism," when the Local Government Board moved to dismiss him from his post for drunkenness. He lived in some style in Killenaule with his English-born wife and their children: by 1901, he owned three houses and employed a cook, a groom-coachman, and a housemaid, all of whom lived in.[6]

Dr. Crean first told Coroner Shee and the jury of his visit to Bridget Cleary on March 13. He had found her, he said, suffering simply from "nervous excitement and slight bronchitis." He had prescribed medicine, but had felt no anxiety about her condition. The two physicians then made a joint "information":

We have carried out an examination of the body of Bridget Cleary. We found the right hip and thigh and lower portion of the abdomen charred and burned, with the internal organs protruding through the burned apertures. The right hand was also burned, the fingers charred and contracted. We found the same condition on the left side of the deceased's body, only not so severe as on the right. The left hand was also burned and the fingers charred. The muscles of the lower end of the spine were charred and burned, and the bones exposed. There was a gold earring in the left ear.

What remained of the body seemed to be well nourished; there was an abrasion on the inner side of the lip at the right side of the mouth, and the tongue on that side was slightly lacerated. On opening the neck we found the tissues slightly discoloured, which might be caused by some person holding the neck, but there were no great marks of violence. On removing the scalp we found extravasated blood [blood forced out of its proper vessel] on the top of the skull; we found the vessels of the brain congested, but no injury to the brain substance. The lungs were slightly congested and the left lung adherent to the wall of the chest; the spleen was ruptured. We removed the stomach and found it healthy in appearance.

It was clear that Denis Ganey's herbs had caused no damage to the stomach tissue. The jury returned a verdict of death by burning:

> We find that the deceased, Bridget Cleary, late of Ballyvad-
> lea, was found dead on the lands of Tullacussane [*sic*], on Friday
> 22nd March 1895, and we further find that death was caused by
> extensive burns, how, or by whom caused we have no evidence
> to show. We further find that the deceased was alive in her own
> house on the 13th March 1895.

The proceedings then concluded. The prisoners would be brought before the magistrates in Clonmel on Monday, March 25, when evidence would be heard about the events leading to Bridget Cleary's death, but meanwhile there was a Sunday to be got through.

A little after four o'clock on Sunday morning, people in the southern half of Ireland were woken by a violent thunderstorm. It was not as severe as in the English midlands, where hurricane-force winds uprooted thousands of trees and knocked down church spires, as well as those symbols of progress, telegraph and telephone wires, but heavy rain continued throughout the morning as people went to church. Fr. Con Ryan came from Drangan as usual to say mass in the old chapel beside the graveyard in Cloneen. Whether or not he prayed for the soul of Bridget Cleary is not recorded, but he did "denounce the outrage in the strongest possible terms . . . and called upon those of his hearers who knew anything of the affair to communicate with the authorities." The parish priest, Michael McGrath, may have made a similar sermon in Drangan, but as the indignantly anticlerical Michael J. F. McCarthy noted later in his *Five Years in Ireland,* McGrath's name was not allowed to appear in print in connection with the case, and so the record is silent about any comment he may have made. McCarthy's book, much of which was concerned with encouraging Irish Catholics toward sturdy, secular self-reliance under the British Crown, also quoted the coroner's remark about "Hottentots," "to his lasting credit."[7]

Fr. Con Ryan's congregation in Cloneen evidently approved of his sermon denouncing the recent events, for the *Nationalist* noted in an editorial on March 27 "how emphatically and how speedily the priest and the people there marked their reprobation of the horrible crime that has darkened the district." "Dark," along with references to Africa, is a word that will recur.

In Clonmel on Monday, March 25, when it was announced that the prisoners would be brought before the magistrates, there were further displays of public revulsion:

> [A]n enormous crowd collected about the county jail and along the streets to the courthouse. They waited for nearly two hours, and when the eleven prisoners finally appeared in the streets, under a heavy police escort, they were greeted with yells, hisses and groans, and the crowd followed them to the court, indulging in all kinds of cries.

This gauntlet of public abuse continued for the entire period of the magistrates' inquiry, which lasted until the end of the following week. Newspapers commented on it, and on April 1 an artist sketched the scene for the London *Daily Graphic* as the prisoners made their way through the streets, escorted by police wearing tall spiked helmets and carrying rifles. At the end of the nineteenth century, faith in the corrective power of the judicial system was at its height, and prisons all over Europe had been reformed, substituting confinement, surveillance, and a strict work timetable for spectacles of punishment. The theatricality of the prisoners' treatment in the streets of Clonmel thus recalled an earlier way of dealing with offenders.[8]

Much of the hissing and groaning was directed at Denis Ganey. His traditional title, "fairy doctor"—uncomfortably close to "witch-doctor"—was enough to single him out for opprobrium in the modern town of Clonmel. The crowd, still hissing and groaning, pressed into the courthouse in such numbers that the resident magistrate, Colonel Richard Evanson, ordered the court cleared of all but the officials and the press.

Richard Charles Evanson, a native of County Cork, was fifty-seven. He was joined on the bench on March 25 by Thomas Cambridge Grubb, JP, a member of a well-known Tipperary Quaker family, before whom the nine prisoners had been brought on the previous Thursday. Grubb was owner of a sawmill and other business interests in Clonmel, and was active in the YMCA.[9] Two other magistrates, Colonel W. A. Riall, JP, of Heywood, Clonmel, and Major George Christian, JP, of Outrath House, Cahir, also occupied seats on the bench for part of the afternoon.

District Inspector Alfred Joseph Wansbrough of Carrick-on-Suir introduced the case. It was he who had organized the week-long search that resulted in the finding of Bridget Cleary's body on Friday. He had gone to Clonmel Prison on that same day and brought away the clothes Michael Cleary had been wearing all week, the light gray tweed suit from which he had attempted to wash the greasy stains. On Saturday, Wansbrough had supervised a search of the house in Ballyvadlea and brought away a spade, a shovel, and other items of evidence: an empty oilcan and a saucepan.

Now aged thirty-eight, Alfred Wansbrough was a native of Somerset and had joined the RIC as a cadet fourteen years earlier, when the Land War was at its height. He had served in Mitchelstown, County Cork, at the time of the infamous "Mitchelstown massacre" in September 1887, when the police shot two men dead and wounded several others during a meeting called to challenge the Crimes Act passed earlier that year. Dublin Castle's long-drawn-out secret investigation into that debacle found officers in the Mitchelstown area suffering from a "very bad state of discipline and morale."[10] The zeal Wansbrough demonstrated in the Cleary case, organizing searches and obtaining sworn "informations" from William Simpson and Johanna Burke, may have been part of a strategy to revitalize his career after Mitchelstown. And his efforts succeeded up to a point: McCarthy's *Five Years in Ireland* publishes his photograph, singling him out for praise as "that able young man . . . who certainly deserves to rise high in the Royal Irish Constabulary." (Alfred Joseph Wansbrough remained at the grade of Sub- or District Inspector for almost thirty years until he retired in February 1920.)[11]

The prisoners had been charged on Thursday, March 21, with ill-treating Bridget Cleary. Now, at the hearing on Monday, that charge was abandoned and the new charge read. Eight of the men, along with Mary Kennedy, were charged "with having on or about the 14th March, at Ballyvadlea, jointly and severally, and with malice afore-thought, feloniously killed and murdered Bridget Cleary"; Denis Ganey was charged with "being an accessory before the fact of the commission of the crime."

DI Wansbrough's prize witness was Johanna Burke. She had been arrested when it became clear that she had lied in her sworn state-ment that Bridget Cleary had left the house in Ballyvadlea in her night-dress on the night of her disappearance. Now, however, she was to be rehabilitated as the principal witness for the Crown. She would give evidence against her own brothers, her uncle, her mother's cousin, and of course against her cousin's husband, Michael Cleary. Even her mother, Mary Kennedy, would be affected by the evidence she and her young daughter Katie would give, although the consequences for Mary would not be as serious as for the men. A strong gender di-vision runs throughout the investigations of this case: the male de-fendants are consistently represented as misguided savages, while Mary Kennedy, Johanna Burke, eleven-year-old Katie Burke, Minnie Simpson, and of course Bridget Cleary herself are presented either as victims or as innocent bystanders.[12] There seems to have been no attempt to question the woman called Johanna Meara, mentioned as having been in the Clearys' house on Friday, March 15, or "Miss Shea," who called there on Wednesday to invite Fr. Con Ryan to breakfast.

In the courthouse on Monday, DI Wansbrough and the mag-istrates questioned Johanna Burke for almost four hours about the events of March 14 and 15. "She had an infant in her arms, and was accompanied by her daughter, who is another witness," the *Irish Times* observed, noting too that she "gave her evidence clearly and intelligently." Intelligence was to be another recurring theme. As commentators on the Cleary case struggled to comprehend what had happened, they returned again and again to the language of social Darwinism. The notion of measurable inherited differences between races and "types" dominated nineteenth-century social thinking.[13] Social Darwinism included the notion, first propounded by the Frenchman Jean Baptiste de Lamarck, and taken up by the English philosopher Herbert Spencer, that acquired characteristics could be inherited. "Intelligence" included what had been learned; it followed that individuals had a responsibility to assist and speed the evolutionary process through education.[14] The prevalence of such views is illustrated by W. B. Yeats's later disenchanted comment on George Moore, whom he met about this time:

> I have been told that the crudity common to all the Moores came from the mother's family, Mayo squireens, probably half-peasants in education and occupation, for his father was a man of education and power and old descent. His mother's blood seems to have affected him and his brother as the peasant strain has affected Edward Martyn. There has been a union of incompatibles and consequent sterility . . . *Both men are examples of the way Irish civilization is held back by the lack of education of Irish Catholic women.*[15] [emphasis added]

Education was thus not merely a civilizing influence; as the means by which human beings were to climb from the lower to the higher branches of the evolutionary tree, it could even influence biology. "Savages," with high cheekbones, protruding jaws, and low morals were to be found not only in Africa, or even in Ireland, but in the white urban underclass of Britain itself. Photography provided important material for study, especially after the invention in 1878 of a dry-plate process, which allowed photographs to be taken at a distance from a darkroom, and mug shots of prisoners allowed the features of criminal "types" to be studied and compared.[16] One English author in 1883 wrote of "a dark continent that is within easy walking distance of the General Post Office [in London]," while John Stuart Mill, mentor of John Morley, the chief secretary for Ireland, had written in 1848 of the English laboring class that "prospect of the future depends on the degree in which they can be made rational beings."[17] Morley's Land Bill was to have its second reading on April 2, and the

Home Rule debate, which was about to be reactivated, would draw much of its rhetoric from the pages of anthropology, a discipline increasingly in favor since the 1880s. Some would draw on research that found no fundamental racial difference between the peoples of the two islands, while others argued that the Irish were essentially a feminine race, unfit for self-government; all would debate the question of whether the Irish were sufficiently "intelligent" to elect their own parliament.[18]

"Intelligence" was the mark of advanced races, at home or abroad; it distinguished them from "savages," was more highly developed in men than in women, and could be discerned readily in a person's physical features. The writings of Italian physician Cesare Lombroso, pioneer of the new discipline of criminal anthropology, offered the possibility that "born criminals" could be identified simply by looking at them:

> At the sight of [a famous brigand's] skull, I seemed to see all of a sudden, lighted up as a vast plain under a flaming sky, the problem of the nature of the criminal—an atavistic being who reproduces in his person the ferocious instincts of primitive humanity and the inferior animals. Thus were explained anatomically the enormous jaws, high cheekbones, prominent superciliary arches, solitary lines in the palms, extreme size of the orbits, handle-shaped ears found in criminals, savages and apes, insensibility to pain, extremely acute sight, tattooing, excessive idleness, love of orgies, and the irresponsible craving of evil for its own sake, the desire not only to extinguish life in the victim, but to mutilate the corpse, tear its flesh and drink its blood.[19]

When Katie Burke came to give her evidence before the Clonmel magistrates, the *Cork Examiner* reported that "she told her story in a remarkably clear and intelligent manner for such a young child, and every word was listened to with intense interest," while the *Irish Times* noted, "*She is a very pretty child, and remarkably intelligent, telling her story clearly and without confusion.*" (emphasis added)

Johanna Burke's testimony took up most of the court's time on Monday and Tuesday. Michael Cleary, standing in the dock with the other prisoners, listened intently as his wife's cousin gave her evidence. He was "a rather good-looking, respectably dressed man, with regular features, but his face was very pale and his eyes had a wild kind of look," according to the *Irish Times*, which also noted that he "seemed to be greatly excited."

At one point, Cleary suddenly shouted, "Excuse me, I cannot listen to this any longer!" This was on Monday, when DI Wansbrough asked the witness, "Did you see [Michael Cleary] throw the lamp-oil on her?" and she answered, "I did."

Colonel Evanson quelled Cleary's interruption, telling him that he would get an opportunity to speak, and Johanna Burke continued with her story about the burning and disposal of the body. She ended that day's testimony with Michael Cleary's finding of his wife's gold earring in the ashes. The court then adjourned, and the prisoners were escorted back to the jail in Richmond Street under a heavy police guard. Again "they were groaned [*sic*] by an immense crowd of people, who had waited patiently for their appearance. They followed the accused to the prison gate groaning."

At eleven o'clock on Tuesday morning the prisoners were again brought from the jail to the courthouse in Nelson Street.

> Though this was half an hour before the time fixed for the opening of the court, large crowds had assembled to see the prisoners, and they groaned them vigorously along the streets to the courthouse. The accused were placed in the dock. The public were admitted to the court. The crowd collected outside the court as on yesterday, eagerly waiting for any fresh bit of information.

When Johanna Burke arrived, with her baby daughter and Katie, the strain she felt was obvious:

> Mrs Burke and her infant and little daughter were brought into court about 20 minutes past 11 o'clock, and on seeing the prisoners she burst into tears, and said something about her mother and cousins. The police tried to quiet her but had to remove her out of court.

Shortly afterwards, Colonel Evanson and Thomas Cambridge Grubb took their seats on the bench.

Tuesday's proceedings continued where Monday's had left off. DI Wansbrough guided a calmer Johanna Burke through the remaining painful details of her evidence, as sworn in her "information" the previous week and read in the Town Hall on Thursday when the original charges had been brought against the prisoners. Colonel Evanson intervened from time to time with questions about Bridget Cleary's demeanor, about the herbs that had been given to her, and about the shilling that had been the subject of dispute between her and her husband. Cambridge Grubb asked only one question about the same episode. Johanna Burke's testimony ended with her responses to a series of searching questions put to her about the circumstances of her cousin's burning: the paraffin oil; the flames; whether or not any of those present had attempted to intervene and if not, why not.

"They were afraid they would be burned themselves," she said. "The blazes reached up to the door of the room where we were." The witness "wept bitterly" as her deposition was read back to her.

Richard J. Crean, the Clonmel solicitor, had been engaged on Monday morning to represent Michael Cleary and Denis Ganey. He now told the court that since the deposition was entirely new to him, and because he had not yet had an opportunity to speak with his clients, he would delay his cross-examination. The prisoners were then invited to question Johanna Burke. Cleary, Boland, and Ganey all declined, and one after another the remaining male defendants agreed that her account had been accurate. Only her brother Michael objected: had she seen him in the house on Friday, or had she seen him at all since Thursday, March 14? he asked. Tall, thin, and tubercular, with brown hair and blue eyes, Michael Kennedy explained to the court that he was trying to establish his innocence: he had not been in the Clearys' house at all on the night of Bridget Cleary's death. His sister bore him out, answering that she had not seen him until Sunday at her mother's house.

Mary Kennedy, at fifty-nine, struck all commentators as pathetic: she seemed old, poor, frightened, and confused, and the *Daily Graphic* artist sketched her with her head covered by a shawl. When it came to her turn to speak, she said simply, "I was in it myself, and saw all that was done, and sorry I was." Asked by William Casey, clerk of Petty Sessions, if she wanted to question her daughter, she answered, "I am too old and weak, and I am frightened, and I can't stand here."

"Would you like to come out here?" Colonel Evanson asked.

"Yes," Mary Kennedy replied, and, as the *Irish Times* noted, "The prisoner, who appeared to be very weak, then came out of the dock, but on coming forward said she had nothing to ask. She was removed back to the dock."

Katie Burke was then examined, and "a thrill of interest went through the court as the little child came on the witness table and was sworn." R. J. Crean asked whether she knew the nature of an oath, and the clerk of Petty Sessions put the question to the child. She replied "that she attended the convent school at Drangan and said her prayers morning and evening. She believed that if she died after telling a lie she would go to Hell."

Tuesday's proceedings ended when Katie Burke's evidence had been heard. One by one again, the prisoners either declined to question her, or agreed that she had told the truth. They were formally remanded for further examination the following week.

The newspapers devoted extensive space to the magistrates' inquiry, and more than one carried editorial comment on the case. On Monday, March 25, just over a week before the debate was to begin on the Land Bill, the unionist *Dublin Evening Mail* began to make a connection between the death of Bridget Cleary and the Home Rule question. Its editorial contended that the people of Ballyvadlea were essentially lawless, and found fault with the local clergy and school-teachers for leaving them "in the moral and intellectual condition of Dahomey":

> The precautions taken by the eleven persons now in custody for the murder of Mrs Cleary seem to leave no doubt that they were all aware that they were engaged in operations forbidden by the law of the land. The law is, of course, not as it would be if the Ballyvadlea people had the making of it. To them it is

British law, foreign-made law, unjustly interfering with their right to manage their own affairs, and running counter to the ideas and the "wants and wishes" of the local "vast majority" of Ballyvadlea. Freely admitting all this, we treat it as of no account. Civilization and humanity are much more precious, whether at Ballyvadlea or elsewhere, than the privilege of self-government, and must not be made the sport of ignorant and superstitious cruelty. We trust that as many as are convicted of assisting in the torments of Bridget Cleary will be met with a punishment as exemplary as that which overtook the savages of Maamtrasna.[20] It is a lying claptrap that says "Force is no remedy." Force is sometimes the only remedy for an evil. At Ballyvadlea it seems that the forces that were no remedy were the schoolmaster and the venerated pastor.

The Clonmel *Nationalist* responded indignantly in a passionate editorial the following day, "The Ballyvadlea Murder Inquiry; Public Horror and Indignation; Tory Slander Again."

We found yesterday that the dreadful occurrence has been utilized editorially by the Tory-Unionist *Dublin Evening Mail* for purposes of political capital and as a suitable occasion to pour forth slander, odium and abuse on Irish people generally; to stir up racial and religious passion and prejudice, and if possible to damage the cause of Home Rule.

The writer drew attention to the displays of "spontaneous popular indignation" in Clonmel, and to the reception of Fr. Con Ryan's sermon in Cloneen on the previous Sunday, but his trump card was the figure of Johanna Burke:

Had [the editor of the *Dublin Evening Mail*] been in Clonmel courthouse he would have seen how the witness, Johanna Burke, separated herself and others from the crime, and did not hesitate to give evidence even against her own mother, brothers, and other relatives . . . [B]efore indulging in unwarrantable comments . . . he should have waited to learn how Mrs Burke,

bearing her infant in her arms, not only told the whole shocking story, but with the spirit of a Spartan woman, sat beside the
witness-table while her intelligent little daughter went over the
gruesome history a second time.

Sparta was an analogy more acceptable to the Catholic middle-
class interests represented by the *Nationalist* than any African country,
as the editorial writer made clear: "What proof is there in all this," he
asked, "of the allegation that the people are 'barbarians,' living in the
moral and intellectual conditions of Dahomey?"

"Dahomey" is the country on the west side of the Niger, which
has been known since 1975 as Benin. Conquered by the French in
1893, the threat it posed to British interests in Africa under its new
and ambitious governor, Victor Ballot, was most easily expressed in
terms of the savagery of its African inhabitants. Anglo-French relations were tense in the last week of March 1895: reports had reached
London that two French expeditions were in the Niger valley within
the sphere of influence of the British Niger Company, and Sir Edward
Grey, undersecretary at the Foreign Office, was preparing to make a
statement in the House of Commons demanding that the French
clarify their position there and in the Mekong and Nile valleys.
Thomas Pakenham's *The Scramble for Africa* describes the events that
led up to the "Grey Declaration" of March 28, 1895. They included
a revolt on January 29 against the Niger Company by the people of
Brass, in the Niger delta, whose trading economy had been devas-
tated by the company's ruthless policy of destroying its competitors.
"Canoe-loads" of prisoners had been killed, cooked, and eaten under the direction of a fetish priest apparently in an attempt to put an
end by ritual sacrifice to a smallpox epidemic that was raging among
the starving people. "Dahomey" in late March 1895, therefore, represented both "darkest" Africa and Britain's near neighbor—fickle,
Catholic France.

In Clonmel, the prisoners were remanded on Tuesday evening, and
the inquiry did not resume until the following Monday. Meanwhile,
however, newspapers on both sides of the Home Rule question got
into their stride. On Monday and again on Wednesday, the *Freeman's*

Journal carried the headline "The Strange Death near Clonmel." An editorial the same evening in the *Dublin Evening Mail* sneered that this seemed "an odd description of a deed which revolts humanity," and continued, "Our contemporary might as well call it 'The Cleary Altercation.'" It raised an eyebrow, too, at the "carefully taciturn" use in the *Freeman's Journal* of the word "liquid" for the urine that had been thrown over Bridget Cleary (although it too managed to avoid naming the liquid involved), and quoted from its sister paper, the *Daily Express,* Johanna Burke's evidence about the Holy Communion that she said Bridget Cleary had not swallowed. "Why does the *Freeman* withhold this very interesting circumstance?" the writer inquired. "Would it embarrass the Government, or anybody in particular?" Only the Parnellite *Independent,* he noted, had included details of the urine, and the Holy Communion.

Earlier, the same editorial had fulminated at length against the chief secretary's Irish policy, and had lumped the Cleary case together with agrarian outrages:

> The horrible event that has occurred at Cloneen will do something to clear the public mind of cant about "coercion" and about the respect due to "popular opinion". . . The principal accused in the Cleary case is reported to have thrown the blame on an old medicine-man named Ganey. How to deal with Ganey, supposing him to be found guilty of having persuaded Cleary that his wife was a witch or a fairy, is a question of exactly the same sort as how to deal with the Irish orators who egg on ignorant peasantry to murder or maltreat landlords, landgrabbers and their employees . . . It would be interesting to know how this revelation from the heart of Tipperary will affect Mr Morley's opinion of Ireland as fit for Home Rule.

On Tuesday, March 26, the *Manchester Guardian* gave a summary of the events up to the finding of Bridget Cleary's body, under the heading "Revolting Affair in Ireland; A Woman Burned to Death." The following day, *The Times* gave a crisp summary, dated March 26, of the story so far:

A special Court was held at Clonmel yesterday by Colonel Evan-son and Mr Cambridge Grubb to hear the case against ten persons, charged with having murdered, by burning to death, a woman named Cleary, who was supposed by the prisoners to be possessed of an evil spirit. The prisoners included the husband and the father of the deceased, and a local herb doctor. It appeared from the evidence of a woman named Burke, who had been nursing Mrs Cleary, that the latter *was suffering from nervous excitement and from a mild attack of bronchitis, and her husband thought she was a witch.* He gave her herbs which he obtained from the herb doctor, the other prisoners holding her while she was forced to take them. The man then called on her to say, in the name of God, that she was not his wife. She was held over the fire to make her say this. *These proceedings were repeated the following night,* when the husband knocked her down, stripped off all her clothes, poured paraffin oil over her, and set fire to her with a burning stick from the hearth. *While she was burning to death* there were present six of the male prisoners and two women, all relatives of the deceased. Some of them remonstrated with the husband, but did nothing more. He told them it was not his wife he was burning but a witch, and that she would disappear up the chimney. He rolled a sheet round the charred body and, with the aid of one of the prisoners, buried it in a dyke near his house. Here the remains were discovered a week afterwards by Sergeant Rodgers [*sic*] of the Royal Irish Constabulary. The prisoners were remanded. They were hissed and groaned as they passed through the streets in custody. [emphases added]

This account, while it admirably summarizes hours of testimony, manages to present the killing of Bridget Cleary as almost leisurely in its deliberateness (see my italics). It suggests that Friday's events were simply a repetition of Thursday's, and that the men and women present would have had the opportunity to intervene. A court, however, takes far longer to hear about a fatal burning than fire takes to kill.[21] Flames exploded from Bridget Cleary's body immediately when her husband doused her with paraffin. In any case, the atmosphere around Bridget Cleary's sickbed on Friday, March 15, had been very different from that of the previous days. We have seen that the food, clothing, and language employed on that day in the Cleary household were significantly different from those used on Wednesday, and especially on Thursday. By Friday evening, Jack Dunne's role was over; life had begun to get back to normal, with informal visiting and chat taking over from the ominous pronouncements and mystifying rituals of the previous days, and, until the final disastrous minutes, the initiative had passed from men to women. If the dramatic action of Wednesday and Thursday had represented a performance by the reactionary forces centered on Jack Dunne—a theatrical last-ditch attempt to assert the value of the old ways by invoking vernacular sanctions against deviance—the play was over. Jack Dunne was nowhere to be seen, and ordinary life was taking up where it had left off; instead of herbs boiled in milk, people were drinking that modern luxury, tea.

One further point deserves comment: *The Times* passes seamlessly from the observation that Bridget Cleary "was suffering from nervous excitement and from a mild attack of bronchitis," to the corollary, "and her husband thought she was a witch." Hidden within the sentence is a huge gap of credibility: a "darkness" that this book is attempting to illuminate. Why his wife's illness should have made Michael Cleary think she was a witch was the exotic mystery around which the law, the newspapers, and public opinion circled in the spring of 1895. The Irish-speaking storytellers of the *Gaeltacht,* who could perhaps have elucidated it, were not consulted. In fact, most interpretations of Bridget Cleary's state had focused on fairy belief, not on witchcraft; they were not accusations, therefore, so much as diagnoses. Commentators, however, preferred to avoid the ambiguous and innocuous "fairy" in favor of "witch." That word's connotation of malevolence and its association with death by burning were guaranteed to whet the appetites of readers.

8

A Funeral, Some Photographs,
More Fairies

KATIE BURKE'S EVIDENCE before the magistrates in Clonmel on March 26 came too late to be included in the next day's newspaper coverage. The *Dublin Evening Mail* reported it on Thursday, March 28, and added a pathetic coda: "The funeral of the murdered woman took place yesterday. No civilian attended. Four policemen were present, and the body was carried on a common car."

The Dublin correspondent of *The Times* next day commented on the ignominy of Bridget Cleary's burial:

> The funeral of Bridget Cleary, who was burned to death near Clonmel, co. Tipperary, in the superstitious belief that she had been carried off by the fairies and an evil spirit put into possession of her body, took place at Cloveen [*sic*] yesterday, and was boycotted by all her relations and neighbours.[1] Not one civilian attended the burial, and the rites of sepulture were performed by four police-constables. There was no hearse, and the coffin was borne by a common car from Fethard. The significance of this will be understood when it is remembered that the Irish peasantry regard a funeral not only as an expression of respect for the deceased and of sympathy with the family, but as invested with a certain degree of sanctity.

A week later, the *Tyrone Constitution* supplied more details, from "a correspondent from Clonmel," including the fact that burial had taken place at night:

It is a remarkable fact that after the inquest none of the neighbours of the deceased offered to undertake the interment of the remains. The relieving officer of the [Poor Law] Union thereupon supplied a rude coffin, and three young fellows, assisted by two policemen, removed the body at night and conveyed it to the Roman Catholic burial place at Cloneen, where they arrived at ten o'clock. One of the lads, with the light afforded by a small lamp, read a portion of the burial service, and the remains of the "martyred woman" were placed in a grave beside that occupied by her mother.

The splendid funeral of nationalist shopkeeper Thomas Kickham, in Mullinahone two weeks earlier, attended by dignitaries and priests, throws Bridget Cleary's wretched burial into stark relief. From the old-style rites with wakes, wake games, and keening women, found in *Gaeltacht* areas until well into the twentieth century, to the elaborate religious ceremonies held for public and private figures today, funerals have for centuries had such central importance in Ireland's social life that it has been termed "a funerary culture."[2] Small wonder that Michael McCarthy used italic type for emphasis six years later when he wrote that "*The police had to bury poor Bridget Cleary that night, by the light of a lantern,*" because "not a single human being, male or female, clerical or lay, would lend any assistance to give Christian Burial to the body."[3]

Refusal to bury a body was one of the grimmest manifestations of boycott in late nineteenth-century Ireland. A confidential RIC report for September 1894 describes the events that followed the death of an emergencyman in north Tipperary:

After the inquest on the remains of M[ichae]l Callaghan, late Caretaker of an evicted farm at Brockagh, a coffin or hearse could not be procured at Borrisokane, the nearest town, and they had to be sent for to Nenagh, which is 13 miles distant. The people did not attend the "Wake" or funeral, and the police carried out the interment.[4]

We remember that William Simpson, too, was the caretaker of an evicted farm. Bridget Cleary, dead by burning, had been his friend, and was rumored to have been his lover. The horror her neighbors felt at her death may have been compounded by their disapproval of her life.

Even the most miserable funeral costs money: Thursday's weekly meeting of the Cashel Poor Law Guardians, reported in the *Clonmel Chronicle* on Saturday, March 30, considered two accounts received. "A man named Aherne" had submitted a bill for five shillings "for the burial of the remains of Mrs Bridget Cleary," while "a man named Ryan" claimed ten shillings "for the conveyance of her coffin to the place of interment at Cloneen." Both bills, certified correct by Mr. Breen, the relieving officer, were ordered to be paid. There is no record of what had happened to the coffee canister containing £20 which Bridget Cleary had kept in the box under her bed, but it was certainly not taken into account when arrangements were made for her pauper's burial. Almost as remarkable as the reluctance of her neighbors to grant her a funeral is the failure of nationalist newspapers to mention the manner, or even the fact, of her burial, although they devoted extensive column inches to the case in all its aspects.

Of course, Bridget Cleary's closest relatives were in prison during the last days of March 1895, and many of the newspapers remained silent about the case from the adjournment of the magistrates' inquiry on March 26 until it was resumed on Monday, April 1. The fine new cottage in Ballyvadlea was standing empty, with furniture and clothing still strewn on the floor after Bridget Cleary's violent death two weeks earlier. William Simpson had the keys—Michael Cleary had asked him to take care of the dog—and the police continued to observe the house.

The RIC's South-Eastern Division was based in Kilkenny, presided over by Divisional Commissioner A.E.S. Heard, whose report on the burial of an emergencyman is quoted above. He ordered photographs taken of the scene of the crime in Ballyvadlea, and on March 26, when the magistrates in Clonmel were finishing their examination of Johanna Burke and her daughter, Constable 43828 Thomas McLoughlin arrived there from Kilkenny with his equipment. The day was fine and dry, and he was able to take pictures both inside the house and outdoors.

Five of Constable McLoughlin's prints survive, each approximately two and a half by three and a half inches.[5] The first shows the Clearys' house, and the stone wall that separates it from the road; the high hedge that conceals it a hundred years later has not yet grown. The door and half door are closed, as are the windows. A wooden barrel, possibly Michael Cleary's handiwork, stands where it will collect rainwater from a downspout at the corner of the left gable.

The second picture shows the room in which Bridget and Michael Cleary slept, at the front of the house, and must have been taken from the doorway that leads into it from the kitchen. A relatively ornate iron bed takes up almost the entire width of the room from left to right, with its head under the window. A mattress or tick, a pillow, and at least one light-colored blanket with three dark stripes near one end can be seen on top of the bed, while a round-topped trunk sits on the floor under it. A small fireplace is visible on the opposite side of the room, and some sort of wooden chest covered with a patterned cloth stands against the wall on the left, between the viewer and the foot of the bed. A round shallow container, perhaps ten inches across by three deep, and apparently containing some pieces of fabric, is propped against the wall on top of the chest.

The third picture is captioned, "Kitchen in M. Cleary's house where Bridget Cleary was burnt." It shows the fireplace on the left, viewed from just inside the front door, with its five-barred grate set between two hobs. A low *súgán* chair stands on either side. Beside the fireplace is a square wooden cupboard, on top of which are a jug and some other objects or utensils. The back windowsill is in the top right corner of the picture. There seems to be a table under that window, for the end of a form projects into the middle of the picture on the right, in an appropriate position. What may be another chair, more elaborate than those by the fire, is at the head of this barely visible table.

The remaining two pictures show "Second Bed-room in Cleary's house" and "Spot where Bridget Cleary's body was found buried." Patrick Boland's bedroom is much rougher than that shared by his daughter and son-in-law. A bed with high, rough-hewn wooden ends takes up most of the space. There are some half-full sacks on the floor, and a large cooking pot on the bed, together with what appears to be a quantity of straw—perhaps part of the mattress. The last photograph—Bridget Cleary's first burial place—shows a hollow surrounded by disturbed earth and vegetation; filled with water, it reflects a small patch of sky.

When Constable McLoughlin had developed and printed his pictures, he stuck them on two sheets of plain white paper, captioned them in ink, and submitted them to the District Inspector Crime Special in Kilkenny, Pierris B. Pattison.

On April 5, DICS Pattison attached a covering note to McLoughlin's report and photographs, and sent the file to Divisional Commissioner A.E.S. Heard. Heard in turn initialed it and sent it to the Constabulary office in Dublin Castle, where it was initialed by the Inspector General, the Undersecretary, the Chief Secretary, John Morley, and finally, on April 20, by the Lord Lieutenant, Lord Dudley.

On April 6, Pattison submitted his own monthly report for March 1895, sending it up through the same line of command. Between 1887 and 1908, Crime Branch Special officers were charged with the gathering and analysis of intelligence about subversive organizations. Pattison's reports are handwritten, on both sides of unruled foolscap paper creased down the middle. He used only the left-hand side of each page, leaving the space on the right blank for the signatures and comments of his superiors all the way up to the Lord Lieutenant.

Pattison's March report starts with accounts of the activities of the Irish National Federation, the Irish National League, and the Unionist Association. It deals with relations between landlords and tenants, and with incidents of boycotting and intimidation, then comes to "Outrages":

The most serious case of outrage that has occurred for some time in the Division took place at Ballyvadea [sic] in the Carrick on Suir District on the 15th March.

The case is a remarkable one and has caused much public interest and local excitement.

A man named Michael Cleary in a state of almost incredible grievance, superstition and savagery, with circumstances of great cruelty burnt his wife to death on a kitchen grate under the belief that he was exorcising an evil spirit. In this extraordinary proceeding he was—more extraordinarily—assisted by several others including the murdered woman's father.

I fear the incident is indicative of a vast amount of ignorance and superstition existent still among some of the Irish Peasantry. It is satisfactory to know that the perpetrators of this outrage are in the hands of the Law.

Pattison's attitude to the "Irish Peasantry" echoes that of the unionist newspapers. "Superstition" is a problematic word: beliefs and practices can appear bizarrely irrational when the system of which they were once part has begun to disintegrate. Fairy tradition, in this respect, has something in common with money, for both are systems through which a variety of transactions can be negotiated, but only for as long as people believe in the system—literally, give it credit— or at least assent to its use. Calling something "superstition" means declaring the currency to which it belongs worthless. Used among equals, the word expresses tolerance for illogical foibles; given a racist or sectarian edge, however, it can mark an unwillingness to consider those to whom it is applied as fully human.

Michael Cleary's actions on March 15 were indefensible and certainly irrational—but so is any such resort to violence. There is no doubt that he was responsible for his wife's death, or that narratives about fairy abduction played a part in his thinking, but "superstition" simply labels what happened; it does not explain it. Certainly, the assertion that one of Bridget Cleary's legs was longer than the other because she was a fairy changeling is unacceptable to the modern mind and can fairly be called superstition, but Pattison and others' use of the word in relation to the Cleary case betrays an arrogant assumption that the logical processes at work were simple. It suggests that Michael Cleary and his neighbors were incomprehensibly different:

that they believed as uncritically in fairies as newspaper readers believed in the postal system, and that all their actions would be guided by that insane belief until it could be eradicated. It gives them no credit for humor or imagination, and shows no tolerance for the way the mind works when under stress. Neither does it take into account the ubiquity of fairy references in nineteenth-century Ireland, or their utility and idiomatic versatility in speech and imagination.

As the Indian social theorist Ashis Nandy has noted, "A plurality of ideologies can always be accommodated within a single life style."[6] When the men held Bridget Cleary down, and shook her, forced her to drink the mixture of herbs and new milk, burned her with the hot poker, and carried her to the fire, both they and the women who complaisantly looked on were exerting their communal power against a woman whose behavior they found unacceptable. Modern though they might have been in some aspects of their lives, Jack Dunne and the Kennedys, men and women, were here reasserting the authority of an older way of life. As they did so, they were also driving a wedge between husband and wife by demanding that Michael Cleary ally himself with the ideology of stigma and control, which fairy legend represented, against his wife. They later claimed that they had merely assisted Cleary or watched him in helpless incomprehension, but their protests do not ring true.

Writing about *sati* (suttee, funeral-pyre suicide by widows) in the context of colonization, Nandy has remarked that in India "[g]roups rendered psychologically marginal by their exposure to Western impact . . . had come under pressure to demonstrate, to others as well as themselves, their ritual purity and allegiance to traditional high culture. To many of them *sati* became an important proof of their conformity to older norms at a time when these norms had become shaky within."[7] If we substitute "oral culture" for "high culture," Michael Cleary's action becomes more understandable, as does the dilemma in which he found himself. Most commentators have seen him as the most "superstitious" of the people involved in his wife's death—the most credulous about the existence and agency of fairies—but in fact he was the best educated among them, and was the one person involved in her torture who had not grown up in the vicinity of Kylenagranagh Fort.

A reliance on the idea of "ignorance and superstition" to explain why Bridget Cleary died suggests that knowledge is the key: that people who know more facts are safer, but this book's argument is that the key is power. Education, of course, conveys power, but the tensions and imbalances that led to Bridget Cleary's death came about as power flowed toward some, leaving others stranded. Jack Dunne was by all accounts very knowledgeable, but in fields whose creditworthiness had all but disappeared. The expertise in negotiating the web of fairy narrative which would have been his symbolic capital in an oral culture had become next to worthless as literacy became general. He was like an elderly immigrant in the world where Bridget and Michael Cleary had learned to hold their own: unable to speak the language, succeeding only in making himself a laughing-stock with his stories. Michael Cleary, for his part, found himself isolated and almost powerless among his wife's family and neighbors, when Jack Dunne at last reacted, rallying them to an older way of thinking. But Bridget Cleary was the one who ended up dead. She had accumulated power, both economic and sexual, it seems, far in excess of what was due to a woman of her age and class, and when the balance tipped, all the anger flowed toward her. Police training, with its orderly categories, could not easily cope with such a seething confluence of motives. Just as "the fairies" provided a convenient label in vernacular culture for everything that could not be otherwise categorized, "ignorance and superstition" were a useful shorthand for DICS Pattison. He did not visit Ballyvadlea, as far as we know, and the Cleary case was simply one item in his March report. Under "General," he wrote: "The farmers throughout the district view the Land Bill with favour."

The journey from Cork to Fethard took five hours by train. While the magistrates in Clonmel were still examining the prisoners accused of wounding and killing Bridget Cleary, a special correspondent from the *Cork Examiner* was traveling to investigate the background to the story. He found a room at Stokes's Hotel in Fethard, where the proprietor, Miss Susan A. Stokes, also ran a grocery and package store and kept horse-drawn cabs and hearses for hire. On the afternoon of

Tuesday, March 26, only hours after Constable McLoughlin had taken his photographs, the reporter set out for Ballyvadlea.

As he was being driven eastward up the Anner valley in the failing light, the journalist's first impression was romantic—and literally colorful: "I beheld the vapourish clouds proudly hurling around the purplish peaks of Slieve-na-mon, and the darkness beginning to obscure the green fields and brown bogs that lie on the slope of the mountain," he wrote.[8]

Slievenamon, in Irish *Sliabh na mBan,* 721 meters high, dominates the landscape north of Clonmel like a great ship sailing westward into the plain formed by the Suir and its tributaries. A stone cairn has long marked the summit (now also topped by a television antenna) while a wealth of legend and song marks the mountain's effect on the human imagination. When the Kilkenny essayist Hubert Butler came to write of the burning of Bridget Cleary in 1960, he began like this:

> You can see Slievenaman [*sic*] from my fields, though it is across the Tipperary border, a pale blue hump with the soft, rounded contours of ancient hills whose roughnesses have been smoothed away by time. Starting after lunch you can climb to the tip and be back by summer daylight, though it is over 2000 feet high. It can be seen from five or six southern counties and is one of the three or four most famous of Irish hills. Finn MacCool lived there and so did Oisin and Oscar, and fifty beautiful maidens, who give it its name, "The Mountain of Women," embroidered garments for them there, or so they say. The top of the mountain to within a couple of hundred feet of the cairn of stones is bare except for an odd patch of sphagnum moss and heather. Below it there is more heather, grazed by sheep, and a few frochan [*fraochán,* bilberry] clumps, but except for some piles of stones that might once have been a house and a rough track for carting turf, there is not much sign of human traffic.[9]

Butler had always assumed, he tells us, that the Clearys' home had been one of these stone ruins; instead, of course, he found that it lay in good farmland on the north side of the Anner valley, and was still habitable when he found it (as it continues to be, forty years later).

But the newspaper coverage at the time of Bridget Cleary's death had made much of the mountain's mythic history and of the "remoteness and isolation" of Ballyvadlea.

The *Transactions of the Kilkenny Archaeological Society* for 1851 include a twenty-eight-page essay on "The Fenian Traditions of Sliabh na mBan." The "Fenians" of the title are not the Irish Republican Brotherhood (founded in 1858), but the original *Fianna,* the legendary band of hunter-warriors led by Fionn mac Cumhaill, whom Butler mentions in the passage above, along with his son Oisín and grandson Oscar. The essay on "Fenian Traditions" is by John Dunne, with some additional notes by John O'Donovan, the most celebrated antiquary of his day. It includes a version of one of the best-known fairy legends in Ireland, still to be heard in both Irish and English: a group of fairy women insinuate themselves into a house where women are spinning late at night, and make free with the furnishings and the people. They are got rid of only when one of the spinners has the presence of mind to call out "Slievenamon is on fire!," and they rush home to the magic mountain.[10] The spinners' narrow escape cautions listeners against working late into the night. Slievenamon also features as *Sidh ar Femun* in the ninth-century tale *Tochmarc Étaíne,* "The Wooing of Étaín"—again, as an otherworld dwelling.[11] Stories like these, well known among antiquaries, helped in the building of theories about the "superstition" of the district.

Hubert Butler's verdict on the "fairy-house" in 1960 was that, "though it suggested poverty, it did not suggest mystery, remoteness, primaeval superstition." The *Cork Examiner* published its special correspondent's description of the same house on Thursday, March 28, 1895. It began, "It is a labourer's cottage, looking out on Slieve-na-mon. There are three rooms, a kitchen and two bed-rooms. Over the latter is a loft, reached by a ladder from the kitchen."

The reporter had walked around the house, and looked in at all the windows as best he could: "[T]he whole house appeared to be in the utmost disorder. It was locked, and looked lonely, as the dog resumed his seat under the half-door, and began once more to wear that aspect of resignation which he bore when the visitors disturbed his watching and waiting."

On the way back to Fethard, the driver of the horse-drawn cab regaled the journalist from Cork with stories of the locality, including the fact that a group of local men had waited with black-handled knives to rescue Bridget Cleary from the fairies on the nights following her death. Another story, already mentioned, concerned "one of the men who are in gaol," whom the driver had met a few months previously:

> [T]his man mentioned that he had a pain in his back, the result of having been taken out of his bed by the fairies and placed in his yard. The driver joked the fellow, but to no purpose. His faith in the people of the forts and raths could not be shaken; there was no night of his life on which he did not hear the fairies outside his house, and sometimes they were playing hurling matches.

Fifty-five-year-old Jack Dunne must be the man referred to here. The Kennedy brothers and William Ahearne, young and unmarried, would have been referred to as "boys," while Denis Ganey lived some distance away and was spoken of by everybody, this journalist included, as "the fairy doctor." If he had meant to refer to either Bridget Cleary's husband or her father, he would surely have said so, for later in his report he is at pains to stress that the defendants are almost all closely related and are not typical of the local population, which he characterizes as being "as deeply religious, and as strong-minded as any to be met with." The reporter continues, "it is doubtful if the standard of general intelligence is as high everywhere, and the intellect of the masses as enlightened, as I have found them to be in South Tipperary." When we read Jack Dunne's account of the fairies who caused his back pain—if the account is his—we must place it in the context of a worldview that the "enlightened masses" who were his neighbors were in the process of repudiating; we must also remember, however, that their ancestors would regularly have described some of their physical ailments in similar terms, at least when speaking colloquially. It is a question of idiom and worldview, not of intelligence.

On Wednesday night, after coming "into contact with all sorts and conditions of men, including those whom one might ignorantly assume at first sight to share in the beliefs of the people who killed Mrs Cleary," the *Cork Examiner* journalist sat in Stokes's Hotel and composed the first of three "letters" to his newspaper. His room was across the lamplit street from the military barracks, whose officers had that day been putting their horses through their paces in preparation for the races to be held in two weeks' time. Downstairs, local people sang the latest songs. Bridget Cleary, he wrote, was "a victim to a sentiment which was deemed extinct and which is nowhere execrated more strongly and laughed to scorn than in the enlightened community in whose midst it bred such an awful result."

This emphasis was an exercise in damage limitation. That day's *Nationalist,* published in Clonmel, had indicated the extent of the offense taken by Catholics and nationalists—readers and potential readers of the *Cork Examiner*—at the Tory newspapers' handling of the story. The *Dublin Evening Mail's* editorial of the previous evening had implicated the whole indigenous population in the crime, drawing a parallel between it and the infamous Lynchehaun case of a few months earlier in County Mayo. On October 6, 1894, in Achill Island, an English landowner, Mrs. Agnes MacDonnell, had suffered grotesque injuries, apparently at the hands of James Lynchehaun, a larger-than-life character and her own former steward. Her house and stables had been burned to the ground, and she had been kicked, beaten, and left for dead, with her nose bitten off. Lynchehaun had been arrested, but had escaped from police custody two weeks later, and remained at large until early January, when he was discovered in a relative's house, hiding in a hole dug under the floor.[12] In March 1895, he was awaiting trial in Castlebar, as the *Mail* reminded its readers:

> There were eleven persons standing by at the burning alive of Bridget Cleary, not one of whom raised a finger in her defence. There were also a number of persons present in the room in which the fugitive Lynchehaun was arrested in Achill. We do not suppose there are many Lynchehauns or witch-burners in Ireland, but neither are there many Mont Blancs or Monte

Rosas in Switzerland. But Switzerland is a mountainous country and the sympathizers with crime are very numerous in Ireland.

"Crime" of course was the catchall word that encompassed every kind of resistance to landlord interests, at the same time as it branded its perpetrators and sympathizers as brutish, apelike, and unfit for franchise. The alternative stereotype, favored by many who advocated the cause of Home Rule, was of the Irish as fey and spiritual.

In his "letter," written in Stokes's Hotel, the *Cork Examiner*'s reporter went on to refer to the recently published *Ballads in Prose* by Nora Hopper by way of placing the recent events in the context of the literary revival:[13]

> This appalling episode proves that fairies are not everywhere discredited, that here and there in this storied island, with its large mass of heathen lore, a few people settled in some remote, wild region (such as I have been visiting), whose image is that of the haunted past, blindly cling to the old traditions, that old traditions die very hard indeed.

He refers to the work of William Carleton and of Thomas Crofton Croker and to a public "which can enjoy the Celtic imaginativeness, seeing no harm in the elusive *leprachaun,* in the gambols on the . . . fairy forts by moonlight, even in the wicked fairy who bewitches the cow and stops the supply of milk." There, however, the reporter parts company with such uncritical readers, warning that

> . . . when the interest passes from the literary or academic domain and becomes more real and active the aspect of the question changes, and changes so seriously that not even the most ardent folklorist amongst us—Dr Hyde, Nora Hopper or Mr Yeats, for example—could defend it, strong as is their attachment to the fascinating fairyland of our country. It is one thing to write fairy tales, telling us how "once upon a time" men and women, horses and cows were bewitched by the inhabitants of the Land of Shee; and it is patriotic to stimulate interest in our

beautiful folk lore. But when the fairies actually play pranks with people, when the bustle of their merry hurling matches is actually heard in the middle of the night, and when all the creatures of the imagination become practical agents in daily life, it is time to pause.

The writer has already stretched facts somewhat in referring to the area around Ballyvadlea as "remote" and "wild." Now, rather as though fairy belief had a geological origin, like radon gas, he adjures his readers to "kindly bear in mind that the foot of Slieve-na-mon witnessed the crime, a desolate bit of hill-side, full of weird suggestion for the Celtic imagination, and that *the persons now implicated are absolutely alone in their unhappy convictions, and are for the greater number members of the same family.*" [my italics] The infection of fairy belief, if it cannot be eradicated, can at least be contained and confined to one family. The Bolands and the Kennedys, along with Michael Cleary, must be isolated so that the wider community may escape contamination.

The writer's mention of Yeats would have had considerable relevance for his readers; the thirty-year-old poet was just becoming a force to be reckoned with, and his first collection, *Poems,* was in press. Yeats's *Fairy and Folk Tales of the Irish Peasantry* had appeared in 1888, followed by *Representative Irish Tales* in 1891, and *Irish Fairy Tales* in 1892. His meditations on fairy lore and its implications for a new kind of Irish identity were set out in *The Celtic Twilight,* published late in 1893. At about the same time *The Bookman* had printed his ballad "The Stolen Bride," a revised version of which would appear in *The Wind Among the Reeds* (1899) as "The Host of the Air." The poem features a young woman, coincidentally named Bridget, who has danced with the fairy folk and eaten their food, and is swept away from her dismayed husband while they distract him with a game of cards:

> He played with the merry old men
> And thought not of evil chance,
> Until one bore Bridget his bride
> Away from the merry dance.

In a note in the *Bookman,* Yeats referred to the oral tradition on which he had based the poem: "I heard the story on which this ballad is founded from an old woman at Balesodare [*sic*], Sligo. She repeated me a Gaelic poem on the subject, and then translated it to me. I have always regretted not having taken down her words, and as some amends for not having done so, have made this ballad."[14]

In fact Yeats told the story in *The Celtic Twilight.* He had heard it, he says there, from "a little old woman in a white cap, who sings in Gaelic, and moves from one foot to the other as though she remembered the dancing of her youth."[15] The legend is familiar in Irish oral tradition, telling of the abduction of a newly married woman by a group of fairies: her husband sees her among them and hurries home, only to find his wife dead. Yeats tells us that, "Some *noteless* Gaelic poet had made this into a *forgotten* ballad, *some odd* verses of which my white-capped friend remembered and sang for me."

The emphases are mine: for Yeats, whose informants in Irish folklore were in fact very few, traditional verbal art was always faint, fragmentary and very old.[16] The Irish song that he heard in Ballysadare (and would not have understood) is almost certainly not forgotten. His account strongly suggests that it was *Ar Mo Ghabháil go Baile Átha Cliath Domh,* "On My Way to Dublin," a song still widely known among singers in the Donegal *Gaeltacht* and elsewhere.[17] In it, a husband tells of leaving his home, where his wife lies seriously ill, to go to Dublin. On his way he meets a seductive woman who asks after his wife and tries to persuade him to come away with her. He refuses to abandon his children, and realizes then that the beautiful stranger is his own wife, stolen by the fairies, who have left a sickly changeling in her place. Like the ballad "Tam Lin," discussed in Chapter 2, with which it has much in common, this song is one of the vehicles through which oral poetry treats of sexual longing, indecision, and loss.

In March 1895, when Bridget Cleary was killed, Yeats was staying at Thornhill, the home of his uncle George Pollexfen, in Sligo. His uncle's servant was the Mayo woman Mary Battle, whom Yeats believed to be clairvoyant, one of his most important sources of information on fairy-belief legend. Like people all over Ireland, she and Yeats discussed the events in Tipperary. He was in no doubt that her understanding of fairy tradition left no room for physical abuse, much less murder:

> The country people seldom do more than threaten the dead person put in the living person's place, and it is, I am convinced, a sin against the traditional wisdom to really ill-treat the dead person. A woman from Mayo who has told me a good many tales and has herself both seen and heard "the royal gentry" as she calls them was very angry with the Tipperary countryman who burned his wife, some time ago, her father and neighbours standing by. She had no doubt that they only burned some dead person, but she was quite certain that you should not burn even a dead person. She said: "In my place we say you should only threaten. They are so superstitious in Tipperary. I have stood in the door and I have heard lovely music, and seen the fort all lighted up, but I never gave in to them." "Superstitious" means to her "giving in" to "the others" and letting them have power over you, or being afraid of them, and getting excited about them, and doing foolish things.[18]

Mary Battle's belief in fairies is not so different from what another time or place might understand as imagination, or spirituality: it is too well balanced by common sense to be pathological. One Yeats scholar who quotes these lines has seen in them a vindication of the "scientific" analysis of Edwin Sidney Hartland, as presented in *The Science of Fairy Tales* (1890), that "a superior stage of evolution is reached in which the cruel *act* becomes a threat or a symbol."[19] There is no evidence, however, that mere threats came later than murderous acts in traditional practice. Hartland, like another famous contemporary, Sir James Frazer, whose essays on "the golden bough" appeared between 1890 and 1915, was applying Darwinian ideas to the study of folklore, presenting human thought as irrevocably evolving from the magical and religious to the scientific.

Yeats was less interested in the scientific, however. He continued:

I was always convinced that tradition, which avoids needless in-humanity, has some stronger way of protecting the bodies of those to whom the other world was perhaps unveiling its mysteries, than any mere command not to ill-treat some old person, who had maybe been put in the room of one's living wife or daughter or son. I heard of this stronger way last winter from an old Kildare woman, that I met in London. She said that in her own village "there was a girl used to be away with them, you'd never know when it was she herself that was in it or not until she'd come back, and then she'd tell she had been away. She didn't like to go, but she had to go when they called to her. And she told her mother always to treat kindly whoever was put in her place, sometimes one would be put and sometimes another, for, she'd say, "If you are unkind to whoever is there, they'll be un-kind to me."

This last observation tallies perfectly with all that we know from Irish oral tradition about changeling belief. True, it was sometimes used to rationalize the exposure, abandonment, and even the killing of children born with disabilities (and probably of some born to unmarried women), as well as death by sudden illness, suicide, or other misadventure; it could be invoked to justify cruel punishment of children or adults; but it also contained that proviso of compassion for those who were temporarily "not themselves."

Journalists writing about the case of Bridget Cleary could not fail to take into account the ideas of anthropologists and literary revivalists. In the weeks that followed her death, various publications would accept and even solicit articles on fairy belief and folklore. One of the pundits, Andrew Lang, was currently engaged with the president of the Folk-Lore Society, Edward Clodd, in a debate about just these questions in the pages of the society's journal. Another, Leland L. Duncan, a fellow of the Society of Antiquaries, visiting County Leitrim that summer, "found the good folk . . . full of the case"; they told him "several little similar tales," which he incorporated in a paper read to the Folk-Lore Society on March 17, 1896. A lively discussion followed, and the paper was later published.[20]

Mary Carty of Drumkeeran told Duncan the following story, which she said she had always heard as fact:

There was a girl living at Kilbride, three miles from Drumkeeran, and she went one day in harvest to mind a baby for a neighbour who was out getting hay, and she was there some time rocking the child. She got sick and cross that night and she was that way for three years. She used to tell the people to come to her at sunset, and she would tell them about their people who were dead; and she said she could show them a certain priest who had died, riding about on a white horse; but the people were afraid to go and see the sight. There was a little boy to whom she took a great liking, and would have showed him more than anyone, only he was kept from her. At the end of three years she got very bad and sick one night, and said goodbye to the people, and said she had to be going to a place called Kilbride near Dublin, that there was a redhaired boy to be taken and she had to be there, and as she was going she would tell them how to get back their own. The mother was to go to a certain little byre upon a hill between twelve and one o'clock at night, to cut a drain round the byre with a black-hafted knife, to get a lot of hen's dirt and mix it up, and between twelve and one to stand inside the byre and throw three dashes of the dirt out of the door; and when that was done she was to shout. The mother did this, and then came home; and in the morning it was their own daughter that got up and began to tell them about people who were dead. She asked for a drink, and when her mother gave it to her she forgot all about the three years and began to talk as of yesterday and of minding the child.[21]

This story carries no hint of burning or other physical assault; instead it tells of a girl's relationship with her mother, explaining three years of "sickness," "crossness," and other difficult and demanding behavior as fairy abduction. The legend features the familiar white horse, along with hen's dirt and the ubiquitous black-handled knife. As in the story told about Bridget Cleary, it was to be used at midnight on a hill in order to defeat the fairies. These motifs make for a satisfyingly vivid narrative, but one that demands no more of the hearer than suspension of disbelief in the existence of a hidden, nearby world of the supernatural. As we have seen, such a willingness to forgo natural scepticism paid rich dividends in terms of access to a shared symbolic universe. In its depiction of the "fairy" impostor's three years among the local community, moreover, this legend offers listeners a charter of deviant behavior; it shows what kind of eccentricities may be tolerated, and how they may be abandoned without loss of face when they have served their purpose.

Another of Duncan's stories offers a clue about a further feature of the Clearys' life that may have disquieted their neighbors. We have already discussed the importance of milk and butter in the symbolic as well as the financial economy of nineteenth-century rural Ireland. Michael Cleary's trade as a cooper gave him access to the most intimate parts of this economy as a manufacturer of tools essential to the production of butter: churns, churndashes, firkins, and the keelers (shallow tubs) in which butter was cooled. Edward McVittie, of Cootehill, County Cavan, told Leland Duncan a legend about a cooper and another man who went to plow a field that bordered on a ringfort:

> They were ploughing some time, about an hour or so; and they heard the noise of churning in the fort, but they could not tell where the noise came from. They ploughed on for a bit, but every time they came up to the fort they heard the sound of the churning. It stopped after a little; and when they had gone down the hill and up again, there was a table there, and the churn staff, with the dash off it, left out to be mended, with cooper's tools laid by. The cooper says: "Here's a job for me; you can plough till I get it mended for them." He set to work, and put the dash on the staff for them, and left it on the table, and went off to the other man to plough; and when they came back, the dash, table and tools were all gone. The sound of the churning went on again for some time after, and then it stopped, and a table was left out with oatcake and butter. The cooper invited the other to take some, but he wouldn't, and said it was not

right. He went over and took some, and satisfied himself, and then went off to his plough again, and when they came back the table and oatcake were gone. When they had their plough-ing and work finished for that day they had to cross a little stream going home. They were riding their horses home, and the cooper went first and crossed the stream, but the horse of his neighbour, who was following him, shied when he was crossing and threw him and broke his neck. It was said that the fairies were angry with him, because he would not take the food they offered him.[22]

In most cases, of course, it is considered highly unwise to take food offered by the fairies. The cooper in this story, like the smiths and midwives who feature in others, is immune from danger when he puts his trade—his special knowledge—at the fairies' service. We remember that Michael Cleary's trade was prospering, and that pros-perity, and especially the possession of money, often led to suspicion and accusations of consorting with the fairies.

Michael Cleary made "butter firkins and other articles for a cream-ery at Fethard."[23] He also apparently supplied local farmers, but it is likely that the creamery which bought his wares was causing resent-ment by usurping the work—and the income—of local farm women. By the 1890s, domestic butter making was being edged out of the market, with much denigration of traditional methods and standards of hygiene, in favor of centralized and standardized production. Women had always kept the income from their own churnings, as they kept the money earned by selling eggs, but when the new creameries contracted to buy the milk or eggs produced on a farm, payment was almost always made to a man: the farmer.[24]

Two days after his first visit to Ballyvadlea, the *Cork Examiner*'s correspondent went there again, this time in the company of William Simpson.

[Simpson] is an intelligent and obliging man. It was he who di-rected the attention of the police to the *boreen* [*bóithrín,* lane] in which the body was found, and he led me to the spot through marshy fields, and up over one of the ditches that line the old path-way. This is grass-grown, and the soil is watery. The hole in which the corpse lay is full of muddy water. It is a horrible spot, desolate and depressing.

Simpson led the reporter to the Clearys' house, where he learned that the dog was called Badger, and the cat Dotey, and saw both animals fed from a pot of potatoes. The reporter made a detailed inventory of the three rooms (as described in Chapter 3), and noted the medicine bottle in the corner, with its printed label. His description accords well with the evidence of the police photographs taken two days earlier.

The car driver for this second expedition was either the same man as on Tuesday, or another with the same taste in stories and jokes. The journalist was interested in the conversation the driver carried on with William Simpson, when Simpson referred to ghost stories told around the neighborhood:

They had been laughing over the fairies and their alleged doings, and the talk drifted on to charms and spells. William Simpson is an eminently practical man. "That's the gate," said he, "where the man in black used to sit. But I have passed it at all hours of the day and night, from six in the morning until six in the evening, and from six in the evening until six in the morning, and never met anything but the cattle I was looking for. The fact of the matter is (added this sceptic), no one can take you away, body and soul, except the police."

Like Bridget Cleary, who was supposed to have tried to bluff her tormenters into thinking that the police were at the window, Simpson here counters the idea of fairies with the equally powerful one of the police. The comparison is not fanciful. It is still to be found in threats to children, which replace "The fairies will get you!" with "The policeman will get you!" As responsibility for the regulation of people's behavior passed more and more from their relatives and neighbors to the jurisdiction of the state, the police had come to replace the fairies as icons of control.

Like the fairies of an earlier imagining, the police in late-nineteenth-century Ireland were everywhere: they communicated secretly from stronghold to stronghold; moved unpredictably about the countryside; observed all that went on in the community and intervened arbitrarily in its life. Among the five hundred or so police officers and men stationed in South Tipperary were many who had grown up in ordinary rural households. They had emerged from six months' training at the police depot in Dublin's Phoenix Park so changed in their habits and behavior that their home communities were left forever in doubt about their real allegiances—much as people mistrusted those said to have been "away with the fairies." The idea of surveillance, monopolized by the state from the nineteenth century, was a long-established part of fairy discourse too: the "good people" were commonly spoken of as eavesdroppers; the hills typically said to belong to them, like Slievenamon, Trooperstown Hill in County Wicklow, and Knockmaa at Castle Hackett, near Tuam, County Galway, are isolated summits that command panoramic views. Kylenagranagh Hill was supposed to be such a fairy place.

For all William Simpson's consorting with the police and the visiting journalist, however, and despite his skeptical laughter about fairies, neither he nor the driver of the horse-drawn cab was prepared to discount all the traditional beliefs current in the area. The driver agreed with Simpson's quip about the power of the police,

> . . . but still there was something in a blue stone wrapped in a petticoat if anything happened to the milk. William Simpson admitted this to be true, but then if you rubbed the cow with your hand or your boot or hat the softening so produced would stop the flow of blood. What about the taking away of the butter though? The question was asked by the driver, and William Simpson's scepticism disappeared. The taking away of butter was a different matter altogether. Everyone knew, indeed, that there was devilment yet in the world, and there was devilment in the taking away of butter.

"Taking away of butter" of course meant not the stealing of butter already made, but the magical spiriting away of the butter "profit," so that however hard one churned, only froth appeared. Even the hard-headed emergencyman—a dairy farmer, after all—allowed that such things could happen.

That night, back in Stokes's Hotel, the journalist sat down again to write his copy for the *Cork Examiner*. He wrote more about the "phantoms and bogies of Irish folk lore," and about people who believed that "Slieve-na-mon in the stillness of the night, or when the storms howled through the hills, looked down on mystical revels." It was hard to believe that such things could still exist so close to the end of the century:

> I cannot help mentioning that as these words are being written in Stokes' Hotel, Fethard—about four miles from the scene of the awful sacrifice—the strains of "Hi Di" from the "enormously successful" modern burlesque "Go Bang" come floating into the room; while only a few minutes ago two peasants could be heard singing "After the Ball." And surely this is the essence of modern civilization in the very heart of the district in which Mrs Cleary was burnt to death for a witch!

"After the Ball" is best known from Jerome Kern's 1927 musical *Showboat,* but it was already a music-hall favorite. Popular music could represent modern civilization in 1895 because it spoke of the revolution that was taking place in communications. This was the year when motion pictures first became available for public viewing, and when Guglielmo Marconi first demonstrated radio transmission.[25]

By the end of the week of Bridget Cleary's funeral, the unionist *Daily Express* in Dublin had sent its own special reporter to Ballyvadlea. This man too traveled around the area, discovering a wealth of detail about the personal history of Bridget and Michael Cleary, their ages and occupations, and the way they had acquired the tenancy of their cottage. First the *Express*'s sister paper, the *Dublin Evening Mail,* and then a chain of other unionist and Tory newspapers, at home and abroad, picked up these reports. Responding no doubt to the *Nationalist*'s angry editorial earlier in the week, this reporter scrupulously noted Fr. Con Ryan's denunciation of the outrage at mass in Cloneen on Sunday. However, he was also the one who first revealed to a voyeuristic readership that "an old man" had pronounced that one of Bridget Cleary's legs was longer than the other. Given the other accounts available, this must have been Jack Dunne.

Like the *Cork Examiner* reporter, the *Daily Express* correspondent found the area around Ballyvadlea to be far more modern and civilized than early reports had suggested. Unlike the nationalist press, however, the Tory papers failed to find any grounds in this for confidence in the political maturity or "intelligence" of the native population in general. On Friday, March 29, the *Evening Mail* again attacked the Home Rule cause:

> A special reporter of the *Daily Express* has gathered some information respecting the "Tipperary Horror," which deepens considerably its political significance. It is not true, as was supposed, that the scene of the crime was a district remote from the influences of civilization or that the alleged perpetrators of it were in an exceptionally savage condition of ignorance . . . Now the question is—are the people of Cloneen or Fethard or of [William] Smith O'Brien's famous Slievenamon, inferior in sense or information to the general body of the Irish peasantry, the constituencies who are to manage Ireland's domestic affairs *vice* [?] an Imperial Parliament . . . ? We put the question especially to Mr Morley . . . Is he still, after the revelations made by the Tipperary horror, inclined to give over Ireland and all her civilization and all her hopes for the future to a peasant-elected Irish Parliament?

The same paper quoted the *Scotsman,* which was bluntly anti-Catholic in its colonialist rhetoric:

> The strange and shocking story . . . reads like a tale of the dark ages of some savage tribe in Africa . . . As the Irish peasants who

are said to have tortured Bridget Cleary to death are no doubt devout Catholics, it may be made a reproach to their religion and their priests that they should be living in such a state of superstition.

And on Sunday, March 31, the London correspondent of the *New York Times* informed his readers:

> As might be expected, the barbarous episode near Fethard, in Tipperary, of a woman being tortured to death by her husband and her male relatives in the process of expelling a witch that had taken possession of her body is being gravely cited by the anti-Irish papers here as evidence of the mental degradation and savagery of the Irish peasant population.

The reporter added, however, that faith in witchcraft was "very general among men in all parts of Great Britain where there have been no modern movements of population."

But even as the media of the English-speaking world turned their attention to South Tipperary, the horror initially felt there was giving way, in certain quarters at least, to black humor and commercial exploitation. On Saturday, March 23, a rumor was started—and at first widely believed, according to the *Cork Examiner*—that Denis Ganey had escaped from his prison cell through the keyhole. And William Simpson, as we have seen, laughed and joked with the car driver about fairy belief, even as they were visiting the scene of Bridget Cleary's death.

The Clearys' cottage and outbuildings were the property of the Cashel Poor Law Guardians, but Simpson was in possession of the keys. The reporter from the *Cork Examiner* had no doubt paid him for his cooperation in admitting him to the house, and he would not be the last journalist to come there. In May the *Nationalist* reported:

> Complaints have reached us that the Crown witness, Simpson, has taken over possession of the labourer's cottage in which Cleary is said to have burned his wife, and that without the authority of the guardians; and that he is at present utilizing his

spare time showing numbers of visitors who go there over the place, &c. It seems to us that no one should be allowed to profit by this horrible transaction. The guardians should take the key of this cottage, and if no suitable labourer will take it, then lock the door.

The Poor Law Guardians attempted to do just that, but William Simpson would not be easily dispossessed. Six months later, when the petty sessions were held in Fethard on Monday, September 23, Darby Scully, JP, of Silverfort, was in the chair. Hugh Sayers, solicitor, appeared for the Cashel Poor Law Guardians, who were suing Patrick Boland and William Simpson for possession of the cottage at Bally-vadlea. The *Nationalist* reported that, "When the case was called, the chairman said they ought to sell the cottage to Madame Tussaud." Sayers immediately rejoined jokingly that "an offer had been made and they were in communication with her." Patrick Boland was in prison and the rent collector testified that William Simpson still held the keys; he was willing to give up the key of the house, but said he "had things" in the outbuildings. An order was made for possession.

The *Nationalist* reported:

The Cashel Guardians have just recovered possession of the famous Ballyvadlea cottage, wherein was enacted that dreadful tragedy known as the burning of Bridget Cleary by her husband for alleged witchery. The cottage has been very much photographed, and since the tragedy, was made a kind of "peep show" by an enterprising neighbour. The decree for possession is against William Simpson, an emergency caretaker, who was one of the principal witnesses against the prisoners at the trial.

But the joke about Madame Tussaud did not die in the Fethard courtroom. On September 28, the *Nationalist* reported on "The Ballyvadlea Cottage: the Alleged Sale to Madame Tussaud":

Our Cashel correspondent writes: "A paragraph appeared in Thursday's *Freeman* to the effect that the guardians of Cashel are in negotiations for the sale of the cottage at Ballyvadlea to Madame Tussaud, of London. Such a statement is untrue. The proposal was only spoken of, as hearsay, by some person at a meeting of the guardians a few months ago, but the mere mention of such a proposition was condemned by every member of the board then present. The matter ended there, and has not since been heard of, however the report got circulation."[26]

The curious visited the cottage and took photographs throughout the spring and summer of 1895 (George Eastman had introduced the Kodak box camera in 1888), and, like the newspapers, the drivers of Fethard's fifteen horse-drawn cabs did good business. The *Nationalist* reported on Saturday, March 30, that "thousands of *Nationalists* containing the report have been re-posted by subscribers to relatives and friends in America, Australia and elsewhere," and that arrangements had been made to bring out a special edition on the following Monday. In fact, special editions appeared both on that day and on the following Thursday, while the *Clonmel Chronicle*'s edition for Wednesday, April 3, included a tabloid supplement on the case.

George Henry Bassett's *The Book of County Tipperary*, published in 1889, lists only three photographers in the county, one each in Clonmel, Cashel, and Templemore. Henry Holborn was then at 8 Main Street, Clonmel; in Guy's 1893 *Directory of Munster* his address is given as O'Connell Street. The *Chronicle* for Saturday, March 30, 1895, carried the following advertisement:

THE FAIRY MYSTERY

By the kind permission of Colonel Evanson and the courteous Police-Officers in charge of the Cottage, I have taken the following PHOTOGRAPHS, Exterior and Interior:-

A Group of Officers; the Glen where the body of Mrs Cleary was concealed; and her present resting-place in Cloneen churchyard. Also, a VIEW OF CLONEEN Copies 1s. each

Holborn Studio, Clonmel

Bridget Cleary's dreadfully abused body had been buried, and the suspects were all in prison. Interest in the case was being kept alive, however, and the reading public was poised to hear the next episode of the case on Monday, April 1, when the magistrates would reopen their hearing.

9

Two Courtrooms

ON MARCH 27, 1895, the *Tyrone Constitution* noted:

> Politically and socially it is a quiet time, as becomes the season
> in Dublin. For once affairs in Parliament are voted to be ex-
> ceedingly slow, and a glance at the columns of the morning pa-
> pers is all that we bestow on that erstwhile attractive portion of
> the newspaper.

Things may have been slow in Parliament, but April 2 was the
date fixed for the second reading of John Morley's Land Law (Ireland)
Bill, for which Irish tenant farmers and supporters of Home Rule
were waiting eagerly. The Land Bill would also be a test for the government in London; the Liberals were struggling to retain the power
they had won on a Home Rule ticket in 1892.

Archibald Philip Primrose, Lord Rosebery, had been Prime Minister for just a year, having succeeded William Gladstone after the
defeat of his second Home Rule Bill in March 1894. Wealthy, enig-
matic, and aloof, Rosebery was forty-eight, and should have been at
the height of his powers. As a young man he had been expected to
have a brilliant career, but the death of his wife, the heiress Hannah
Rothschild, in 1890, had left him shattered, and so severely did he
suffer from insomnia that when the Liberals returned to government
two years later he had only reluctantly agreed to resume office as Foreign Secretary. He had accepted the premiership when offered it by
Queen Victoria, but now, in March 1895, following a severe attack of

influenza, he was so weak that newspapers throughout Britain and Ireland carried almost daily bulletins on his health, with solicitous reports of his inability to sleep. On March 19, he was "unable to do much yet in the way of attending to his public duties." Two days later the *Dublin Evening Mail* announced that "Lord Rosebery has had no relapse, and the suggestions of his probable resignation are officially declared to be absurd"; by March 28, however, his progress was still "very slow."

There was a further complication: Lord Rosebery's name was being mentioned in connection with the case of criminal libel being brought by Oscar Wilde against the boorish and eccentric Marquess of Queensberry.[1] Best remembered in modern times for the rules of boxing he drew up in 1867, Queensberry was notoriously belligerent. He was incensed at Wilde's increasingly public relationship with his son, Lord Alfred Douglas, and had insisted on dragging the issue into the public arena. Douglas's older brother, Viscount Drumlanrig, had been Lord Rosebery's private secretary, but had died the previous October in what was reported as a shooting accident. His death was widely believed to have been suicide, however, and Queensberry was among the many who believed that a homosexual relationship with Rosebery had been the source of his older son's distress. A letter Queensberry wrote to his former father-in-law shortly after his son's death described the prime minister as a "snob queer." As Richard Ellmann puts it, "The conviction that one son had died in a homosexual scandal resolved Queensberry to make sure that a second did not die the same way." It was common knowledge that he hated the prime minister as much as he did Wilde.[2] Queensberry's vendetta against Wilde was laden with danger both for Rosebery's government and for the cause of Home Rule, and rumors about it had been building in London during the weeks when Bridget Cleary's disappearance and death had been talked of all over Ireland.

On February 18, Queensberry left a card at the Albemarle Club in London, where Oscar Wilde and his wife Constance were both members, addressed to "Oscar Wilde, posing somdomite [*sic*]." Wilde received the card ten days later, and was persuaded to take legal action. Queensberry was arrested on March 2, and after a week of discussions his solicitor Charles Russell briefed the barrister (and union-ist MP) Edward Carson, to defend him. Queensberry was committed for trial on March 9, at a hearing packed with inquisitive spectators. Letters he had written were mentioned, but not read, for fear of com-promising certain "exalted personages" whom they named. On March 18, a grand jury returned a true bill for libel, allowing Queensberry to be tried at the Old Bailey. Although the grand jury's business was conducted in private, one of its members happened to be "a distin-guished French journalist who had lived in England for many years."[3] He immediately alerted newspapers in France to the contents of those controversial letters. By early April, the story of Rosebery's re-puted entanglement with Queensberry's eldest son had spread from the watering places of France to the clubs of London, and more rev-elations lay ahead.

Edward Carson, who challenged Wilde's counsel to disclose the contents of Queensberry's letters, was not only a consummately able barrister, he was the protégé of Tory leader Arthur Balfour, and Chief Secretary Morley's most formidable opponent in the House of Commons. As we have seen, he had already described Morley's Land Bill as "a revolutionary monster" and vowed to oppose it strenuously. Born in Dublin in 1854, Carson had been a student at Trinity Col-lege in the 1870s, at the same time as Wilde. There, he had seemed dull alongside his brilliant and flamboyant contemporary, but he was to astonish those who underestimated him. In 1887, as a young legal officer of the Crown in Ireland, he was assigned to prosecute William O'Brien and local farmer John Mandeville in Mitchelstown, in the case that led to the so-called "Mitchelstown massacre."[4] His career since then had gone from strength to strength.

In moving the Land Bill's second reading, John Morley drew calls of "Oh!" from the benches and cheers from nationalists as he de-plored what he characterized as the unconstructive criticisms made by unionist and landlord interests since its introduction. Carson, he said, "had made a speech filled with the rather mechanical and auto-matic violence which was sometimes thought forensic, and which Irish lawyers had at command [oh, and laughter], but which neither helped any question forward nor kept any question back [nationalist cheers]." The Irish landlords he called an "irreconcilable junta, which was always violent and unteachable, and always wrong [oh]—which always fought proposals of this kind with blind and rather stupid desperation [oh]."

Carson replied only briefly, but pledged that he and his party would fight the bill at every step to the very end, and the debate was adjourned.[5]

The next day, April 3, Carson was on his feet again, this time in the Old Bailey, as counsel for the defense in *Regina* v. *Queensberry* at the Central Criminal Court. The trial caused a sensation in London, as Carson's examination revealed more and more details of Wilde's lifestyle. As the *Dublin Evening Telegraph* noted on April 5: "The Wilde case has attracted the largest and most heterogeneous crowd to the Old Bailey that has been seen there for many years. It is largely a fashionable crowd—minus the ladies—and it includes many persons well known in theatrical circles." The paper devoted a full column to the case, and notwithstanding its own nationalist allegiance, commented admiringly on Carson's skill.

The libel trial continued for two days, as Wilde's dignified defiance crumbled under the onslaught of Carson's righteousness. By noon on Friday, Queensberry had been acquitted, leaving the way open for the public prosecutor to pursue a criminal case of indecency against Wilde. He was arrested the same evening at the Cadogan Hotel on Sloane Street.

Carson's courtroom victory over Wilde, an avowed advocate of Home Rule, was a triumph also for those who opposed the Irish Land Bill. Thursday's *Dublin Evening Telegraph* illustrated the extent to which Carson might now control the bill's fate. The paper reported at length on a by-election speech made at Lambeth Baths by the nationalist Irish MP John Dillon, on behalf of the Liberal candidate L. P. Trevelyan. Dillon used the opportunity to drum up support for the Land Bill, boasting of the drop in crime in Ireland under Morley's administration:

Where are all the blood-thirsty prophecies of Mr Balfour, Mr T. W. Russell and Company, who declared that the Irish were a race of wild beasts who should be kept down by coercion? The record can never be obliterated that the Irish people, while they resent coercion—and shame on them if they did not [hear, hear], and will always struggle against it, and against the denial of liberty—while they are treated like human beings and like men entitled to treatment like yourselves, will respond to that treatment as you do [cheers].

The Land Bill now before Parliament is demanded by nine-tenths of the Irish people in Ireland . . . The English members do not understand, and they do not want to take the trouble to understand this great question, but they will vote as they are told by Mr Carson, QC.

In fact no vote was ever taken on Morley's Land Bill, for the Liberal government resigned in June. Few histories of the period refer to the bill, or indeed to Rosebery and Morley's time as prime minister and chief secretary for Ireland respectively. In early April, however, they were still in power, and their carefully prepared Irish Land Bill was an urgent and important matter.[6]

That Wilde's downfall was seized on as propaganda by those opposed to Home Rule is well known. Like Charles Stewart Parnell before him, he was an upper-class Victorian Irishman, publicly accused of sexual irregularity. If such potential leaders among the Irish could not be relied on to set an example, the argument ran, what hope could there be of morality and "intelligence" among the rank and file of the electorate?

The case being heard in Clonmel courthouse by Colonel Evanson and the other South Tipperary magistrates, and now being reported throughout Ireland and Britain and beyond, provided another plank for the same platform. On Monday, April 1, crowds had again gathered when the nine male defendants were marched through the streets to the courthouse, and the building was packed long before the proceedings began. Mary Kennedy, brought by train from Limerick, arrived a little after the men. The court was to hear the evidence of William Simpson and of Fr. Cornelius (Con) Ryan. The prisoners, the *Irish Times* reported, "on being put into the dock presented a rather unconcerned appearance. They chatted, smiled, and exchanged patches of snuff."

William Simpson was the first witness called. His testimony related to the night of March 14, and corroborated that given by Johanna and Katie Burke. They had had ample time to make sure their stories agreed, and in fact it would later emerge that Simpson had coached Johanna Burke in what she was to say.[7] Asked what so many people had been doing in the Clearys' house on that evening when Bridget Cleary was forcibly dosed with herbs and new milk, Simpson said, "They were there to hunt away the witches and the fairies. The door was open for that purpose. I don't know that they came for that purpose, but when they were there they were at that work. I went to see Mrs Cleary." Simpson also gave it as his opinion that it was Jack Dunne who had said, "Make down a good fire and we'll make her answer."

District Inspector Wansbrough led Simpson carefully through the testimony that he had already given in the form of a sworn "information" before Bridget Cleary's body was found. After Simpson described how Bridget Cleary had been held over the fire, Acting Sergeant Egan gave evidence; he had followed Michael Cleary home to Ballyvadlea from Drangan on March 16. He produced a striped flannel nightdress, which he had obtained by climbing through a window of the house at about ten o'clock that same night. Simpson identified it as the one the dead woman had been wearing on the Thursday night. He told how Johanna Burke and Mary Kennedy had removed it, and dressed the sick woman in a clean dry nightgown after the men had returned her to her bed.

The court adjourned for lunch when Simpson's narrative arrived at midnight on Thursday, the time when Bridget Cleary was said to have been brought back from the fairies. Questioned in the afternoon, he told of spending the rest of the night with others in the house after Patrick Boland and the four Kennedy men had left for the wake in Killenaule, of his last visit to Bridget Cleary on the morning of the day she died, and of Michael Cleary's vigil on Kylenagranagh Hill, apparently waiting for his wife to reappear on a white horse.

Richard J. Crean, solicitor for Denis Ganey and Michael Cleary, cross-examined Simpson, trying to establish that Cleary's instructions about the way the herbs were to be administered had come from Jack Dunne, and not from Ganey. None of the other prisoners, except William Ahearne, was represented. The *Irish Times* described Jack Dunne and Patrick Boland as "extremely odd-looking types of countrymen." As we know, the two men were first cousins; both belonged to the generation of laborers born before the Famine, who had never learned to write; they would almost certainly not have been sufficiently at ease in the world of literacy to hire solicitors.

Dr. John J. Hanrahan, another Clonmel solicitor, appeared for William Ahearne. Simpson agreed with him that his client had been forced to hold the candle in Bridget Cleary's bedroom, adding that "Ahearne was a delicate boy and did not work." He also told the bench that he had not seen Michael Kennedy take any part in the proceedings, and that Bridget Cleary had not struggled when she was held over the fire. (This was when he recalled her saying "Are you going to make a herring of me? Give me a chance!")

The rest of Monday afternoon was spent in taking the evidence of Fr. Ryan. He had visited the house twice, although he had been sent for three times. He had also met and spoken to Michael Cleary in the chapel in Drangan on the day after Bridget's killing, when Cleary had been so distressed and had wept so loudly and so bitterly that the priest had been afraid of him. District Inspector Wansbrough asked the priest, when he had described his visits to the house, "Is it possible that you heard nothing of these proceedings about witchcraft?"

"Up to the time I heard nothing—absolutely nothing."

"Don't you think that very extraordinary?"

"No, I do not. The priest is very often the last to hear of things like that generally, I should say. I heard a rumour on the Saturday after that Mrs Cleary had disappeared mysteriously. I had no suspicion of foul play or witchcraft, and if I had I should have absolutely refused to say Mass in the house, and have given information to the police at once."

District Inspector Wansbrough returned to the same line of questioning after hearing about the priest's conversation with Jack Dunne in the chapel yard. A native of Somerset in England, and a Protestant, he seems to have had difficulty in grasping the nature of the relationship between Irish Catholic priests and their parishioners, where much of the communication that took place was protected by the seal of the confessional: "Will you say how, that foul crime having been revealed to you, you took no steps whatever to bring any of those criminals to justice, or to inform the police?" Fr. Ryan had, of course, alerted the police in Drangan to the situation in Ballyvadlea on March 16, immediately after he spoke to Michael Cleary, but he cannot have told them he suspected murder.

"I told the police that I suspected that there was foul play from something Dunne had said, or that probably he could be able to give every information."

"But did he not tell you that she was burned to death?"

There was no answer, and here Wansbrough apparently gave up: "It is a very extraordinary thing, but I had better leave it to the court to judge. It is no evidence, and I will ask no further questions."

The day's proceedings were almost at an end, but Fr. Ryan attempted to clarify his position: from Cleary's demeanor he had thought the man's mind was going astray, so he had reported the matter to the police and requested them to look after him.

Tuesday saw a continuation of the hearing, with testimony from Minnie Simpson, farmer Thomas Smyth, and two police officers, DI Wansbrough and Sergeant Patrick Rogers, who had been in charge of the party that found the body.

Wansbrough testified that he had visited the Clearys' house when he heard of Bridget Cleary's disappearance. His calling it "a new labourer's cottage" reminds the reader again of how the landscape had changed in the ten years or so since the Poor Law Guardians had begun to implement the provisions of the Labourers (Ireland) Act of 1883. The cottage in Ballyvadlea does not look particularly old at the end of the twentieth century; at the end of the nineteenth, despite a certain amount of weathering, as shown in Constable McLoughlin's photograph, it must have appeared strikingly new.

When Sergeant Rogers and Constables Somers and O'Callaghan had found Bridget Cleary's body on March 22, Wansbrough had gone to the spot to view it. He had also apparently ordered measurements to be taken, for he informed the court that the body had been lying 1,050 yards across the fields from the Clearys' house. He had seen the postmortem examination carried out, and had heard the finding of the coroner's inquest. He gave evidence of having searched the house on March 23, and produced a spade and shovel:

> The spade was a comparatively new one and the handle was stained with oil, as though carried by some person with an oily hand. It appeared to be paraffin oil. The shovel had on it traces of black, boggy soil, similar to that on the ground in which the body was found buried.

The court heard from Sergeant Rogers about the finding of the body, and the presiding magistrate complimented the police on their work: "Colonel Evanson said that the magistrates wished to express their high opinion of the prompt action by District Inspector Wansbrough and the men under his command, particularly in finding in this very unfrequented spot the body of this unfortunate woman."

Six years later, Michael McCarthy devoted several pages of his *Five Years in Ireland* to Wansbrough's intrepid search for Bridget Cleary:

> Railway stations are watched, farmhouses and outhouses are searched; fields and woods and brakes are tried in all directions; ponds and rivers are dragged! . . . At length . . . District-Inspector Wansbrough rightly concludes that she must be dead. If Bridget Cleary's body was not discovered, no further effective proceedings could be taken. No crime could be laid to the charge of those people whatever. It seemed a hopeless quest that the police now entered upon. Thousands of square miles of country to search for one poor half-burned body lying in a few feet square of earth! No assistance, no clue, though so many people around them knew everything.[8]

McCarthy starts with the railway stations, as did many of the newspaper commentators. The black lines of the railway map, radiating from cities and towns, were a powerful image of the logical, linear, hierarchical thinking that underlay the work of administrators, scientists, and educators. Throughout Europe and North America in the second half of the nineteenth century, the coming of the railway signaled an end to barbarism and the coming of civilization. Fresh fish, eggs, flowers, and vegetables could be transported from the farthest outposts into the centers of population, and money could be sent back in exchange, while daily newspapers carried the language, culture, and values of the metropolis insistently outward.

In McCarthy's commentary, it is as though an impenetrable membrane separated the authorities from the people of the countryside; he implies that the police would have had to turn over every square foot of soil in South Tipperary in their search. A barrier did exist between metropolitan and vernacular culture, and the prevarications of fairy narrative were part of it, but certain individuals moved freely across it. The *Cork Examiner* reported that William Simpson had led the police to where the body was buried, as he later led the paper's own special reporter. In all these accounts, Simpson emerges as an individualist and something of an opportunist; his must have been a tough personality to sustain such an ambiguous position.

Before Tuesday's proceedings finished, District Inspector Henry Hawtrey Jones of Clonmel produced before the court the gray tweed suit Michael Cleary had been wearing at the time of his arrest. It had been taken from him in the jail on the day his wife's body was discovered, and Jones pointed out greasy stains and spots on the legs of the trousers and on the right sleeve and front of the coat. The police had bought new clothes for Cleary: the register of communications received at Dublin Castle in 1895 carries a terse summary of a requisition received: "6153: April 2, Tip. Expenses, purchase of clothes for prisoner M. Cleary."[9]

Colonel Evanson announced on Tuesday that the court would not sit the next day. The RIC county inspector for Tipperary South Riding, based in Clonmel, had already sent a telegram to Dublin Castle: "Clearys case is likely to end on Thursday there will be an adjournment over tomorrow which is fair day here. Case cannot end today. Two sol[icito]rs represent some of accused."[10] On Wednesday April 3, therefore, the day when Oscar Wilde and Edward Carson's courtroom confrontation began in London, the actors in Clonmel's drama were resting. Clonmel's fairs on the first Wednesday of each month were famous, and the town was crowded with people buying and selling horses, cattle, and sheep. The *Clonmel Chronicle* published its tabloid supplement, detailing Monday and Tuesday's evidence in the Cleary case. The *Dublin Evening Telegraph* on the same day published a "specially contributed" article headed, "The Tipperary Horror: Changelings."

The writer, identified only as "X," drew heavily on Yeats's *Fairy and Folk Tales of the Irish Peasantry,* with references to writings by the twelfth-century Giraldus Cambrensis, Edmund Spenser, Dr. John Anster, and Thomas Crofton Croker, and to "Sir Walter [Scott]'s fine ballad of *Tam Lin.*" He quoted *The Faerie Queene:* "Such, men do changelings call, so changed by fairies' theft," and Dr. Anster: "I crossed my brow; I crossed my breast, but that night my child departed! / They left a weakling in his stead / And I am broken hearted." From Lady Wilde, via Yeats, came the lines, "Burn, burn, if of the devil, burn / But if of God and the saints, be free from harm." The writer also explained: "The Irish 'forts' have always been sacred to the 'good people,' and hence it is that those round ditches which surrounded the ancient Irish villages still survive in hundreds, though it must be a thousand years since the last was erected."

This writer's knowledge of folklore and field monuments reflects the importance of antiquarian study in Ireland at the end of the nineteenth century. When Michael McCarthy came to write of these matters five years later, however, he showed less scholarly detachment. On first mentioning the word "fort" in connection with the Cleary case he explained:

[L]et me say at once that it means a ring fence, or double ring fence, of simple earth, thrown up in ancient times by the Danes or other settlers in Ireland after the manner of a Zulu Kraal. The South of Ireland is studded with them; and though they are often most inconveniently situated on tillage land, and though their destruction presents no features of difficulty whatever, beyond merely levelling the fence, they have been preserved; from

a superstitious dread of ill-luck to anyone who ventured to destroy them. I am informed that people in Ballyvadlea believe
that a person being near this fort at night is liable to be struck
with rheumatism, paralysis, and soforth! Those accursed
unlovely and useless remains of barbarism should be levelled to
the ground by every man who wishes to see Ireland prosper. I
myself know a score of farmers who have these forts on their
land: all farmers of the best class, comfortable, rational, hospitable, intelligent, keen men of business; yet, not one of them
has the courage to remove these nuisances from their holdings,
although they continually grumble at the inconvenience they
cause.[11]

The *Atlas of the Irish Rural Landscape,* published in 1997, shows the
extent to which ringforts have been cleared from the landscape over
the last hundred years (see Chapter 3). By contrast, two anecdotes
that Patricia Lysaght recorded in 1976 and 1989 in County Laois,
some seventy miles north of Ballyvadlea, illustrate their continuing imaginative importance.[12] These narratives are set in an indeter-
minate, but not particularly remote, past. They serve to mark one
ringfort as a sacred place—a site about which stories containing important truths are told—and as a reference point for social control.
The storyteller, Jenny McGlynn, referred to the site near her home
as the "Rusheen," describing it as "a bit of a hill with a rath on top
of it, covered with bushes." Both her narratives about it—and more
examples could be adduced from all over Ireland—recapitulate an
analogy we have already noted, between landscape and the human
body. If men disturb the integrity of the fort, injuring the body it
represents, or if they penetrate its interior without permission, they
themselves suffer mutilation, either personally, or vicariously through
a farm animal.

The first story tells of a man who cut a stick from the Rusheen to
drive cattle:

> . . . and when he was going through the gate with his cattle a
> little man handed him one of the cattle's tails and said: "There's
> a lash for your whip." And one of the cows' tails was cut off.

> You know, if you do harm on them, or their property, they will do harm on you. I mean, that was a big loss to that man, the tail gone off his cow on the way home to be milked.

We remember that land agitators often cut the tails off cattle belonging to "land-grabbers" and "emergencymen"; the fairies presided in oral narrative over all damages that could not be securely located either in culture or in nature.

The second of Jenny McGlynn's stories concerns a workman who "cleaned up" the Rusheen to prepare it for tillage, not knowing it was a rath: "And he went and he cut old thorny bushes out of the way for to make room to till. And he got a splinter in his hand. And the hand decayed; he had to have the hand taken away."

Brought up against the impatient rationalism of a Michael McCarthy, stories like these are easily labeled superstition, but they were never designed to be told to such as him, or to the journalists or lawyers involved in investigating the death of Bridget Cleary, unless for entertainment. Told to a sympathetic and familiar audience, however, who were prepared to suspend skepticism in the interest of pleasure and wisdom, they were packed with meaning. As Jenny McGlynn said in 1989, "Keep them in doubt; it keeps the stories going; it keeps the old traditions alive!"[13] In the benign environment of neighborly storytelling, there is nothing dangerous about fairy legends; on the contrary, they serve many of the purposes for which the modern world uses warning signs and safety regulations. Television programs on health education and child care often use narrative too to communicate their messages. However, fairy belief is a powerful imaginative tool, with the same potential for misuse as mind-altering drugs and other therapies. In nineteenth-century rural Ireland, it was a currency, capable of being used for either good or ill. Traditionally, its use for evil was called *piseogaíocht,* "superstition," but this negative charge came to be applied to all its aspects.

To educated people in 1895 who read newspaper accounts of Bridget Cleary's death, keeping these old traditions alive would have seemed both pointless and irresponsible. (The exceptions were literary Protestants with a taste for mysticism, like Yeats and George Russell.) Meanwhile most, but by no means all, the people who told legends of the fairies were Catholic. Among Protestants, Catholicism itself was widely believed to have a contaminating effect on the body politic, especially after the declaration of papal infallibility in 1870. This distrust had been expressed vividly in Germany: when three small girls in the German village of Marpingen reported a series of apparitions of the Virgin Mary in 1876, the result was a kind of popular hysteria of devotion that confirmed the polarization of Catholics and National Liberals. Revulsion at Catholic backwardness, superstition, and "darkness" was expressed in Germany in terms of disease: "Religious orders were 'outgrowths of diseased aberrations of human social drives'; action should be taken against them as one would act against 'phylloxera, Colorado beetle, and other enemies of the Reich.'" The response of the Prussian state on that occasion was a crackdown by police and military.[14]

Far from advocating an ecological principle of "live and let live," or welcoming and sheltering diversity, the progressive mind of the late nineteenth century advocated a ruthless hygiene that would exterminate—or at least remove from use by potential subversives—everything not dreamt of in its own philosophy. As though to illustrate a parallel between homosexuality and fairy belief, even as both were being repudiated in courts of law, the word "fairy" as a term for a homosexual man first occurred in print in 1896.[15] Often well-meaning but unimaginative people were devoting their energies to eradicating things that went on between consenting adults, whether they were having sex or simply telling each other stories. Like Oscar Wilde, insouciantly bandying words with Edward Carson in Great Marlborough Street Courthouse in London, the smiling and snuff-taking defendants whose case was being heard by the magistrates in Clonmel represented a challenge to the rectitude of progress.

The prosecution's case was not a strong one: its witnesses were the relatives and neighbors of the defendants, and possible coconspirators, while Johanna Burke, who had herself been arrested earlier, was effectively a stool pigeon. Solicitor John J. Hanrahan was a Doctor of Laws, admitted to practice in 1889; Richard Crean had been admitted to practice in 1887; neither would have forgotten his legal training in that time. District Inspector Wansbrough had been conducting the prosecution, but now the police seem to have felt they needed legal support. Late on April 2, the RIC in Dublin Castle sent a memo to the undersecretary: "Request from Clonmel for either the Crown Solr. or the Sessional Crown Solr. to attend on the 4th."

The Crown Solicitor was Michael Gleeson, of Peter Street, Nenagh, fifty-three miles away. The undersecretary replied, "The Crown Solicitor has been instructed to attend and to place himself in communication with the C[ounty] I[nspector] in Clonmel."

When the magistrates resumed their hearing in Clonmel on April 4, Michael Gleeson was present to prosecute. He and Colonel Evanson conferred about the need to hear medical evidence, but the physicians could not be present until the following day. Thursday's proceedings were brief, therefore, with Acting Sergeant Egan giving evidence about what he had observed when he followed Michael Cleary home from Drangan and later climbed through the window of his house.

On Friday morning, both Dr. Crean and Dr. Heffernan appeared. William Crean gave evidence about his visit to Bridget Cleary, and then both he and William Heffernan testified as to their findings in the postmortem examination. Michael Gleeson questioned them closely about the dead woman's symptoms and their later findings, then closed the case for the Crown.

Richard Crean now proposed to examine two witnesses on behalf of Denis Ganey. They were not called, however, for Colonel Evanson announced that the magistrates had not heard any evidence against the fairy doctor. With Gleeson's agreement, he then discharged him, and after more than two weeks in custody Ganey was allowed to go free on Friday morning. Faced with the physicians' Latinate vocabulary and their evidence based on the postmortem examination—the medical gaze penetrating the body's deepest secrets through dissection after death—the court had found the fairy doctor and his traditional healing neither culpable nor sinister, merely irrelevant.[16]

John J. Hanrahan, William Ahearne's solicitor, made an unsuccessful attempt to have his client discharged too: Ahearne was a "delicate boy of sixteen" who had been sent by his mother to the Clearys' house and detained there against his will. He could not possibly have prevailed against the older men, and the only evidence against him was that he had held a candle while a harmless medicine was being administered. Unlike Ganey, though, and like all the other defendants, Ahearne had been in the house on Thursday evening during Bridget Cleary's torture. The fact that, along with Jack Dunne and Michael Kennedy, he had been elsewhere on the night when she had actually died counted for little with the court.

When the depositions of the various witnesses had been read over, with a break for lunch, Michael Kennedy said he wished to examine a witness. Edward Anglin was sworn. He was the Drangan farmer for whom Kennedy worked as a laborer, and he confirmed what the young man had said: that Michael Kennedy had been in his employment for the last two years, and that on the evening of Thursday, March 14, he had asked for his wages in order to take money to his mother. Kennedy had sent for his employer through the police, but both Anglin and Colonel Evanson seemed to be at a loss as to the relevance of his testimony. Michael Kennedy explained, however, that he wanted to establish what he had been doing in Ballyvadlea: he had gone there on the Thursday to give money to his mother, but he had not been there at all on the Friday.

Until now, the hearing had been occupied with the testimony of docile witnesses—they were either educated, or at least literate, like William Simpson, the two physicians and the police, or compliant and well schooled, like Johanna and Katie Burke. Now at last, after almost four days of testimony, the prisoners were asked, one after the other, if they had any statement to make. Michael Cleary was literate, but not docile. He had interrupted Johanna Burke in court the previous week. Now the other prisoners were removed from the dock and he began to speak:

Yes. This is in reference to Johanna Burke. She stated in her evidence that I threw paraffin oil on my wife. I threw no paraffin oil on my wife, nor neither was there paraffin oil in the house on the occasion at all, only what she herself put out of a bottle into a lamp that was lighting. She stated also in her evidence that I placed my wife on the fire. I have not placed my wife on the fire, nor neither would I have done so. I would sooner put myself on the fire than put her on the fire. Her [Johanna Burke] and her family often made an attempt to injure both me and my wife. We were not great [close] at all, only for about the last twelve months. Both her and her brothers left no stone unturned to injure both me and my wife, and they never got a chance of doing so till they got a chance of destroying my wife, and anyone in the country who wished to tell the truth would tell that. I worked here in this town of Clonmel four years ago, and her father, who is dead now, and herself, who is alive yet, when they could do nothing to me were running away with [destroying] my character behind my back to my wife. Her father used to say, "Ah! It's seldom he will come home to ye now. He have plenty of women where he is. Seldom will do him to see her." [Johanna Burke] used to go on another occasion, previous to that, and fall on the road and say I put a rope before her to kill her. Her father used to leave no stone unturned to get the law of me for it [to have me charged], and to know [see] if she could prove it. So this is the wind up of the whole of it. I have no more to tell. That leaves me with a broken heart behind her.

Michael Cleary's protestations are not unusual: women are often injured or killed by men who claim to love them.[17] His outburst is remarkable not so much for its self-justification and its paranoid accusations, as for its vivid communication of all that the civilized structure of question, answer, and cross-examination cannot accommodate: it speaks of a domestic history of mistrust and backbiting going back over several years, and the ability of malicious words to lodge poisonously in the memory. "We were not great at all," he said, using the same phrase as Gretta Conroy does in James Joyce's story "The Dead." His words are a direct translation of the Irish *Ní rabhamar mór le chéile ar chor ar bith*. To be "great with" someone is to like them, or get on well with them. To be "very great" is to be in love.

Newspapers described Cleary's testimony, like that of his father-in-law, Patrick Boland, and of Mary Kennedy, who spoke after him, as rambling and incoherent: "[Cleary], on being asked what he meant by saying, "We were not great," said, in a disjointed way, that Pat Boland was an uncle to the boys, and Pat Boland's wife and the prisoner's wife were not "great," and Pat Boland's wife or the boys did not come into his house, except when they wanted a smoke."

Michael Cleary may have said "Pat Boland's wife" (who would have been Bridget Cleary's dead mother) when he meant Richard Kennedy's wife Mary, or the court stenographer may have made a slip. It is possible that "the boys" were his wife's brothers, but whatever combination of people he had in mind, it is clear that, for Michael Cleary, relations within his wife's extended family were not good.

Bridget Cleary's father, Patrick Boland, was called next, the other prisoners again being kept outside the courtroom. Those listening for official purposes had little patience with his way of speaking, which was conversational and narrative by turns. His statement shows us the helplessness of this elderly, illiterate countryman in the face of unfamiliar authority, at the same time as it vividly conveys the scene of his daughter's torture and death. The events of Wednesday and of Thursday night seem to be mixed in his account, unless the men carried Bridget Cleary to the fireplace on Wednesday as well as on Thursday, but his memory of words spoken is clear and, read in the context of what we already know, perfectly coherent. His is an oral narrative, free from the influence of writing. Like his sister Mary Kennedy and his cousin Jack Dunne, and like oral storytellers everywhere, he quotes direct speech extensively:

Patrick Boland, who said he was getting a weakness, and whose voice could not be heard well from the dock, was allowed to sit in the witness box to give his statement. He said the first night that she was burned they brought her down and they put her on the fire when she was not taking herbs. Says Jack Dunne, "We'll make you speak."

They brought her down and they put her across the fire. Said Cleary to me, "Have you any faith? Don't you know it is with an old witch I am sleeping?"

I said, "You are not. You are sleeping with my daughter."

They brought her down and they put her on the fire. There was no fire I may say. Said Michael Cleary, "Call your daughter now in the name of the Father, Son and Holy Ghost, and I have her in spite of the world." So then I was sure I had her when he said it. Then the same people brought her up and put her on the bed, and she was as well as ever that morning. That is all I have to say about that night.

The night after that his father was dead, and a man came to tell Michael Cleary that his father was dead. He sent to the wake, and himself did not go at all. I went to the wake then, and when I came home in the morning I went to the bed and spoke to her. She was grand then, and there was no one in with her but Mary Boland [Kennedy]. She was grand until the night after, when we were taking a cup of tea, and he asked her to eat a bit of bread along with him, and she said she would. He gave her a small little bit, and she ate two bits; she would not eat a third, and he caught her then and knocked her; he thought to put it in her mouth in spite of her. "Ah," says he, "I'll make you take it, you old witch," throwing her across the fire; and that is all I know about it.

I had to run away from the house. To make a long story short, he burned her. I have no more to say, but that himself burned her. Father Ryan told me to tell the truth about it when I was going to confession to him. That's Father Ryan in the jail [i.e., not Fr. Con Ryan of Drangan]. Cleary then asked Patrick Kennedy to bury her along with him, and Patrick Kennedy said he couldn't, but he persuaded him. He went along with him and buried her.

Boland then addressed the presiding magistrate:

Would your worship allow me to go home? I am only half a mile from it, and I am willing to come back any time you like. I want to go home, for because I am losing my sight. The sergeant can see me every day, because I am only a half mile away from him, and could you see your way to be decent towards me? I would be very grateful to you.[18]

Colonel Evanson told Boland that he would hear the court's decision later.

When Mary Kennedy made her statement, the journalists found it similarly inaudible and incomprehensible, and by the time the court adjourned she had told her story only as far as Thursday night. Like her brother, Mary Kennedy recalled events vividly into an immediate narrative that tells us not only what people did, but what they said and how they felt about each other. Two days before she died, Bridget Cleary had told her that her husband "was making a fairy of her, and that he had tried to burn her three months ago." She had told her aunt as well that "if her mother were alive she would not be this way."

On Friday morning, when Edward Carson at the libel trial in London was winding up his remorseless attack on Oscar Wilde in his speech for the defense, the Clonmel court's business began an hour earlier than usual, so as to be finished that evening. First, the statements made by Cleary, Boland, and Mary Kennedy on the previous evening were read over, their fellow defendants not having heard them yet. When Michael Cleary heard what Patrick Boland had said, he reacted with another impassioned outburst:

> I would make an objection to that statement. There is not one word of truth in it, and, if I am to get justice between them, they are all one. If I will not get justice here I will get it in heaven. They are all one there, and no one of them has told the truth. They are all a lot [all one lot, all related]. They are after doing their best, and their father is the worst to do the like of that on me. If I am going to get justice—I don't care whether I will or not—I will get it in another place. It is their badness and dirt. I did not do it, but they did it, and buried her.

Johanna Burke attempted to say something then, and Cleary reacted angrily. Newspapers differ at this point in their reports, reminding us that all the evidence presented to their readers (and to us) was dependent for its accuracy on the careful listening of the stenographers; when exchanges became heated, detail could escape. According to the *Irish Times,* Cleary turned on Johanna Burke: "You had your say," he said. "You need go no further than Fethard for your character!" He then turned to his fellow prisoners and added, "I will satisfy them that I am not cowardly like ye, ye dirty set. I never laid a finger on her." In the *Cork Examiner,* however, we read:

> Johanna Burke, one of the witnesses in the case, who occupied a seat in the court, addressed a remark to Cleary, who again excitedly said—"I am satisfied whatever way it goes. I am not cowardly like ye. I never laid a finger on her, and never would," and addressing the other prisoners in the dock, he said, "It is only her brothers and first cousins could do such a thing as that."

Cleary's reference to his wife's brothers stands out: nobody else had mentioned them.

Mary Kennedy took up her position in the witness box again, to continue her statement, but this time the other prisoners remained in the dock. She told of the Friday, three weeks earlier, when she had spent most of the day at the Clearys' house, of the various conversations that had taken place, and then of her own harrowing experiences that night, when Michael Cleary pushed her aside as he stood over his wife's burning body. Her story took a long time to tell, and occupied many column inches in Monday's *Irish Times* and *Cork Examiner.* At every stage, she named the speakers and participants, and gave her version of their words. It was not a summary, such as a literate witness might give; rather, it was a dramatic reenactment. When she had finished, instead of signing her deposition, she marked it with an X. Mary Kennedy was followed on the witness stand by her cousin Jack Dunne, and then in turn by her sons, Patrick, James, Michael, and William.

Dunne's statement was long too. "He is an old man, but spoke intelligently," according to the *Irish Times.* Like Mary Kennedy, Dunne made considerable use of direct speech, but he also gave details about the various days and times involved (we remember that there was a clock in the Clearys' kitchen):

He said that he went up to Michael Cleary's on Wednesday, and asked him what way was his wife. Cleary said that she was only very middling, and that the priest and doctor was with her. He (Dunne) went up to see her in the bed, and said to Cleary that she was not too bad. Cleary said, "I have something here which I'll give her, and 'twill make her better."

"What are they?" said he (Dunne).

Cleary replied, "They are herbs I got from a woman in Fethard."

He (Dunne) saw the herbs given to her. He remained for about an hour, and then went home. Cleary then sent word to him by a neighbouring woman to have him go up to the house, that he could not depend on the lot that were about him. He (Dunne) then went up, and Cleary said, "I have something now that will cure her. I have herbs that will cure her. 'Twill be very hard to make her take this. You must assist me with this."

They gave it to her then, and they sat down by the fire for a few minutes. William Ahearne then came and asked him was he going home, and he (Dunne) said he was. Cleary said he should not go, as he wanted him for another start. This was about 8 or 9 o'clock at night. James, Pat, and William Kennedy then came in. Then Cleary said, "I think it is time for us to give her this." He had it in a pint. Then four of them caught her. He (Dunne) had a hold of her by the head.

It was very hard to make [her take] it. Cleary told him (Dunne) then that after taking that she should be brought to the fire. They did so; they held her over it, but they did not burn her. He (Dunne) thought it was part of the cure. Cleary asked her, "In the name of the Father, Son, and Holy Ghost, was she the wife of Michael Cleary."

She said she was, and Cleary said she should answer that three times. He asked her again, and she said she was. He called Pat Boland then to ask her three times was she his daughter, which he did. When that had been done they put her on the bed again, and the four boys of the Kennedys went to the wake.

He (Dunne) went home with Ahearne, and he went to see Mrs Cleary the morning after. On the way he met a man named Lahy, who told him that Bridget Cleary had broken away and gone away in the middle of the night. He did not credit it, and he went up to the house. There he met Pat Boland, crying.

He (Dunne) asked, "What ails you, Paddy?"

"'Tis Bridgie is gone away," said he.

"Where did she go, Paddy?" asked he (Dunne).

"I don't know," said he.

Cleary was standing in the yard, and also said that he did not know, that he was stretched on the bed and he saw her going out with two men.

He (Dunne) asked, "Why did you not follow her?"

"It was no use for me," said he. "Ten men would not keep her." He told some other fibs which he (Dunne) did not credit, and which were not fit for publication. He said, "She was always talking about Kylenagranagh. She used to be meeting an egg-man on the low road about a mile and a half."[19]

"Well," said he (Dunne) "come on with me; there is no place that I don't know, and we'll make her out." And they went on then, and there was a boreen with a large furze ditch, and he (Dunne) told Cleary to go on one side and he would go to the other, for fear she might be hid in that place; so they did; and they went on till they came to Kylenagranagh House. They searched around, and searched all the [out]houses that they got open. They then went out in the old kitchen garden. There was an old [out]house there, and they searched it. He (Dunne) then said, "She is not now in Kylenagranagh. We are in the open field now. What must happen her [sic]?"

"Oh," said Cleary, "Don't ever speak of it. She was burned last night."

He (Dunne) asked him, "You vagabond, why did you do it?"

Cleary replied, "She was not my wife. She was too fine to be my wife. She was two inches taller than my wife."

He (Dunne) said, "Go now and give yourself up to the authorities and to the priest, and get yourself punished. You'll have no living on this earth."

And Cleary said, "I'll cut my throat or do something to myself before night."

He (Dunne) told him that it was only nonsense, to go and do what he told him, to deliver himself up to the police and the priest. "Well, I will," said he, "if you come along with me."

Dunne had clearly been paying attention to the direction of questioning, and told his story so as to minimize his own part in torturing the sick woman. At the same time, he emphasized the way he had helped Michael Cleary to search for his wife, and had then urged him to give himself up to the authorities in Drangan: his testimony continued with his account of his, Cleary's and Michael Kennedy's meeting at the chapel with the two priests, and of their walk back to Ballyvadlea. Dunne's evidence covered the events of Wednesday, Thursday, and Saturday; he had not been in the house on Friday, the night Bridget Cleary died.

Patrick Kennedy, eldest of the four brothers, had helped Michael Cleary to bury his wife's body. The *Irish Times* gave a short account of his statement. He began by saying that he wanted to speak the truth, and ended: "I have no more to say. I am not steady this good start [while]. I am cracked after it, for to see my first cousin burned. I am under the care of Dr Crean for six years. That is as true as God is above me."

Patrick's brothers, James and William, told roughly the same story, but Michael Kennedy spoke only about Thursday and Saturday, and about Thursday said he could remember little, because he had fainted: "He was subject to fits; he was sent home from foreign climates for them."[20]

Last to be called was William Ahearne, who confirmed the evidence given by William and Minnie Simpson. "They were no relatives of his," he said. "He knew no more about it." Crown Solicitor Gleeson then addressed the court:

There could be no question, he submitted, that the parties present on the night of the 15th would be returned for trial on the charge of the murder. They were all abettors, whether in the first or second degree, and none took any overt act to prevent the death of this woman. With respect to those concerned in

the occurrence of the 14th only, they had it on the medical evidence that the injuries by the shock then caused might have
caused death on the night following, and that would be for a
jury to determine. Consequently, he submitted that these also
should be returned on the same charge.

Gleeson complimented DI Wansbrough on the diligence, patience,
and skill with which he had conducted the case, and the alacrity with
which he had put it forward. The magistrates took just over half an
hour to decide that, notwithstanding differences in their degree of cul-
pability, the nine remaining prisoners should be committed for trial
at the summer assizes.

Most newspapers fall silent about the Cleary case between this decision in early April and the July assizes. Some, however, continued to
publish essays and correspondence about fairies, changelings, and the
like, reflecting the sober discussions of antiquaries and folklorists that
continued to rumble on. A short article by Lady Gregory appeared in
the *Spectator* on April 20. She confirmed that "here in the West the
belief in fairies, always of a malevolent sort, is still very deeply
rooted," giving examples of matter-of-fact attributions of death and
illness to fairy intervention. Quoting the words of one old man who
had pointed out a "ring-shaped rath" to her and her husband as
"where the fairies do be," she suggested a connection with the "New
Woman"—the sort of bicycle-riding bluestocking frequently carica-
tured in the newspapers of the day: "[H]e was on his way back from
'burying his first cousin's wife,' but seemed resigned to her loss, as she
was from the County Clare, 'and the Clare women are a great deal
cliverer than the Galway women, and that makes them a great deal
crosser.'" This is a recurring theme: "cross" women—those whose
anger or assertiveness made them difficult for men to deal with—were
often the ones said to be away with the fairies, as were those "clever"
ones whose special skills set them apart. The American folklorist Jeremiah Curtin published his *Tales of the Irish Fairies* in 1895. On page
158, he mentioned an old man who believed "his afflicted daughter

was a creature substituted by fairies for his own daughter. His daughter was a 'quiet honest girl' and this one had 'the tongue of an attorney.'" In Lady Gregory's example, sharp tongue and "cleverness" are expressly linked, as they seem to have been in the remarkably strong-willed Bridget Cleary.

On April 21, the *New York Times* picked up another article on superstitious belief from the *Spectator*, noting that many letters and comments had been received on an initial, "contemptuously tolerant," essay, which had prompted the writer to open up the whole subject again "in a week in which an Irishwoman has been slowly roasted to death because she was, in her relatives' belief, bewitched." The writer attacked the popular piety that was such a feature of contemporary Catholicism:

> There is an impression, especially, it is said, among Catholic priests on the Continent, that the superstitious mind is potentially the religious mind, and that it is a pity to disturb or impair a tendency which makes for good. We do not believe there is any truth in that theory. The most unscrupulous are often the most superstitious, while a man of genuine religious feeling can hardly be superstitious at all.

On April 27, the *Illustrated London News* printed an essay on "Witchcraft in Modern England," in which the writer referred to the recent exercising of the public mind about the so-called "witch-burning" in what he described as "a lone district of Tipperary":

> The horrible story has led to statements concerning the prevalence of belief in witchcraft and allied superstitions among the Irish; statements followed by angry denials. Except on the ground of "another injustice to ould Ireland," there is no warrant for the anger and probably none for the denial. For belief in witchcraft is very far from extinct in the British Isles; it lurks in out-of-the-way districts in every part of the so-called civilized world. Its decay among the intelligent classes is comparatively recent.

On May 25, the same periodical published an essay by Andrew Lang on the subject of "Changelings," which began with a reference to "the late melancholy events in a peasant family of Tipperary," and offered examples from various cultures and periods. It concluded:

> In the recent Irish tragedy it is not unlikely that the unfortunate woman really had developed some hysterical change in character. But she did not wholly disappear into fairyland, therefore what was left in her place was a changeling. Catholics ought to have called in the aid of a clerical exorcist, when all would have been well. But "the priest is often the last to hear of these things," and recourse was had to the prescriptions of ancient folklore. Peasants are not alone here. As I write comes in the advertisement of a book, "Demon Possession and Allied Themes," by Dr. Nevius, "for forty years a missionary to the Chinese." "This book is based . . . upon a large collection of thoroughly sifted and authenticated facts, showing that demon possession is a common experience of our own day." I cannot criticize a work which I have not read, but I wish that a form of Dr. Nevius's theory had not prevailed in Tipperary.

Lang, whose debate with Edward Clodd on the subject of fairy belief has been mentioned, was author of the immensely popular *Red, Green, Yellow,* and several other, *Fairy Books.* By the time the prisoners had been sentenced, he had read Nevius's book. He referred to it in a letter to *The Times* (July 19) where he echoed the hope already expressed by Clodd that Michael Cleary's sentence might be mitigated, out of pity for the "invincible ignorance" which had caused his crime.

Perhaps the most unusual intervention in this discussion was the six-page essay by E. F. Benson, which appeared in the widely read monthly the *Nineteenth Century* for June 1895, under the title "The Recent 'Witch-Burning' at Clonmel." Best remembered for the "Mapp and Lucia" novels, "Fred" Benson was twenty-seven, and had recently begun to make a name as a popular novelist. He was the son of the Archbishop of Canterbury and lived with his parents in Lambeth Palace. A charming and witty aesthete, and something of a

snob, he was not in the habit of commenting on the painful questions of the day; nor did his world of public-school types and frivo-
lous fiction have much to do with the fey poetic mysteries favored by
such as Yeats. His essay, which quotes Tylor, Lubbock, and other contemporary anthropologists, is all the more surprising in that he had
no known interest in or connection with Ireland. He was, however,
homosexual, at least by inclination, and uncomfortably close to the
circles in which the disgraced Oscar Wilde was known to have
moved; Lord Alfred Douglas had stayed in his rooms in Athens the
previous year, and they had traveled in the same party in Egypt. Benson had become deeply interested in archaeology while a student at
Cambridge, and had worked on excavations in the Middle East. It was
an interest he shared with Oscar Wilde. Wilde was found guilty of in-
decent acts on May 25, and sentenced to two years' imprisonment
with hard labor.

Benson's priggish but humane essay, written at about the same
time, put forward a view of the Tipperary case that contrasted strongly
with both the bloodthirsty editorials of the Dublin unionist papers
and the pained distancing of the nationalists.

> There seems to be no doubt, if we examine the motives which
> appear to have led to this crime, that the ten persons, nine of
> whom are to be tried on the capital charge of wilfully murder-
> ing Bridget Cleary, in the recent case of witch-burning at
> Clonmel, acted . . . honestly, and, as they undoubtedly appear
> to have believed, for the best.

He went on to adduce examples from Patagonia, from northeast India, from Vancouver in Canada, and, inevitably, from Zulu and Hottentot culture, to demonstrate that the defendants had acted "strictly
in accordance with a primitive and savage superstition." This was
"not a case of witch-burning at all," he contended, "and ought to be
called manslaughter rather than murder":

> That such superstitions should still be believed in a Christian
> country, and by men who by religion are Christians, is appalling

enough; but the remedy for such a state of things is not to be found in the hangman's noose, nor yet, perhaps, in the convict prison, and one cannot but feel that it would be in the spirit of that wise and merciful law which ordains that boys under a certain age may not be hanged for capital offences to spare these men, even if they are condemned; for children they are if, as can, I think, be proved, they have acted under the influence of such superstitious fears, as surely as the savage who fears his own shadow is a child.

Benson's biographer, Brian Masters, has described the "panic of emigration" among homosexual men in England at the time of Oscar Wilde's trial, noting that "in later years Fred distanced himself from Wilde and his disgrace, managing deftly to express compassion and disapproval with the same voice."[21] Benson's passionate plea for clemency for the Tipperary defendants, focusing as it did on another sensational Irish story, may have been an attempt to deflect attention from his own connection with the Wilde case. With its sympathy for the misguided and misunderstood Michael Cleary, and its retelling of the sort of narrative for which Sir William and Lady Wilde were known, it reads like a masked or coded commentary on the fate of their son.[22]

Benson's essay did not find favor with the Folk-Lore Society. Its council, under the presidency of Edward Clodd, directed that an analysis be printed in its journal *Folk-Lore* of all the evidence in the Cleary case, "so as to preserve the relevant facts in a form accessible to scientific students." This essay, which was based on reports published in the *Irish Times,* ran to over eleven pages.[23] The writer ended:

It would only seem necessary to add a protest, in the interest of the due administration of the law, against the article by Mr E. F. Benson in the *Nineteenth Century* for June last. Some of Mr Benson's interpretations of the evidence before the magistrates are disputable; but whether they are right or wrong is not the point. The article in question was published before the trial. It was an attempt to influence public opinion upon a case that was still *sub judice*. And, however unlikely to reach the jurymen who would have to try the guilt of the prisoners, it ought not to have been published at that time.

The case was over by the time this appeared in December, but when Benson published his essay, Mary Kennedy was still in Limerick's women's prison, and the eight male prisoners were in Clonmel, awaiting trial.

On June 21, 1895, two weeks before the Clonmel summer assizes, Lord Rosebery's government finally resigned after being defeated by seven votes in a snap division on the question of the supply of cordite explosive. John Morley's Land Bill was abandoned, and in the general election which followed, he lost his seat. When the new Conservative and unionist government took power in July under Lord Salisbury, the question of Home Rule for Ireland, which had so exercised newspaper editors over the previous months, faded once again.

10

Trial and Imprisonment

ON WEDNESDAY, July 3, 1895, as nationalist politicians in Clonmel were seeking nominations for the forthcoming general election, the grand jury for Tipperary South Riding was being sworn in at the courthouse. At the summer assizes the next day, Michael Cleary, Patrick Boland, and Mary Kennedy were to stand trial for the murder of Bridget Cleary, along with Jack Dunne, William Ahearne, and Mary Kennedy's four sons.

On Thursday morning, for the first time since April, the prisoners were marched through the streets from the prison to the courthouse under heavy police escort. Crowds gathered to watch them as before, but this time there was no hissing or groaning. At half past eleven, Mr. Justice William O'Brien took his seat on the bench and heard a roll call of the nineteen grand jurors. A former reporter on the *Cork Examiner,* he had risen from what Michael McCarthy calls "a very humble position in life" to a seat on the bench. He was one of a handful of Catholic judges in Ireland, a Liberal nominee to the bench; thirteen years earlier he had been trial judge in the dramatic Phoenix Park murder case.[1]

The judge's long-winded opening speech lasted almost fifteen minutes, and dealt, as was customary, with the general state of law and order in the county. "There was an unusually large attendance of the public," the *Irish Times* noted, "representing all classes of society." Mr. Justice O'Brien was pleased to observe, he told his listeners, that by comparison with twenty criminal offenses reported in the constabulary returns for the corresponding period in 1894, only twelve had been reported in 1895, of which none indicated danger to the public peace. In his by-election speech the previous spring, John Dillon MP had noted similar statements by judges in Killarney, Ennis, Boyle, and Castlebar, attributing the ongoing changes to the chief secretary's policy of suspending coercion and introducing a new Land Bill.[2]

Only when the judge had been speaking for a full five minutes did he come to the subject of the case before the court. He described Bridget Cleary's death with emotion and incredulity, he referred to belief in witchcraft as widely attested, even in other parts of the United Kingdom, and among "statesmen, philosophers, judges, kings," but made the distinction that in the Ballyvadlea case it seemed to have been blended with religion. Bridget Cleary herself he described with chivalrous indignation, adapting lines from *Macbeth:*

> [A] young woman at the opening of her life . . . a young married woman, who suspecting no harm, guilty of no offence, virtuous and respectable in all her conduct and all her proceedings, from those, of all others, who were bound to protect her—from the hands of her own husband, who swore at the altar to cherish and protect her, and from her own father—has met her death under circumstances which remind us of the lines:
> > "Pleading like angels, trumpet-tongued,
> > Against the deep damnation of her taking off."

A grand jury's task was not to try cases, but to determine whether or not the evidence warranted the indictment of the defendants, and to bring in a true bill in connection with each charge. Mr. Justice O'Brien impressed on the jurors that although a charge of murder might be commuted to manslaughter "where life was taken away in the course of a sudden quarrel or under the influence of a sudden passion," this would not apply where life had been taken as a result of belief in witchcraft.

In the event, after more than an hour's deliberation, the grand jurors found a true bill for murder against Michael Cleary, Patrick Boland, Mary Kennedy, James Kennedy, and Patrick Kennedy, but found no bill against John (Jack) Dunne. On an indictment for wounding, they found a true bill against the same parties, and also against John Dunne, Michael Kennedy, William Kennedy, and William Ahearne. The trial could now begin, and three Queen's Counsels, Ryan, Curtin, and Malloy, instructed by Crown Solicitor Gleeson, appeared to prosecute.

Michael Cleary was placed in the dock. He appeared in "a well-worn suit of clothes," and wore a flannel shirt without a collar. "From his appearance," the *Irish Times* remarked, he "might well be regarded as a matter-of-fact sort of person."

"Not guilty," Cleary replied at once, on being arraigned, and, following an application by his solicitor, R. J. Crean, Dr. John Boursiquot Falconer, a barrister from Dublin, was assigned to defend him.

Stating the case for the prosecution, Mr. Ryan QC told the jury that it was their privilege, if they were satisfied, to bring in a verdict for manslaughter. He himself would have been glad, he said, if he could have felt it his duty to charge the defendant not with the capital offense, but with manslaughter. If Michael Cleary and the other defendants were to be found guilty of murder, they would be hanged. In England a year later, as Oscar Wilde would record in his eloquent poetic critique of the penal system, *The Ballad of Reading Gaol,* that was to be the fate of Charles Thomas Wooldridge:

> The man had killed the thing he loved,
> And so he had to die.

Wooldridge, a trooper in the Royal Horse Guards, had killed his wife by cutting her throat with a razor, and the fact that he had borrowed the razor and waited for her in the road was taken as evidence of premeditation. Wooldridge was thirty when he was hanged; his wife had been twenty-three. Like Bridget Cleary, she was young and attractive, and was said to have done something to arouse her husband's jealousy. In their case, however, no exotic belief system could be invoked in mitigation, and the law took its course.[3]

Johanna Burke was the first witness called at the July assizes. In answer to questions put by Mr. Malloy QC, she told her story much as she had done in the spring, starting with the events of Thursday, March 14, and continuing through Friday and Saturday. The judge also questioned her from time to time, and in answering him she added more detail to the evidence already given. Before she had left the Clearys' house on Saturday, the morning after her cousin's death, she said, Cleary had told her that he was going to America, "and that he would not see her wanting for a shilling, but would see her and Mrs. Cleary's father all right."

The extent to which ordinary communication between accused and witnesses went on, even after outbursts of horrific violence, was remarkable. Newspaper commentators found it inexplicable. Lawyers and magistrates also asked repeatedly why nobody had intervened to stop the torture and killing of Bridget Cleary, and young William Ahearne's solicitor had had to remind the magistrates at the petty sessions that for "a youth of his age to put his mind or strength against those of so many others of more mature years . . . would be a proceeding similar to that of a first year's medical student expostulating with a professor of the College of Surgeons for his treatment of a patient." The increasingly individualistic culture of the metropolitan nineteenth century assumed that each person was autonomous, guided from within by an independent and authoritative moral sense, which might be more or less developed, according to the individual's place on the continuum between savagery and civilization. This view left little space for the compelling reality of the social group in a more traditional society, with all the trade-offs that are necessary to maintain it, or for the extent to which poor and powerless people must depend on those close to them, even if the relationship is oppressive.

The legal system found in Western societies today, which was also the one at work in Clonmel in 1895, endeavors to identify culprits and apportion blame. The legal systems of oral cultures, on the other hand, are more concerned with restoring equilibrium.[4] It may be useful to view fairy belief in Ireland as a sort of vernacular system of ethics: a way of laying down rules, defining sanctions, and, very occasionally, implementing them. Belonging, as it does by definition, to groups of people whose economic and family ties constrain them to live almost within sight and earshot of each other, it resists strict codification and invasive exegesis; its terms of reference are fluid, slippery and often ambiguous. Nevertheless, as long as the system is not discredited, everything in the environment, from landscape features to calendar custom to household hygiene, illness, birth and death, works to reinforce it. Attributing tragic events or criminal actions to the fairies could work as a face-saving mechanism that would allow ordinary, indispensable social interaction to proceed, something that could not be achieved through accusation and confrontation. Bridget Cleary's economic or sexual behavior may have been causing offense to her neighbors and relatives, but the strategy they had employed to discipline her was not indictment, but diagnosis.

Johanna Burke's examination had not finished when the court adjourned at a quarter to seven on Thursday evening. The jury was sequestered for the night, and the accused were returned to the prison: "Cleary was removed to the jail under a strong force of police, who carried fixed bayonets. Large crowds of people thronged the streets to see the prisoner, who wore a haggard appearance all through the day's proceedings." The *Irish Times* added a grim item of recent information: "News has reached Clonmel that the house of the Kennedys, near the scene of the occurrence, was burned down maliciously last night, it is stated, by some of the neighbours to prevent their return again to live in the district, in case of their being acquitted."

The little thatched "cabin" at Ballyvadlea bridge, where Mary Kennedy had lived since her marriage, had been burned to the ground. As with the nonfuneral given to Bridget Cleary, some clearly wanted it known that their idea of community did not include Mary Kennedy and her sons. It was a demonstration of power, and also an unequivocal declaration that not everybody in Ballyvadlea thought alike. The blackened, burned-out site may have been a message to those who consorted with emergencymen. It remained to challenge anyone who might still suggest that something in this very landscape made belief in fairies inevitable. Ironically, the weapon used to exterminate the fairies from this part of the landscape was fire: the same as had been used to banish the purported fairy changeling from Bridget Cleary's kitchen a few months earlier.

The court resumed its business on Friday, July 5, with Johanna Burke again in the witness chair. Dr. Falconer cross-examined her about Jack Dunne's involvement in the treatment of Bridget Cleary and about Michael Cleary's sending for the priest. He also attempted to elicit more information about the fairy belief centered on Kylenagranagh, but was robustly halted by the judge: "I will not allow a question as to where fairies are supposed to be. They may be supposed to be in this courthouse. We are not here acting a play, but to inquire into matters of fact!" Mr. Justice O'Brien himself asked the witness about the communion host that Bridget Cleary was supposed to have taken out of her mouth and rubbed in the blankets, and the examination concluded. Katie Burke was called then, and gave her evidence as before.

No further witnesses were called in the case against Michael Cleary. Dr. Falconer requested permission to withdraw his client's plea of "not guilty" of murder and instead plead guilty of manslaughter. The judge demurred. The jury, he said, had the power to return a verdict of manslaughter, but he had no power to direct them, and the Crown's consent was also required. Mr. Ryan told the court, however, that under the circumstances he was agreeable, and the judge withdrew his objection. "I will put the issue paper to the jury," he said, "and let them say 'Not guilty of murder, but guilty of manslaughter.'"

Dr. Falconer's plea bargaining succeeded. The jury retired and found Michael Cleary guilty of manslaughter. Sentence was deferred until the other charges had been heard, and Cleary was removed from the courtroom.

The court did not proceed with the charge of murder against Patrick Boland, Mary Kennedy, James Kennedy, and Patrick Kennedy: as reported by newspapers, its next business after Cleary was found guilty of manslaughter was the charge of misdemeanor against the eight remaining prisoners. They were charged with having, on March 14, unlawfully and maliciously wounded Bridget Cleary. There was a second count of assault on Bridget Cleary, occasioning her actual bodily harm.

One by one the defendants denied the charges, looking, according to the *Irish Times,* "as if they had not suffered by their incarceration." Jack Dunne said he had not been at the house on the night Bridget Cleary died, but was told that the charges related to the previous night. First Johanna Burke, then William Simpson, gave evidence. Simpson detailed the part played by Jack Dunne, Patrick Boland, and three of the Kennedy brothers in carrying Bridget Cleary to the fire on Thursday night. Patrick Boland challenged him, denying that he had held his daughter over the fire, although he agreed that he had questioned her, at her husband's request, as to whether or not she was really his daughter. When she had said she was, he said, he had put his two hands under her and swept her off the fire, saying that she was no fairy. The old man added:

> I had no one in the world to turn to but my daughter. Her mother and myself gave her a good trade. She was only twenty-six years of age, and she was a fine milliner, and able to give us a bit of money, and when her mother died she was the only one I had in the world to look to. It was not me that should ever have put a finger to her.

The court heard evidence from Minnie Simpson, wife of William Simpson, and from Alfred Joseph Wansbrough, the RIC District Inspector. Colonel Evanson, who had presided at the petty sessions as resident magistrate, was also called, but when it transpired that examining him would involve reading out twenty-eight pages of depositions, Mr. Ryan QC declined to do so; instead he entered a *nolle prosequi* against William Ahearne, who was immediately discharged. Ahearne had been in prison for over three months, although his only crime had been to hold a candle for his older and stronger neighbors.

When the Crown's case had closed, Patrick Boland and Jack Dunne again denied having had act or part in the burning of Bridget Cleary, and Mr. Justice O'Brien charged the jury. His words echoed the social-Darwinist rhetoric of the newspaper reports, but he adapted it to the concerns of educated, conservative Irish Catholics:

This most extraordinary case demonstrated a degree of darkness in the mind, not of one person, but of several, a moral darkness, even religious darkness, the disclosure of which had come with surprise on many persons. He had followed the evidence with care to try and find a solution of the real motive that led to the death of this unhappy woman, and although he was not entirely satisfied with the evidence as to the previous relations of the prisoner Cleary with his wife, nor as to the medicines, as they were called, which Cleary employed for the purpose of retaining his wife from the evil and preternatural companionship she was supposed to have entered into, he should at the same time say that there were many things in the case which, possibly, further inquiry as to the relations between Cleary and his wife might have brought to light. That, however, was practically out of consideration on this trial. There was no instance of remonstrance against violence to her proved to have been uttered by anybody, a fact which almost passed human comprehension.

The case was still a considerable mystery as the trial came to an end, but the intense drama of the proceedings had dissipated when Michael Cleary was found guilty of manslaughter. When the jurors retired, they took just three-quarters of an hour to find John Dunne, Patrick Kennedy, James Kennedy, and William Kennedy guilty of wounding. They found Patrick Boland, Mary Kennedy, and Michael Kennedy guilty too, "but not as guilty as the four others," and recommended them to mercy. Michael Kennedy had insisted all along that he had had no role in his cousin's ill-treatment or killing, and his sister's evidence had borne him out, but his failure to intervene to save her had made him guilty in the eyes of the court.

Passing sentence, Mr. Justice O'Brien first addressed thirty-two-year-old Patrick Kennedy. He regarded him, he said, after Michael Cleary, as the most guilty of all, and sentenced him to five years' penal servitude. Jack Dunne was sentenced to three years; the judge made it clear that he felt him to be equally guilty with Kennedy— "with you it would seem the idea originated"—but imposed a lighter sentence, "partly because the sentence I have passed on Patrick Kennedy would consume the greater portion of the life that nature has allotted to you." Jack Dunne was fifty-five; Mr. Justice O'Brien himself was more than ten years older.[5]

James and William Kennedy were each sentenced to a year and a half's imprisonment from the time of their committal in April. Unlike Jack Dunne and their older brother, therefore, they would not be transferred to a convict prison, but would serve their sentences in Clonmel. The same was true of Patrick Boland and Michael Kennedy. Each received six months' imprisonment, Kennedy's with hard labor, although the judge acknowledged that he was perhaps the most innocent "so far as any actual proof [was] concerned."

When he came to fifty-nine-year-old Mary Kennedy, Mr. Justice O'Brien, instead of sentencing her, set her free. Michael McCarthy, himself a barrister who had taken a keen interest in the case, says the judge spoke "tearfully":

> I pass no sentence on this old woman. Nature has decreed a sentence upon her not far distant, and I will not abridge the remainder of your life by sending you to gaol. I will order your discharge, however grave my disapprobation of your conduct, and I am not uninfluenced in that course by the misfortune which has befallen so many members of your family as a result of this great crime, and by the reparation which your daughter, Johanna Burke, has made by the evidence she has given.[6]

The notion of "the law" as an injured or offended abstract body, to which "reparation" can be made by docile and compliant behavior, is reminiscent of the Catholic teachings of the time; it would, however, have been incomprehensible in terms of the ethical system represented by fairy legend, which claimed no monopoly on morality, but instead represented moral decisions as negotiations between rival claims.

All the prisoners were removed from court, and Michael Cleary was brought forward to be sentenced. His counsel, Dr. Falconer, addressed the judge, echoing his references to "reparation" and to "the state of darkness in which the man was sunk." In this line of argument, he made clear, he had his client's full approval. To his points about ignorance he added the notion of heredity:

> [I]n addition to the ignorance and superstition, and the mental and religious darkness in which the parties were steeped, there existed in the prisoner a hereditary disposition to believe in superstition, because, according to the evidence of Mrs Burke, the deceased woman had said to him, "Your own mother sometime went with the fairies, and that is the reason you want to make a fairy of me."

Michael Cleary's treatment of his wife during her illness had been exemplary, Dr. Falconer said. "What occurred at the end, and which was the consequence, as he had said, of darkness and ignorance, he would have to expiate by remorse during the remainder of his life."[7] He appealed to the judge to be lenient.

Cleary's sentence, when it came, was not lenient, but rather such as would express the degree to which the judge believed him guilty. Mr. Justice O'Brien was by no means convinced that all the talk of fairies was not a cloak for ordinary murder; he had judged the case on the evidence brought before him, however, and found, in short, that Michael Cleary had burned his wife alive. Before pronouncing sentence, "amid a scene of painful silence" in court, the judge indulged in a last romantic and chivalrous reverie on the dead Bridget Cleary as bride. He compared her implicitly to the virgin martyrs of early Christianity, devotion to whom was such a significant feature of middle-class Irish Catholic culture after the Great Famine:

> I rest upon the fact that you inflicted on the woman whom you had taken to be your wedded wife, and sworn before the altar to cherish and protect—that you took her life away by a form of cruelty which the fortitude of the martyrs has been found alone able to resist, and which is generally regarded as the most cruel and painful of human afflictions—by burning her alive— for dead she was not at the time you threw the paraffin oil over her—dead beyond a doubt she was not. And your wicked hand

> sent her to another world in the very prime of her life. The young woman confided to you her affections and her love, and you most wantonly and cruelly and bitterly betrayed her.

The judge's attitude seems to indicate that he felt the evidence was more consistent with murder than with manslaughter. He had deliberated, he said, about whether or not he was justified in imposing less than the "extreme sentence" of death on the man who stood before him; he sentenced him instead to twenty years' penal servitude for manslaughter.

Michael Cleary, the *Clonmel Chronicle* reported, "wept bitterly while his lordship was speaking, and when being removed from the dock shouted out that he was innocent." This time, when the prisoners were marched through the streets back to jail, the crowds "groaned and hooted vehemently."

Coming from a rural district only recently brought under the influence of state agencies, and just becoming literate, the men from Ballyvadlea now found themselves in an environment of maximum record-keeping and control. The prison system functioned through timekeeping and paperwork. Marks were awarded daily for compliance with rules, subtracted for breaches, scrupulously totaled, and carried forward in a complex system of human accountancy. The regime of surveillance and control of bodies had found architectural expression in new prisons based on Jeremy Bentham's *Panopticon*. The east wing of Kilmainham Jail in Dublin, now a museum, and location for numerous prison films, was one such. Cells were ranged in three tiers around the outer walls, opening onto galleries, while the skylit interior stood empty except for a central staircase: a single warder could stand in the middle and observe the doors of all the cells; a prisoner never knew when he was being observed through the judas window in his door.

At the end of the nineteenth century, a new "scientific" dimension was being added to the treatment of prisoners, as the writings of Cesare Lombroso were read and digested by lawyers, prison officials, and the interested public. As we have seen, Lombroso was the criminal anthropologist who claimed to be able to distinguish "born criminals" by a supposedly scientific evaluation of their physical characteristics. Printed forms supplied to the prison service in the 1890s provided for criminals to be weighed, measured, photographed, and subjected to minute physical examination. This sort of record-keeping had the advantage of providing reliable evidence of identity, especially in the case of habitual criminals, who often used aliases (the use of fingerprints was still in its infancy, and fingerprint evidence was not accepted in an English court until 1902); it also made data available for scientific study.

The names and other details of the nine men originally arrested had been entered in the General Register of Prisoners when they were brought to Clonmel Prison on March 21, 1895, and numbered 109 to 117. Each of their records shows age, height, hair color, color of eyes, complexion, weight in pounds, place of birth and of last residence, occupation, religion, education, date committed, offense, name of committing magistrate, and sentence. A space is provided for further remarks.

In Limerick Female Prison, Mary Kennedy was also weighed and measured, and made to strip almost naked for inspection. In the prison's General Register of Prisoners she is No. 599. A further entry, dated March 29, includes under "marks on person," "deft up front teeth," which seems to be the clerk's shorthand for defective (or missing?) teeth. Another, on April 7, notes "For trial at assizes Tipperary S[outh] R[iding]." The final entry is undated, but must refer to July: "Charged with wounding. Rt Hon Wm O'Brien. Found Guilty and ordered to be Discharged."

When Michael Cleary, Jack Dunne, and Patrick Kennedy returned to Clonmel Prison following their conviction and sentencing on July 5, new records were begun. Cleary became Convict 866; Dunne, following in alphabetical order, was C867; Kennedy was C868. The men would be in the care and control of the prison service for some considerable time, and the files that were now opened for them were designed to stand up to wear and tear. The printed form entitled "Penal Record of Convict" consisted of several pages ruled into boxes and columns, reinforced with cloth and bound together with brass rivets. Lest the paper develop cracks with use, at the bottom of the first page ran the warning, "This Document is not to be folded."

During their time in Clonmel, all three men were assigned to "picking rope junk," a fact recorded in the box marked "Statement shewing date of Reception, and Trade followed at each Prison." Junk was the cut-up discarded rope that prisoners picked apart to make oakum, the substance so often mentioned in prison songs and literature. Oakum was used in caulking between the planks of wooden ships, and featured strongly in the British prison system:

> We tore the tarry rope to shreds
> With blunt and bleeding nails;
> We rubbed the doors, and scrubbed the floors,
> And cleaned the shining rails:
> And, rank by rank, we soaped the plank,
> And clattered with the pails.[8]

The three men sentenced to penal servitude spent a last week in Clonmel Prison after their trial, waiting while the necessary documents were processed for their transfer to Mountjoy Prison in Dublin. On Monday, Michael Cleary sent a letter to his widowed mother, addressing it to Mrs. Bridget Cleary, Cashel Street, Killenaule. Its contents are not preserved, but as with almost every move a convict made, it was noted in his record. The record also noted that on June 29, the Saturday before his trial began, Cleary had been guilty of "communicating." He may simply have spoken to another prisoner, but by order of Prison Governor Oxford, he spent twenty-four hours on bread and water in his own cell. The blue record-sheet, with columns for Date of Offence, Offence, Punishment and By Whom Punishment Ordered, accompanied him to Mountjoy, and later to Cork, back to Mountjoy, and finally to Maryborough (now Portlaoise) Prison, but there were no further breaches of the rules.

Richard Ellmann records that Oscar Wilde's oakum pickings in Wandsworth Prison were skimpy, reading this as a sign of his failure to adapt to the prison regime. Michael Cleary may have found it more congenial. Unlike Wilde, who was totally unused and unsuited to manual labor, he was accustomed to heavy work. He may also have found that the prison routine of gates, sirens, bells, and strict time-keeping was one with which he was already familiar. According to his own evidence, Cleary had worked in Clonmel as a cooper until about 1891. Bassett's *Book of County Tipperary* for 1889 does not show any firms specializing in cooperage, but prints a full-page advertisement for the brewery of Thomas Murphy and Sons, and devotes a page of description to it. Originally built in 1798, the brewery had been rebuilt after a fire in 1829 and modernized throughout the nineteenth century; it occupied a two-acre site on the bank of the Suir, and employed two hundred people. The advertisement shows a large, rectangular, six-story building, with castellated roof and a single entrance gate in the middle of its longest wall: "[I]mprovements have been introduced into the several departments to keep pace with the progress of inventive skill. As a result it would not be easy to find a concern more perfectly organized and equipped." Murphy's of Clonmel embodied one of the ideals of the nineteenth century: the factory as hive of industry, each worker occupying a preordained place for maximum efficiency. Such factories were organized in ways remarkably similar to prisons. Both required enclosure, partitioning, and surveillance; the same principles were applied in schools.[9]

The factory, like the prison, the school, and the workhouse, was a place where ambiguity had been eliminated. It would be hard to imagine an environment more different from the traditional rural world represented by Jack Dunne, Patrick Boland, or Mary Kennedy, where people young and old might walk to a wake along country roads long after midnight, where certain places were known as sites of things not spoken of or where absences and desertions might be explained as fairy abductions. The legends people told were a means through which many of them resisted centralized kinds of discipline until long after the 1890s.

Thomas Murphy's brewery in Clonmel employed a number of coopers:

The casks are made on the premises, and the department from
which they are turned out contains a saw mill, and is not the
least interesting of the features. At the Dublin Artisans' Exhibi-
tion, in 1885, a first-class certificate was awarded for the excel-
lence of the cooper-work sent from here.

If Michael Cleary was not himself employed at Murphy's during his
time in Clonmel, he certainly would have known people who were.
In prison, once he settled down, his conduct was uniformly "good."

The blue "Medical History" sheet which formed part of Cleary's
penal record describes him as "stout & strong," and gives his weight
on first admission to Mountjoy on July 12, 1895 as 167½ pounds. His
height was measured in Clonmel at five feet nine and a half inches,
corrected in Mountjoy, with Victorian precision, to five feet nine and
a quarter. He had gained almost fourteen pounds in weight during
his months in Clonmel Prison, evidently getting back to normal after the ordeal of his wife's illness and death, but he still had a way to
go: his weight stabilized at around 176 pounds, where it remained
until his reception at Maryborough in 1901. In 1910, when he was
finally released from prison, he weighed 189 pounds.

A penal record of the time includes a full page devoted to "Description of the Convict," with space for photographs, the first of
which was to be taken "on first reception," the second on release on
license. (Two further spaces allow for the possibility that the convict
may forfeit his license and be imprisoned again until final release.)
Michael Cleary's hair was light brown, his eyes blue, his nose and
mouth large, his complexion fresh. Officers in Clonmel and Mountjoy also entered particulars of his "distinctive marks or peculiarities":
"Small scar on left forearm; Cut mark on right eyebrow; 3 cuts on 1st
finger left hand; Thumb-nail left hand broken; Hair thin on top and
front." The first of Michael Cleary's mugshots was taken with a mir-
ror at his shoulder, so that it shows his full face and profile in the same
image. He looks resolute and calm, gazing straight at the camera, his
hands laid flat on his chest, so that they too appear in the picture. Instead of the full beard he wore when the *Daily Graphic* artist sketched
him in the dock, he simply looks as though he has not shaved for sev-

eral days; his partial baldness makes his face a perfect oval. By the time of his release, his hair is gray, and he has lost more of it, but a long strand is brushed across the top of his head. Once again, he wears a full beard and mustache.

Only one photograph survives on Jack Dunne's penal record, taken at the time of his release from Maryborough Prison on license in October 1897. It shows a heavyset man with a white beard. He had been transferred to Maryborough, about fifty miles from his home, in late July 1896. There his occupation was given as "labourer," although the medical officer assessing him on his reception noticed that he was suffering from a ventral hernia and defective vision in both eyes, and issued him glasses. He had also lost several upper front and lower side teeth. He could read, but not write, and in July 1897 a note was sent to the General Prisons Board in Dublin Castle stating that "John Dunne is not learning a trade." In Mountjoy, where he had spent the previous year, he had graduated from picking rope junk only to "winding yarn." The description of Dunne's physical condition on arrival in Mountjoy was one of four available to the officer assessing him: "fat." His height was five feet three inches. His weight in Clonmel had been recorded at 176 pounds, but by the time of his arrival at Mountjoy it had gone down to 160. The only detail of his appearance noted in Clonmel—and therefore perhaps the most conspicuous one—was that his right leg was shorter than his left, the result of a fracture.

On March 3, 1896, Jack Dunne submitted a petition for early release to the Lord Lieutenant. Special blue foolscap sheets, ruled with a broad margin on the left-hand side for official comments, were issued to prisoners for the purpose of writing petitions. A printed notice at the bottom of the page read:

Only one prisoner may memorial [make a case] on this paper. The petition which must be legibly written on the ruled lines and not crossed, must be couched in proper and respectful language, and any complaint must be made as soon as possible after the occurrence which gives rise to it.

The paper is printed with the appropriate opening for a prisoner's petition: "To His [Excellency] The Lord Lieutenant of Ireland: The Petition of————Humbly sheweth————." John Dunne's is handwritten, probably by J. Craig, warder, who witnessed it, and signed with the petitioner's mark, an X.

By July, he had received no response, and the deputy governor of Mountjoy made inquiries of Dublin Castle. The papers had been sent to Mr. Justice William O'Brien for his opinion, but the judge was now out on circuit. The judge's report, scrawled on four sides of foolscap paper, came at last, on August 3. It confirms the impression given by reports of the trial, that Mr. Justice O'Brien believed Bridget Cleary had been killed deliberately:

> Sir,
>
> John Dunne to whom the accompanying memorial relates was tried for his part in the somewhat memorable crime that attracted so much attention at the time known as the Tipperary Witchcraft case. The Crown accepted a verdict of manslaughter on the indictment for murder against the husband. So far as he was concerned, I formed the conclusion from the trial that the only parties bewitched were the authorities, who had allowed, what I thought a deliberate and wicked design to kill his wife, to be confounded in their minds with superstition. Dunne was an elderly man either a labourer or a small farmer, and the impression left on my mind of the trial was, not that he was an accomplice in the husband's design, but that the idea of witchcraft, started from him, through superstition and folly, and was made a pretext by the husband for making away with the woman. What was proved concerning him was that he certainly took a leading part in the incantations or orgies that were supposed to be a remedy for witchcraft. He was proved to have been seen holding the woman down in the bed with others while the husband was trying to force her to take some kind of decoction, and to have suggested taking her to the fire, and to have assisted in putting her to the fire, under some horrible idea that she would be forced to confess herself a witch and that the

supposed spell would be put an end to. It seemed to be plain that he was considered to have a special knowledge in sorcery. Whether he was the tool of the husband, or was the person who put the idea of witchcraft either as a delusion or a pretext into the husband's head, or whether the latter sought him out for the purpose, could not be said with any degree of certainty. But he did not take any part in the atrocious act of the husband in throwing the paraffin oil on the unhappy woman, under the idea or pretext of quickening the exorcism, which in all probability was the cause of her death. The sentence indicated my opinion formed at the time that amongst the minor agents in the tragedy, he was the person most responsible for the occurrence. But I recollect he declared that he did not intend to harm the woman, and he certainly appeared to be an ignorant and humble countryman. In so unusual a kind of case, ordinary grounds of judgement fail me to give an opinion on the sentence as appealed or to question whether the idea might have been that he was not doing anything wrong, or even that he was doing the woman [good], was an excuse for conduct that was cruel to her herself, and may have been accessory to her death.[10]

I have the honour to be etc., [signed] William O'Brien

Dunne's petition was refused. In September 1896, Dunne again petitioned the Lord Lieutenant, this time asking that the time he had spent in prison awaiting trial be counted as part of his sentence. Again the response was negative: "Let the law take its course."

Jack Dunne, like Michael Cleary, had sent one letter while in jail in Clonmel, although he could not have written it himself. It was addressed to his wife, Catherine Dunne, Cloneen, Fethard, County Tipperary. Her reply, signed "Kate Dunne," arrived in Mountjoy on October 9, 1895. He sent her five more letters from prison in 1896, including a "Reception Form" sent on July 30, 1896, and received a total of six from her. Probably, like him, she was unable to write, but had someone write on her behalf. Mysteriously, a letter received in the prison on June 20, 1896 from Dunne's wife was "declined"; the medical record shows only that he was "costive" that week, and that a dose of castor oil was prescribed.[11] His last letter to her, posted three days after Christmas 1896, was returned on January 9 marked "Deceased."

This seems to have been the only notification Jack Dunne received of his wife's death. He immediately set about petitioning the Lord Lieutenant again. He was by now about fifty-seven, although there is some confusion about his age, and he may have believed himself older.[12] This petition, and the last, appear to have been written for him by a warder called P. Egan. He asks again to have his sentence reduced by the amount of time he had spent in Clonmel Prison, and continues:

> Petitioner makes this humble appeal to His Excellency particularly on account of the death of his wife which has very recently occurred and as he was the occupier of a house and small portion of land at the time of his conviction and it was held for him by his wife until he would be released and as he has no one now to look after it for him he will be homeless when his time is complete if His Excellency should not be graciously pleased to take his pitiable case into consideration and allow him the above time or such reduction in his sentence as His Excellency may consider fit.
>
> Petitioner is now an old man in declining years and this affliction has prayed [sic] on his mind to such an extent that he fears he will not be able to complete his time.
>
> Petitioner humbly begs leave to state that he had no criminal part in the case for which he was convicted or never intended injury to the person but as he visited the place persons who were badly disposed towards him proved certain things against him and he now once more humbly and with great confidence implores that his Excellency will look with mercy and compassion on him under the sad circumstances to which he has been subjected and grant him his humble request for which he shall, as in duty bound, ever and sincerely pray.
>
> John X Dunne his mark

This petition too was refused, and Jack Dunne remained in prison until he had accumulated the requisite 6,570 marks that would make him eligible for release on license. The license was granted on September 15, 1897, signed and sealed by Gerald Balfour, Chief Secretary, and Jack Dunne went home to Cloneen, with a prison gratuity of £1 6s 4d, on October 2. If convicted of any other offense, he would be required to serve the remaining 274 days of his sentence. In the meantime, he was to report monthly to the local police, to retain the license for production if required, and to be of good conduct. This meant, among other things, that he should "not lead an idle and dissolute life, without visible means of obtaining an honest livelihood." As we have seen, according to the census returns for 1901, he appears to have found laboring work on Skehan's farm in Ballyhomuck.

Patrick Kennedy and Michael Cleary were still in Mountjoy when Dunne was released. Cleary was shortly to be transferred to Cork, and Kennedy had graduated from picking rope junk to shoemaking. Looking at his record, it is not difficult to understand how Michael Cleary had been able to dominate him as he had on the night of Bridget Cleary's death: Kennedy's photographs show a timid-looking man of slight build with large, apologetic eyes, and the record shows that on admission to prison he could neither read nor write. The *Irish Times* described him in April 1895 as tall and good-looking, but he measured just five feet seven and a half inches, and weighed 147 pounds. Regulations stated that a prisoner's physical condition was to be "described as far as possible by one of the following terms: 1st, *Stout and Strong.* 2nd, *Fat.* 3rd, *Spare but Muscular.* 4th, *Spare and Weak.*" Kennedy, "spare but muscular," fell into the third category. He had lost one upper front tooth, and had a cut mark under his left eye; his record also mentions a "varicocele, left testicle." Whereas Jack Dunne and Michael Cleary's general health is described as "good," Kennedy's is given as "fair."

Kennedy made 111 visits to the prison doctor in Mountjoy between July 30, 1895 and April 3, 1897, by which time the blue medical record form was full. The page on which it would have continued has not survived. Most visits are annotated "Rept visit." Most entries record that he was "costive," and many mention seconal; some have "*H. Oleosis,*" showing that castor oil was prescribed. On April 21, 1896, a note was sent to the General Prisons Board, "Complains that he got syphilis twice, the second time through tobacco given outside." The reply is initialed on the same day: "I believe that he is labouring under a delusion as to the syphilis. He is under observation as to his mental state." On December 30, 1898, a note on the record of his petitions reads "Does not feel well in his inside." On that occasion, he was "referred to Dr. Woodhouse."

In April, Patrick Kennedy had told the magistrates that he had not been "steady" for some time and had been under the care of Dr. Crean for six years. His brother Michael was subject to fits, and their youngest brother, William, had "got a weakness" on the night of Bridget Cleary's death. Seconal, which was prescribed repeatedly for Michael Kennedy in prison, is a barbiturate. In addition to tranquilizing him, it would have made him costive, or constipated: hence the castor oil.

But Patrick Kennedy's years in prison were not simply a catalogue of physical miseries, for he learned to read and write in the prison school. The entry "Illiterate," made when he was first admitted to Mountjoy, was crossed out three years later and replaced with "R & W." In July 1898, a petition apparently in his own hand went to the Lord Lieutenant, appealing for a reduction in his sentence. Two earlier petitions on his behalf, in February 1897 and February 1898, had been written by a prison warder. On October 1, 1898, Kennedy was transferred to Maryborough and assigned to laboring. On February 3, 1899, Governor Sheehan sent a memo to "The Chairman, General Prisons Board, Dublin Castle":

In compliance with instructions on file 2639/96 I beg to report that convict C868 Patrick Kennedy will become due for release on Licence on 3rd April next.

   He states he will take his discharge for Ballyvadlea, Co. Tipperary and requests that his gratuity which will amount to about £5.2.0 may be paid him on release to enable him to get his land (about 1½ acre) tilled and crops sown and also to assist to maintain himself before he gets employment as a labourer.

This man has not been previously convicted. He is a quiet, well disposed and deserving prisoner. His conduct in Prison has been very good, and I have no doubt but that he will lead a sober & industrious life.

He is one of those concerned in the Tipperary Witch-burning case.

The reply is dated the following day: "Governor. The balance of gra-tuity can be paid in the usual way—which will involve a delay of only a few days . . ."

Patrick Kennedy had spent just over four years in prison when he was released on April 3, 1899. He had grown a luxuriant mustache, which probably concealed his missing front tooth.

In December that same year, John Condon, governor of Mary-borough Prison, received a letter from Patrick Kennedy:

> Kilburry House
> Cloneen
> Fethard
> Co. Tipp.

Dear Sir

I lost my Licence Paper Sir I shall thank your Honour if you would oblige me by sending me another

Patrick Kennedy C 868

On the back of the page he has written, "Sir I wish to enform you that Im going on well."

Kennedy was employed on the notorious farm from which Henry Meagher and his wife had been evicted in 1880, and whose tenant had required police protection for years afterward. By the time of the 1901 census, the ten-room Kilburry House was occupied by a new owner, farmer George Lysaght, unmarried, aged twenty-eight, a member of the Church of Ireland. Patrick Kennedy was still there, one of four laborers or "farm servants," and still unmarried at thirty-five. His letter to the prison governor suggests pride in his own progress, but no congratulations are recorded. Sergeant Edmund Dowling of Cloneen reported that his "conduct since his release has been very good & I find him very industrious & sober since his arrival in the SubDistrict." On December 19, 1899 came an order from the General Prisons Board in Dublin Castle (recorded in red ink): "Send a duplicate copy of licence to the D.I., R.I.C., Carrick-on-Suir, asking that it may be handed to the holder, with a severe caution."

Michael Cleary, meanwhile, was back in Mountjoy. Like Patrick Kennedy and the notorious James Lynchehaun from Achill, who was also in Mountjoy during this period, he had worked as a tailor during his first months there. He and Lynchehaun had been defended at their trials, ten days apart, by the same barrister, Dr. Falconer. Lynchehaun's former teacher, Brother Paul Carney, in a manuscript biography of his former pupil written about 1904, noted that the tailoring workshop at Mountjoy was underground, offering little fresh air or exercise, but more importantly, from the authorities' point of view, no chance of escape.[13] For Michael Cleary there must have been a particular irony in finding himself, as punishment for killing his wife, sitting working a sewing machine.

Before being transferred from Mountjoy, however, Cleary was promoted to an altogether more congenial employment: his own trade of coopering. On his return from Cork in June 1898, he was registered as a carpenter, and this appears to have been his work for the remainder of his time in prison. The medical record shows that his health was generally good; he complained occasionally of piles, and of constipation, and was dosed with castor oil, but there is nothing to indicate the kind of anxiety and hypochondria that evidently plagued Patrick Kennedy. Cleary was given spectacles in February 1901—at forty-one, he was probably becoming far-sighted—and in July he applied to be exempt from school. A governor's memorandum requested a report from the schoolmaster, and the reply came on July 27, signed M. O'Sullivan, Schoolmaster: "Convict Michael Cleary C866 is not fully up to the required standard in Arithmetic; but will be in a short time." In November of the same year, Cleary was transferred to Maryborough.

By November 7, Cleary had served nine months in separate confinement at Mountjoy, followed by a total of six years, seven months, and four days as a working prisoner. A photograph taken at this time shows a handsome, strong-featured man with a stern expression. From February 1902, Cleary was allowed an extra half-pound-daily ration of bread.

James Lynchehaun was transferred to Maryborough Prison in July of that year, and Cleary may have worked alongside him, for prisoners were employed on the building of a new prison wing. Lynchehaun was plastering on the top floor when he discovered a way to gain access to the roof garden, and on September 7 he escaped from his cell, made his way to the roof, climbed down four stories to the prison yard, and got over the outer wall with the aid of planks and scaffolding left by the builders. He made his way to America without being recaptured, his intrepid escape becoming a matter for songs and legends, as well as indirectly for J. M. Synge's *The Playboy of the Western World,* first performed in 1907.[14]

Michael Cleary could obviously be trusted not to attempt an escape. Copious official correspondence records that when working on a roof in the prison on September 2, 1904, he fell, breaking his left arm. He seems to have recovered from the fracture, and continued to work as a carpenter, but in the years that followed he had several problems with his hands, specified in December 1906 as "eruption on palms." In July 1907, syphilis ointment was prescribed for him, with no further details supplied.

In April 1905, Michael Cleary petitioned for a remission of his sentence "on the grounds of good conduct in prison and that his crime was committed when his mind [was] upset by trouble and want of sleep." An official noted: "This convict's conduct has been most exemplary during the 9 years he has been in Prison. A remission of his sentence is a matter for his Excellency the Lord Lieutenant. Prisoner may petition if he thinks he has a case calling for the clemency of the Crown." Cleary had been writing petitions on the regulation blue paper since July 1901. In a careful copperplate hand, with occasional blots and crossings-out, these documents poignantly recall the effort that must have gone into them, as the prisoner sat with dip pen and inkwell, under the eye of a warder, writing the painful story of his crime. His spelling is erratic, as is his punctuation, but the writing is fluent and vivid as it wavers between the flowery "proper and respectful language," which must have been taught to prisoners by schoolmasters and warders, and his own spoken idiom. One petition, written in June 1905 and quoted at length in Chapter 5, runs to three foolscap pages.

Michael Cleary was approved for special privileges from January 18, 1907. On October 5, 1908, he was approved for the intermediate class and by 1910 was in the special class, entitling him to one week's remission on the governor's recommendation. The time was approaching when he would be eligible for release on license. Apart from a single letter at Christmas in his first year, the only correspondence he had received during his time in prison had been from his mother.[15] Twice a year, in summer and winter, he wrote to her in Killenaule, and she wrote back, or had somebody write for her. In July 1902, she sent two photographs that may have been taken during celebrations marking the coronation of Edward VII on June 26. Michael Cleary received his mother's last letter on January 10, 1907. In August, the letter he wrote to her came back. The entry in his penal record is in red: "Returned by Postal Authorities marked 'Deceased.'" Cleary was photographed again that year, full face and profile. At forty-seven, after twelve years in various prisons, he is a strikingly good-looking man, his eyes still bright and proud as he stares at the camera, wearing a dark prison jacket and a regulation checked muffler.

In March 1910, in response to yet another petition, the Lord lieutenant allowed two months of Michael Cleary's sentence to be remitted. In April, the governor of HM Prison, Maryborough, submitted his record to the General Prisons Board announcing that Cleary would soon have the required number of marks (43,824, together with 6 forfeited for remission) to qualify for release on license, and recommending him for one week's extra remission. The week was granted; the license was ordered, and after fifteen years Cleary prepared to be set free:

The petition of Michael Cleary C866

Humbly sheweth I am to be released on licence from this prison on the 28th inst after serving a sentence of 20 years PS I am going to Liverpool on release where I entend following my trade as Cooper. I would feel for ever Grateful to your Excellency if you would be so kind as to discharge me from prison without a licence. This would give me an opportunity of getting employment and not being exposed to my fellow workmen as a man discharged from a Convict Prison and under police suprvision I was never bfore in prison and I faithfully promise if granted this concession I will never return to prison again

Your Excellencys
most obedient Servant M. Cleary

Michael Cleary was released on license from Maryborough Prison on April 28, 1910, and went to Liverpool. His gratuity on release amounted to £17 13s 4d: less than his wife had kept in the coffee canister in the trunk under their bed fifteen years earlier. On October 14, 1910, a black-bordered letter was sent from the office of the Secretary of State, Home Department, Whitehall, to the undersecretary, Dublin Castle:

Sir,

With reference to your letter of the 5th May last in the case of Michael Cleary, I am directed by the Secretary of State to inform you that this man emigrated from Liverpool to Montreal on the 30th June last.

I am,
    Sir,
Your obedient Servant,
H. B. Simpson

Epilogue:
When Does a True Story End?

> Are you a witch or are you a fairy,
> Or are you the wife of Michael Cleary?

A CHILDREN'S RHYME, still well known in South Tipperary, shows that Bridget and Michael Cleary have not been forgotten. In the hundred or so years since they first became notorious, however, they have been reduced to caricature. The house where they lived is called "the fairy cottage," "the place where they burned the witch." Local tradition has absorbed the sensational headlines of the late nineteenth century, and Bridget Cleary is sometimes spoken of as "the last witch burned in Ireland," although the changeling belief on which her tragedy pivoted was significantly different from witchcraft as it is usually understood, and it was never suggested that Bridget Cleary had had dealings with the devil.[1]

The story did not end, of course, when Michael Cleary sailed for Canada. Other actors in this drama lived on too, many of them in South Tipperary. The Index to the "Chief Secretary's Office Registered Papers," at the National Archives of Ireland, shows several entries during 1895 relating to the death of Bridget Cleary. A considerable number of CSORP records were lost in a fire that followed an attack on the Custom House in Dublin in May 1921, and the documents to which these entries refer could not be found, but the Index shows correspondence between Dublin Castle and the RIC in Tipperary, regarding clothing and other expenses for Johanna and Katie Burke, Crown witnesses. After the trial in July, correspondence dealt with their protection, and, in August 1895, Dublin Castle consulted Crown Solicitor Gleeson for his opinion. On February 21, 1896, the CSORP Index has a further entry, "protection to the Burke family witnesses in the Cleary murder case."

It appears that the RIC found lodgings for Johanna Burke, with or without her family, about twelve miles from her home. On December 9, 1895, she sent a reply from Springfield, New Inn, County Tipperary, to a letter her brother Patrick Kennedy had sent her while still in Clonmel Prison. In January, and again in July 1896, letters were mailed to her on his behalf from Mountjoy, c/o Sergeant Hopkins, RIC, Springfield, New Inn, Cahir, but her reply to the July letter, which her brother received on August 5, came from Clonmel Union. The Crown's star witness seems by then to have been living in the workhouse. The final, poignant mention of Johanna Burke comes on October 9, 1896: "Tipperary S[outh] R[iding]—Case against Mich[ae]l Burke, deserting his wife & children."

About the time when he was first judged able to read and write, Patrick Kennedy wrote to his mother: on July 1, 1898, and again on October 15 and November 4 of the same year. The address he gave was Glenconnor, Clonmel, the home of Colonel Richard Evanson, the resident magistrate. In 1901, when the census was taken, Evanson's was the only inhabited house in the townland of Glenconnor, apart from one where his groom lived. It was a first-class house, with twenty-three rooms and fourteen outbuildings. Evanson, by then aged sixty-three, lived there with his forty-five-year-old wife Agnes Elphinstone Evanson, born in India, their four children, and three women servants. Mary Kennedy's own house had, of course, been burned down before she was set free by Mr. Justice O'Brien at the July assizes in 1895. The resident magistrate, who had treated her kindly during the petty sessions, seems to have found a place for her on his own extensive property. By 1901, however, there was no trace of her in Glenconnor.

Mary Kennedy's granddaughter, Katie Burke, does appear in the 1901 census. On November 21, 1898, Patrick Kennedy wrote a letter to "Miss Kate Burke (niece), c/o Mr. Richard Hunt, Brumsick, Clonmel." Brunswick is a townland near Clonmel, where the 1901 census shows household No. 3 as headed by Richard Hunt, farmer, aged fifty, a member of the Church of Ireland. His house had six rooms with three windows in front. It was of stone or brick construction with a slate roof. He shared it with his wife Sarah, aged thirty-nine; their children, John, Hannah, Susie, Edward, Maria, and Sarah, aged from eight years to eight months; and servants called William Hahescy (or Halesey?), twenty-two, and Kate "Bourke," aged sixteen. Kate was unmarried and could read and write; between December 4, 1898 and February 26, 1899, her uncle Patrick received four letters from her. At the 1911 census, the children Edward and Maria Hunt, who should have been aged fifteen and fourteen, are not mentioned, but Richard, aged five, and Louisa, two, are. William, the farm servant, appears again, though this time his name is spelled Hasy, but Kate is not included, nor is any maid's name given.

As we have seen, Jack Dunne and Patrick Kennedy were both employed as laborers near Ballyvadlea in 1901. James Kennedy too must have returned to the area to work, for his brother Patrick wrote to him on February 26, 1897, c/o Mr. Patrick Smith, Ballinard, Cloneen, Fethard. Denis Ganey returned to Kyleatlea in April 1895, and died there some years later.

More is known about the subsequent lives of some of these people than I have written, but it is not the business of this book to pry into or make public the family affairs of people yet living, and so my narrative ends just after the turn of the twentieth century. The wider importance of this story lies in the clash it illustrates between two different world views, two ways of dealing with troublesome people, two ways of accounting for the irrational, at a time of profound social, economic, and cultural change. The intolerable pressures that were brought to bear on Michael Cleary, to make him behave as he did, were not personal or domestic only. The kitchen in Ballyvadlea was another crucible: a microcosm of a larger world in which political and economic issues exerted inexorable influences on the lives of individuals. Like the people of Easthampton, Long Island, in 1658, or of Salem, Massachusetts, in 1692, the people of Ballyvadlea in 1895 were playing out a drama whose larger parameters were not of their own making.[2] The land question scarcely concerned them, yet it was responsible for William Simpson's presence among them, while John Morley's Land Bill and the history of the Home Rule debate profoundly affected the way newspapers treated their story. Courts and newspapers alike depicted the men involved as brutish and dangerous, the women as victims or bystanders, as the gender stereotypes of metropolitan Victorian Britain were applied to rural Ireland, further obscuring the issues that had been at stake. The rich imaginative and metaphorical resources of fairy legend, which carried meaning so effectively in oral culture, emerged into the harsh world of money and newspapers as tattered and pathetic superstitions: foolish and meaningless. Only poets like Yeats and George Russell would take them seriously now, until the new independent Ireland instituted its Folklore Commission and carefully filed and cataloged them.

Fairy legends have been denigrated as superstition, and trivialized in ethnic stereotypes; like any other art form, however, they carry the potential to express profound truths and intense emotions. As we have seen, they are particularly well suited to the expression of ambivalence and ambiguity. No psychologist has built a theory of therapy from them, as far as I know, yet they are resonant with awareness of mental and emotional turmoil. The model of society they offer is firm, yet forgiving: flexible enough to accommodate transgression. In the late twentieth century, artists in media other than oral storytelling have begun to rediscover fairy legends and fairy places. Some of Marian O'Donnell's landscape installations are like latter-day ringforts, while Éilís Ní Dhuibhne's feminist fiction and drama use ideas about fairies to explore issues from housework to maternity hospitals. Poet Nuala Ní Dhomhnaill, whose Irish-language poetry has been translated into English, Japanese, and many languages besides, has perhaps given the richest reading of these legends. The issues she treats are both personal and political, ranging from lyrical fantasy to uncompromising violence: her poems open out the shocking underside of familiar, innocuous fictions.

Cases of marital violence and of women killed by their husbands in their own homes are not unusual. The story of Bridget Cleary is firstly one of "domestic" violence. Like all such stories, it is made up of the histories and personalities of the people involved and of their circumstances. Michael Cleary comes across to us as intense, hard working, and taciturn; Bridget Cleary as articulate, clever, strong willed, and proud. Their society was highly patriarchal.

After seven years of marriage, the Clearys had no children. Across Europe, rates of marital fertility had fallen steeply in the second half of the nineteenth century, but Ireland had barely begun to follow suit by 1895. Having children was a form of insurance against poverty in old age, and a childless marriage was unusual, even shameful.[3] It was customary to attribute infertility to the wife, especially among the better-off, whose farms and businesses were passed from generation to generation in the male line, but Michael Cleary cannot but have felt a certain stigma too.

Erving Goffman's classic study, *Stigma: Notes on the Management of a Spoiled Identity*, illuminates the issues involved for the person marked as discreditably different, and for the "normals" who surround him or her:

> By definition, of course, we believe the person with a stigma is not quite human. On this assumption we exercise varieties of discrimination, through which we effectively, if often unthinkingly, reduce his life chances. We construct a stigma theory, an ideology to explain his inferiority and account for the danger he represents, sometimes rationalizing an animosity based on other differences, such as those of social class.[4]

The fairy-belief tradition that is pejoratively called superstition might more positively, if less felicitously, be labeled a vernacular stigma theory. It is precisely a way of labeling people as not quite human, and serves to rationalize the ambivalence or hostility felt towards those who are different, as the Clearys certainly were. In Jack Dunne's insistence on his own diagnosis of Bridget Cleary's illness as fairy abduction, moreover, and his choreographing of the ordeal to which she was then subjected, we can read an attempt to deal with his own stigma as a lame, childless, poor, and illiterate countryman.

After Bridget Cleary had been killed—and unlike Mr. Justice William O'Brien, I cannot imagine that her killing was either deliberate or premeditated—there remained the problem of what to say. Jack Dunne, accustomed to his marginal position, knew immediately that this was a case for the "authorities" of church and state: their involvement could not be avoided, so it was best to come as clean as possible before them. He, who had been so adamant about the need for fairy medicine, persuaded Michael Cleary to walk with him to Drangan and give himself up. He even enlisted the priests to mediate on his behalf with the police. Michael Cleary was different. He had worked in Clonmel, and could read and write. He was a self-employed artisan, not a forelock-tugging laborer; he was making money; his standard of living was rising, and he had come to expect to be treated with respect, as his attempts to have Dr. Crean call on his wife show clearly. What he had done in causing his wife's death was entirely inconsistent with the self he had been in the habit of presenting to the world, and it appears that he cracked up under the strain of trying to account for it. When his wife's remark about his mother and the fairies on Friday night left him at last entirely isolated, unable any longer to sustain the self he had thought himself to be, he had reached for the nearest and most obvious weapon, a stick from the fire. Now he reached for the nearest narrative: his wife was with the fairies, but all was not lost, for he would rescue her. At midnight on Sunday she would ride a white horse out of the fairy fort of Kylenagranagh, and he would be there, with a black-handled knife.

Bíonn dhá insint ar gach scéal, agus dhá ghabháil déag ar amhrán [there are two ways of telling every story, and twelve ways of singing a song]. *The Burning of Bridget Cleary* is not a work of fiction. All the characters mentioned in the preceding pages lived, and all of them spoke, or were reported by their contemporaries as speaking, the words I have attributed to them. Except where I state otherwise, I have relied on reputable contemporary documents, often corroborated by oral tradition, for information about people's appearance, actions, and circumstances; I have not knowingly invented any detail of fact (and see my note on sources after this Epilogue). Nevertheless, story is the medium through which I have chosen to present my research on the many strands of culture and history that go to make up the case of

Bridget Cleary. Throughout this book I have argued, following Walter Benjamin, that narrative has the power to convey ideas, and to offer them in resilient, subtle forms that can resist the sometimes brutal logic of the loudest voice. Everyone who tells a story offers an interpretation of the facts narrated, however, and the way the dots are joined profoundly affects the picture that appears, so I must take responsibility for this story. Many of the decisions that go into the shaping of a narrative are conscious and deliberate; some are dictated by tradition; others are necessarily unconscious. I have tried to be objective, and to weigh judiciously all the evidence I found, but this has been an interdisciplinary study and, in working to build as complete a picture as possible, I have sometimes ventured into territory that was new to me; I have also undoubtedly been influenced to a greater extent than I am aware of by my own preoccupations and preconceptions.

Experts in various fields have helped me to interpret parts of the evidence that related to their work, and I have drawn gratefully on the discoveries and insights of many who have gone before me, for the burning of Bridget Cleary has been the subject of journalism, essays, scholarly articles, and works of literature and other media.[5] It has also been the lifetime study of people like Brendan Long, former editor of the Clonmel *Nationalist,* whose rich acquaintance with his native county I could not hope to emulate, and of local residents such as Patrick Power and Michael Moroney, who have generously shared with me their knowledge of the Cleary case. I hope my acknowledgments in the Notes and after this Epilogue will give a sense of my debt to those who have helped me, both directly and indirectly, without holding them in any way responsible for the use I have made of their material, and that if I have inadvertently left out the names of some who have enlightened me, I will be forgiven. I hope too that my telling of this story will be seen as a positive contribution to a discussion which will certainly continue. Many people were hurt and damaged by the events of March 1895, and memories are long in rural areas, so the discussion has been understandably muted, but time is a healer; the materials are in the public domain, and it has certainly been my experience that learning more about the case of Bridget Cleary has clarified the difficulties faced by everyone concerned and shown the story as the sort of human tragedy in which nobody is entirely to blame, or entirely innocent, and there are no winners.

ACKNOWLEDGMENTS
AND SOURCES

THIS BOOK began life in Cambridge, Massachusetts, in 1993, as a chapter in a projected academic work on Irish fairy legend, but as my research progressed, it became clear that the full story of Bridget Cleary's death had never been told, and that any attempt to do it justice would necessarily bring in many different aspects of Irish studies. Luckily, I was in an environment hospitable to interdisciplinary approaches, among colleagues and friends whose commitment to fresh ways of reading old material was an inspiration. Adele Dalsimer in particular, to whose memory this American edition is to be partly dedicated, encouraged me to write this as a story, and to trust that whatever scholarly analysis I had to offer could be conveyed through narrative. *Ní bheidh a leithéid arís ann:* There will never be another like her. Back in Ireland, I benefited from the accumulated knowledge and wisdom of my colleagues in various departments and faculties of the National University of Ireland, Dublin (University College Dublin), and other institutions, of independent scholars, librarians, archivists, and antiquaries, and of many individuals in South Tipperary. I have been honored by invitations to deliver lectures, stimulated by students and other audiences, and blessed by the loving kindness of friends and family who have allowed me to talk about this book at great and tortuous length for hours at a time. To those who read drafts of the book, in whole or in part, and offered me their comments, I am especially grateful.

It is a pleasure to record my thanks to the librarians and archivists of the following collections, many of whom shared their specialist knowledge of the documents of this case: the Allen Library, O'Connell Schools, Dublin; O'Neill Library, Boston College; Cashel & Emly

Diocesan Archives, St. Patrick's College, Thurles, County Tipperary; Widener Library, Harvard University; National Archives of Ireland, Dublin; National Library of Ireland, Dublin; MetÉireann, Dublin; the Library, and the Department of Irish Folklore, National University of Ireland, Dublin; Tipperary County Library, Thurles; Tipperary Heritage Trust, Tipperary Town.

Where no other source is given, accounts of the magistrates' hearing and of the trial are taken from contemporary newspapers, principally the *Irish Times, Freeman's Journal, Cork Examiner, Nationalist* (Clonmel), *Clonmel Chronicle, Daily Express, Dublin Evening Telegraph,* and *Dublin Evening Mail.* These accounts are frequently identical, being derived from a common stenographer's record, but vary in the spelling of proper names and in punctuation; they have therefore been silently edited in places for the sake of clarity and consistency.

Information on weather in 1895 is from handwritten daily records kept at Birr Castle (about fifty miles from Ballyvadlea) by Robert Jacob, and preserved in the library of MetÉireann, the Irish meteorological service, Glasnevin, Dublin, where they have been checked against records in *Symons's Monthly Meteorological Magazine.*

Details of the health, personal appearance, height, weight, and hair color of the people accused of Bridget Cleary's killing are taken from their prison records in the National Archives of Ireland, Bishop Street, Dublin, with corroborative notes from contemporary newspapers.

Information about the commercial life of South Tipperary at the end of the nineteenth century has come from Thom's *Directory* for 1895, from Francis Guy, *Directory of Munster* (Cork, Guy, 1893) and from George Henry Bassett, *The Book of County Tipperary* (Dublin, 1889), republished as *County Tipperary 100 Years Ago* (Belfast, Friar's Bush Press, 1991). These are supplemented by details from George A. de M. Edwin Dagg, *Devia Hibernia: The Road and Route Guide for Ireland of the Royal Irish Constabulary* (Dublin, Hodges Figgis, 1893).

Information about the deliberations of the Cashel Poor Law Guardians is from their minute books, kept in the Tipperary County Library, Thurles.

Baptismal records for Drangan and Cloneen are held at Tipperary Heritage Trust, Tipperary. I was allowed to consult them by courtesy of Fr. Christy O'Dwyer, Diocesan Archivist, St. Patrick's College, Thurles, and of Ann Moloney, Tipperary Town.

The series of biographies in Irish by Diarmuid Breathnach and Máire Ní Mhurchú, *Beathaisnéis a hAon—Beathaisnéis a Cúig* (Dublin, An Clóchomhar, 1986–97), has been invaluable.

The *Dictionary of National Biography* was the major source of information on British statesmen and other public figures.

I am grateful to Comhairle Bhéaloideas Éireann for permission to quote at length from Seán Ó hEochaidh, Máire Mac Néill, and Séamus Ó Catháin (eds), *Síscéalta ó Thír Chonaill/Fairy Legends from Donegal* (1977).

The following pictures in the plate section have been reproduced by kind permission of the National Archives of Ireland, Bishop Street, Dublin, where the originals are held: photographs of the Clearys' house, Ballyvadlea; mug shots from the prison record of Michael Cleary; mug shot of Patrick Kennedy; and Michael Cleary's petition from 1905.

I thank my colleagues in the Department of Modern Irish Language and Literature, the National University of Ireland, Dublin (UCD), for facilitating research leave; the Department of Celtic Languages and Literatures, Harvard University, and the Irish Studies Program, Boston College, for generous scholarly hospitality; audiences at American University, Washington DC, the American Conference for Irish Studies annual meetings, the National Library Association of Ireland, the Synge Summer School, Rathdrum, County Wicklow, the Yeats Summer School, Sligo, and Waseda University, Tokyo, for stimulating discussions; the Tyrone Guthrie Centre, Annaghmakerrig, County Monaghan, for an idyllic writing environment, and my students at UCD, Harvard, and Boston College, for keeping me thinking.

I owe an enormous personal debt to the following, and hope this book will in some measure repay them for the help they have given me and the interest they have taken in it: Cormac, Ken, Maryrose, Rosaleen, and Stephanie Bourke, Marcus Bourke, George Bornstein, Noreen Bowden, Tony Butler, Brenna Clarke, Kathleen Clune, Brother Thomas Connolly, Pat Cooke, John Cooney, Goretti and Michael Corway, Carol Coulter, Maura Cronin, Monica Cullinan, Liz Butler Cullingford, Brendan Dalton, Mary E. Daly, Molly Daly, Mary Darmody, Michael Doherty, Gráinne Dowling, John Fleetwood Senior, Sheila and Denis Foley, Roy Foster, Luke Gibbons, Nicky Grene, Fiana Griffin, Ruth-Ann Harris, Michael Hayes, Jörg Hensgen,

Norma Jessop, Declan Kiberd, Gabriel Kiely, Lee Komito, Ivan, Jacob, Tom, and Vera Kreilkamp, Susan Lanser, Rena Lohan, Gerard Long, Bernard and Mary Loughlin, Maria Luddy, Gerard Lyne, Tom McArdle, Margaret MacCurtain, Jerusha McCormack, Lucy McDiarmid, Dave McDonagh, Thomas McGrath, John MacMenamin, Breandán Mac Suibhne, Fidelma Maguire, Elizabeth Malcolm, Gerard Mills, Michael Moroney, Joanne Mulcahy, Bríona Nic Dhiarmada, Nuala Ní Dhomhnaill, Éilís Ní Dhuibhne, Siobhán Ní Laoire, An Bráthair Liam P. Ó Caithnia, Proinsias Ó Drisceoil, Rev. Christy O'Dwyer, Diarmuid Ó Giolláin, Cormac Ó Gráda, Philip O'Leary, Liam Ó Mathúna, Kevin O'Neill, Tim O'Neill, Nial Osborough, Barra Ó Séaghdha, Beth Parkhurst, Deborah Pogson, Patrick Power, Pauline Prior, Tom Quinlan, Mick Quinlivan, Joan Radner, Tríona Rafferty, Lily Richards, Catherine Santoro, Dóirín Saurus, Lisa Shields, Will Sulkin, Mia Van Doorslaer, Jonathan Williams, and Wendy Wolf.

Angela Bourke
Dublin, May 10, 1999

NOTES

I: Laborers, Priests, and Peelers

1. Kevin Whelan, "The Catholic Parish, the Catholic Chapel and Village Development in Ireland," *Irish Geography,* vol. 16 (1983), pp. 1–15; and "The Catholic Church in County Tipperary, 1700–1900," in William Nolan and Thomas McGrath (eds.), *Tipperary: History and Society: Interdisciplinary Essays on the History of an Irish County* (Dublin, Geography Publications, 1985), pp. 215–55. See also William J. Hayes (unpublished paper), "A Review of Church Building in the Archdiocese of Cashel and Emly from the Penal Times," copy in Cashel Diocesan Archive, Thurles.

2. National Archives, Dublin, Penal Record, 1897/110.

3. Local farmer Mr. Patrick Power of Tullowcossaun remembers hearing that his grandmother had just been "churched" following the birth six weeks earlier of a baby daughter, and that she had met Jack Dunne as she left the confessional. The baby in question was Mr. Power's aunt, later Mrs. Gleeson, of Drangan Post Office. (Taped interview with the author, Ballyvadlea, July 1997.)

4. For the RIC, see W. J. Lowe and E. L. Malcolm, "The Domestication of the Royal Irish Constabulary, 1836–1922," *Irish Economic and Social History,* vol. 19 (1992), pp. 27–48; for coercion, L. P. Curtis Jr, *Coercion and Conciliation in Ireland, 1880–1892: A Study in Conservative Unionism* (Princeton, NJ, Princeton University Press; and London, Oxford University Press, 1963).

5. George A. de M. Edwin Dagg, *Devia Hibernia: The Road and Route Guide for Ireland of the Royal Irish Constabulary* (Dublin, Hodges Figgis, 1893), p. 344. Dagg was an RIC District Inspector, based in Lisnaskea, County Fermanagh.

6. James O'Shea, *Priest, Politics and Society in Post-Famine Ireland: A Study of County Tipperary, 1850–1891* (Dublin, Wolfhound, 1983), pp. 26, 38.

7. For a comparison between vernacular and more modern spirituality, see Margaret MacCurtain, "Fullness of Life: Defining Female Spirituality in Twentieth-Century Ireland," in Maria Luddy and Cliona Murphy (eds), *Women Surviving: Studies in Irish Women's History in the Nineteenth and Twentieth Centuries* (Dublin, Poolbeg, 1990), pp. 233–63. See also S. J. Connolly, *Priests and People in Pre-Famine Ireland, 1780–1845* (Dublin, Gill and Macmillan, 1982), Chapter 3, "Popular and Official Religion"; and Lawrence Taylor, *Occasions of Faith* (Dublin, Lilliput, 1996).

8. O'Shea, *Priest, Politics and Society,* p. 21.

9. *Ibid.,* pp. 13–24, 73.

10. *Ibid.,* p. 82.

11. His brother Michael (1846–1902) was Dean of St. Patrick's Diocesan College, Thurles, 1874–1878; his cousin was Archbishop Harty. See Walter G. Skehan, *Priests of Cashel and Emly* ("the Skehan Index") (Thurles, Cashel and Emly Diocesan Trust, Ltd, 1991), R37 and R132. Obituary, *Nationalist,* December 23, 1916.

12. Tom Inglis, *Moral Monopoly: The Rise and Fall of the Catholic Church in Modern Ireland* (2nd ed., Dublin, University College Dublin Press, 1998), suggests, p. 148, that visits to the sick offered opportunities to gather information about families and individuals, and were an important means by which the Church in nineteenth-century Ireland disseminated the culture of "respectability."

13. Lowe and Malcolm, "The Domestication of . . .," p. 30: "The Irish police did not formally disarm until disbandment in 1922, but the carbine became progressively less visible. From the 1870s, most regular policing and patrol duties did not call for firearms."

14. Mary E. Daly, *The Buffer State: The Historical Roots of the Department of the Environment* (Dublin, Institute of Public Administration, 1997), p. 203, describes this act as "a landmark in Irish housing legislation." Boards of guardians were to use low-interest Exchequer loans to build cottages on half-acre plots for rent to rural laborers, whose rents would be subsidized by rates.

15. O'Shea, *Priest, Politics and Society,* pp. 104–11.

16. Newport: RIC Divisional Commissioner's report, Western Division, June 1895 (National Archives, Dublin); Clonagoose: Patrick

C. Power, *History of South Tipperary* (Cork and Dublin, Mercier, 1989), p. 179.

17. The GAA was at first regarded by the RIC, and by many of the Catholic clergy, as a front for secret revolutionary activities. In the spring of 1895, however, the Archbishop of Cashel, Thomas William Croke, endorsed it publicly, announcing that he did not consider that the association had anything to do with secret societies. By June, District Inspector Pierris B. Pattison, Crime Branch Special, South-Eastern Division, could write in his secret monthly report to Dublin Castle, "It seems to me that there are two forces at work on this association—one the I[rish] R[epublican] B[rotherhood] anxious to work it up and use it as a political power, the other the Priests and moderate men who would like to see it thrive from a purely athletic point of view." (National Archives, Dublin)

18. Ordnance Survey of Ireland, Tipperary 6", sheet no. 63. Site and monument record: Constraint Map, 1906. SMR detail, 1992. Site no. 35.

19. This Michael Cusack was not the founder of the GAA (1847–1906), but a namesake and contemporary, who was a native of Drangan. He was a noted member of the IRB and died in 1909. See Liam P. Ó Caithnia, *Micheál Cíosóg* (Dublin, An Clóchomhar, 1982) pp. 42–3, 278–9; O'Shea, *Priest, Politics and Society,* pp. 82, 170.

20. Details from Mullinahone Barracks Diary, in the Allen Library, O'Connell Schools, Dublin. I am grateful to An Bráthair Liam P. Ó Caithnia and to Brother Thomas Connolly for affording me access to this manuscript, which covers the period July 9, 1864 to September 11, 1885. It seems to be a transcribed record of station correspondence (including orders marked "confidential" and "Return this paper sealed under double cover"), rather than the day-by-day record for which the bound notebook was issued. For the eviction of the Meaghers, see also Power, *History of South Tipperary,* pp. 184–5, and O'Shea, *Priest, Politics and Society,* p. 104.

21. E. Estyn Evans, *Irish Folk Ways* (London, Routledge and Kegan Paul, 1957), pp. 118–19, notes that souterrains (often found within ringforts) were sometimes used for hiding stock to avoid confiscation in lieu of arrears of rent, for storing explosives in the early 1920s, and for other illegal activities such as poteen-making.

22. Lucy McDiarmid and Maureen Waters (eds.), *Lady Gregory: Selected Writings* (London, Penguin, 1995), Introduction, p. xvi.

23. Michael Quirke is not listed as a Clonmel Town Councillor either in George Henry Bassett, *The Book of County Tipperary* (Dublin, 1889) or in Francis Guy, *Directory: Province of Munster* (Cork, 1893), although Guy lists a grocer and vintner of this name on pp. 60 and 152. Guy, p. 71, also lists a Michael Quirke, farmer, in Ballyvadlea.

2: Fairies and Fairy Doctors

1. Douglas Hyde, "The Necessity for Deanglicizing Ireland," in Sir Charles Gavan Duffy, *The Revival of Irish Literature* (London: T. Fisher Unwin, 1894). For a discussion, see Declan Kiberd, *Inventing Ireland* (London, Jonathan Cape, 1995) pp. 140–5.

2. James H. Delargy, *The Gaelic Storyteller, With Some Notes on Gaelic Folk-Tales* (Chicago, American Committee for Irish Studies, 1969). Reprinted from *Proceedings of the British Academy,* vol. 31 (1945).

3. For a lively and readable account of the Commission's work, see Bríd Mahon, *While Green Grass Grows: Memoirs of a Folklorist* (Cork and Dublin, Mercier, 1998).

4. Gearóid Ó Crualaoich, "The Primacy of Form: A 'Folk Ideology' in de Valera's Politics," in J. P. O'Carroll and John A. Murphy (eds.), *De Valera and His Times* (Cork, Cork University Press, 1986 [1983]), pp. 47–61.

5. For the significance of Elias Lönnrot's *Kalevala,* see Olli Alho, "Culture and National Identity," in Bo Almqvist, Séamas Ó Catháin and Pádraig Ó Héalaí (eds), *The Heroic Process: Form, Function and Fantasy in Folk Epic* (Dublin, Glendale Press, 1987) pp. 265–78, and other essays in the same volume.

6. During the same period, however, Francis James Child, Professor of Mathematics at Harvard University, developed the method still used for the systematic cataloging of ballads in *The English and Scottish Popular Ballads,* 5 vols. (New York, Dover, 1965 [1882–98]).

7. The best collection of transcribed and translated Irish-language texts is Seán Ó hEochaidh, Máire Mac Néill and Séamus Ó Catháin (eds.), *Síscéalta ó Thír Chonaill / Fairy Legends from Donegal* (Dublin, Comhairle Bhéaloideas Éireann, 1977). For discussion see Peter Narváez (ed.), *The Good People: New Fairylore Essays* (New York, Garland, 1991), especially (for the English-language tradi-

tion), Patricia Lysaght, "Fairylore from the Midlands of Ireland," pp. 22–46. For North American reflexes, see Barbara Rieti, *Strange Terrain: The Fairy World in Newfoundland* (St. John's, ISER Books, 1991).

8. This story is also found in the apocryphal Christian literature of the late Middle Ages, associated with the Harrowing of Hell.

9. Bengt Holbek, *Interpretation of Fairy Tales: Danish Folklore in a European Perspective,* Folklore Fellows Communications, No. 239 (Helsinki, Suomalainen Tiedeakatemia/Academia Scientiarum Fennica, 1987), p. 198.

10. Geoffrey Grigson, *The Englishman's Flora* (London, Paladin, 1975 [1958]), pp. 84–9.

11. For an example from oral storytelling (which does not name the plant, although it mentions both the time of year and the need to collect it before sunrise), see my translation of Éamon a Búrc's *"Bean Óg a Tugadh sa mBruín,"* "A Young Woman Taken by the Fairies," [in "Language, Stories, Healing," pp. 299–314], in Anthony Bradley and Maryann Gialanella Valiulis (eds), *Gender and Sexuality in Modern Ireland* (Amherst, University of Massachusetts Press, 1997), pp. 311–12.

12. Anjana Ahuja, "Plants on the Wild Side," *The Times*, August 10, 1998. I am indebted to Liam Ó Mathúna for this reference. Cf. Nicholas Williams, *Díolaim Luibheanna* (Dublin, An Gúm, 1993), pp. 90–4.

13. Biddy Early, ?1798–1874. See Lucy McDiarmid and Maureen Waters (eds), *Lady Gregory: Selected Writings* (London, Penguin, 1995), pp. 57–74, 77–88; Nancy Schmitz, "An Irish Wise Woman," *Journal of the Folklore Institute,* vol. 14 (1977), pp. 169–79; Edmund Lenihan, *In Search of Biddy Early* (Cork, Mercier Press, 1987); and Meda Ryan, *Biddy Early, The Wise Woman of Clare* (Cork, Mercier Press, 1978).

14. For delirium caused by pyaemia, (blood poisoning) see Jo Murphy-Lawless, *Reading Birth and Death: A History of Obstetric Thinking* (Cork, Cork University Press, 1998), p. 151; for anorexia, see my "Fairies and Anorexia: Nuala Ní Dhomhnaill's 'Amazing Grass,'" *Proceedings of the Harvard Celtic Colloquium,* vol. 13 (1993), pp. 25–38.

15. For a discussion of oral traditions about power struggles between healers and priests, see Pádraig Ó Héalaí, "Priest versus Healer:

The Legend of the Priest's Stricken Horse," *Béaloideas,* vols. 62–63 (1995), pp. 171–88.

16. Censuses were taken in independent Ireland in 1926, 1936, and 1946, and at five-year intervals thereafter.

17. Sir William Wilde, 1815–76. See Lady Wilde, *Ancient Legends, Mystic Charms and Superstitions of Ireland* (London, 1888); *Ancient Cures, Charms and Usages of Ireland* (London, 1890).

18. *Cnaí* in Irish has roughly the same semantic range as "consumption" in English; Wilde's *cuirrethe* should probably read *ciurrethe,* for modern Irish *ciorraithe:* maimed, mutilated (esp. when disability is attributed to the evil eye); *millte,* "ruined," sometimes carries the sense "blighted by the fairies."

19. Sir William Wilde, *Census of Ireland Report, 1851* (1854), part v, vol. 1 (Dublin, 1856), p. 455.

20. W. R. Wilde, *Irish Popular Superstitions* (Dublin, McGlashan, 1852), p. 28.

21. Thomas Crofton Croker, *Fairy Legends and Traditions of the South of Ireland* (London, John Murray, 1828), vol. 1, pp. vii–ix.

22. *Folk-Lore Journal,* vol. 2 (1884), pp. 190–1. This account was quoted by Edwin Sidney Hartland, *The Science of Fairy Tales: An Inquiry into Fairy Mythology* (London, Walter Scott, 1890). For other cases, see S. J. Connolly, *Priests and People in Pre-Famine Ireland, 1780–1845* (Dublin, Gill and Macmillan, 1982), pp. 100–101 (and n. 34, p. 298).

23. Clinical notes and cases, *Journal of Mental Science,* vol. 34, no. 148 (January 1889), pp. 535–9. I am indebted to my cousin, Dr. Pauline Prior, for this reference.

24. See Joyce Underwood Munro, "The Invisible Made Visible: The Fairy Changeling as a Folk Articulation of Failure to Thrive in Infants and Children," in Narváez, *The Good People,* pp. 251–83.

25. "The Storyteller" (written 1936), Walter Benjamin, *Illuminations,* Hannah Arendt ed. and introd. (New York, Harcourt Brace and World, 1968), pp. 89–90.

26. Ó hEochaidh, etc., *Síscéalta ó Thír Chonaill,* pp. 56–61. The places mentioned are in southwest Donegal, near Kilcar.

27. For coding in folkore, see Joan N. Radner (ed.), *Feminist Messages: Coding in Women's Folk Culture* (Chicago, University of Illinois Press, 1993).

28. Walter Scott, *The Minstrelsy of the Scottish Border* (Edinburgh, Kelso,

1802; repr. London, Alexander Murray, 1869), pp. 439–81; the "Introduction to the Tale of Tamlane" is subtitled "On the Fairies of Popular Superstition." *Tam Lin* is No. 39 in Child's *The English and Scottish Popular Ballads,* vol. I, p. 335ff.

29. E. B. Lyle, "The Ballad *Tam Lin* and Traditional Tales of Recovery from the Fairy Troop," *Studies in Scottish Literature,* vol. 6, no. 1 (1968), pp. 175–85 (p. 177). For Irish versions of the ballad, see Edith Wheeler, "Irish Versions of Some Old Ballads," *Journal of the Irish Folk Song Society,* vol. 1, nos. 2 and 3 (1904), pp. 41–9, especially pp. 47–8, "Lord Robinson's Only Child"; Hugh Shields, *Narrative Singing in Ireland* (Dublin, Irish Academic Press, 1993), pp. 67–8, 216.

3: Reading, Sewing, Hens, and Houses

1. Michael J. F. McCarthy, *Five Years in Ireland: 1895–1900* (London, Simpkin, Marshall, Hamilton, Kent; Dublin, Hodges Figgis, 1901), p. 144.

2. *Census of Population: Ireland, 1841, 1851* (HM Stationery Office). In 1841, there were 21 houses in Ballyvadlea, with a total population of 57 males and 61 females. In 1851, after the Famine, there had not been much change: 56 males and 56 females, in 19 houses. (During the same period, many townlands in poorer areas, such as west Kerry, lost half or more of their population.) In 1851, the Poor Law Valuation for the townland of Ballyvadlea was £179 15s 0d. Its population fell steadily from then until the end of the century (*Pobal Ailbe: Cashel and Emly, Census of Population, 1841–1971* (Thurles, Archbishop's House, 1975).

The original census documents for 1901 are held in the National Archives, Dublin. Nine dwelling houses are recorded on form N for Ballyvadlea, of which five (Nos. 1,2,3,4, and 6), are marked as inhabited.

3. James O'Shea, *Priest, Politics and Society in Post-Famine Ireland: A Study of County Tipperary, 1850–1891* (Dublin, Wolfhound, 1983), p. 119, calls the laborers "that forgotten class"; John W. Boyle reviews the literature in his essay "A Marginal Figure: The Irish Rural Laborer," in Samuel Clark and James S. Donnelly Jr (eds.), *Irish Peasants: Violence and Political Unrest, 1780–1914* (Manchester, Manchester University Press, 1983), pp. 311–38. With the 150th

anniversary of the Great Famine of 1845–49, a large body of new work has appeared, which pays more attention to the social history of the laboring class.

4. Mary Carbery, *The Farm by Lough Gur: The Story of Mary Fogarty (Sissy O'Brien)* (Cork, Mercier Press, 1973 [1937]). Narrated as autobiography, but written long after the events it describes, by a person who was not present, this is a romantic, even sentimental, account, but it is generally accepted as presenting an authoritative picture of the social world of the Catholic "strong farmers" of the time.

5. Quoted in O'Shea, *Priest, Politics and Society,* p. 125 (rags) and p. 120 (begging).

6. Carbery, *Farm by Lough Gur,* p. 58.

7. A reporter from the *Cork Examiner* who visited the area after the discovery of Bridget Cleary's body described it (March 29) as "a little thatched cabin." On the same day, another reporter, from the Dublin *Daily Express,* called it a "hut," and gave its location as about fifty yards from the house where she died. However, Patrick Power in 1997 pointed out its site to the author as beside the crossroads at Ballyvadlea bridge.

8. The Drangan Parochial Register shows a daughter called Bridget born to Patrick Boland and Bridget Keating and baptized in February 1867, but this would make her twenty-eight at the time of her death, which contradicts information from several other sources. It was a common practice to name a second infant after one who had died, so I retain Bridget's age as twenty-six.

9. Walter G. Skehan, *Cashel and Emly Heritage* (Abbey, 1993), p. 201.

10. Tom Inglis, *Moral Monopoly: The Rise and Fall of the Catholic Church in Modern Ireland* (2nd ed., Dublin, University College Dublin Press, 1998), pp. 151–8.

11. *Census of Ireland for the Year 1901* (HM Stationery Office), Summary Tables, p. 23: "Occupations of Females." 44,513 women were classified as "Milliner, dressmaker, staymaker," of whom 43,208 could read and write, while a further 664 could read only. 4,417 were aged 45–65; 816 were 65 and over. By contrast, there were 56,196 in the category "Shirtmaker, seamstress," the majority presumably employed in the northern factories which made shirts for the British Empire (5,852 were Presbyterians, almost all of whom

were in Ulster). Of these, 9,119 were aged 45–65, 2,803 were over 65, and 4,894 could neither read nor write.

12. *Cork Examiner,* March 30, 1895.

13. George Henry Bassett, *The Book of County Tipperary* (Dublin, 1889), repr. as *County Tipperary 100 Years Ago* (Belfast, Friar's Bush Press, 1991), carries an advertisement for Butterick paper patterns, p. 414, but makes no mention of the Clonmel Sewing Machine Depot. It is listed, however, in Francis Guy's *Directory: Province of Munster* (Cork, 1893), p. 61.

14. *Woman's World,* vol. 1 (1888), p. 555.

15. Bassett, *County Tipperary,* p. 67. For street lighting in County Tipperary, see also Michael O'Donnell, "Lighting the Streets of Fethard, 1870–1914," *Tipperary Historical Journal,* 1998, pp. 128–32.

16. Professor Mary E. Daly, personal communication.

17. For discussions of the poultry industry in this period, and how state and cooperative attempts to reform it affected power relations in the rural community, see Joanna Bourke, "Women and Poultry in Ireland, 1891–1914," *Irish Historical Studies,* vol. 25, no. 99 (1987), pp. 293–310; "Poultry-Rearing," Chapter 6 in her *Husbandry to Housewifery: Women, Economic Change, and Housework in Ireland, 1890–1914* (Oxford, Oxford University Press, 1993), pp. 169–98; Patrick Bolger, *The Irish Co-operative Movement* (Dublin, Institute of Public Administration, 1977); and S. J. Connolly (ed.), *The Oxford Companion to Irish History* (Oxford, Oxford University Press, 1998), s.v. "Poultry" (Jonathan Bell). Quotes from *Royal Commission on Labour: The Agricultural Labourer, Ireland . . . Reports,* pp. 64–8; E. Anderson, "Irish Poultry and Poultry-Rearing," *Irish Homestead,* September 4, 1897 (both in Bourke, "Women and Poultry," p. 294).

18. See Bourke, "Women and Poultry," and compare the attitudes to hens, eggs, and women expressed in Tomás Ó Criomhthain's *An tOileanách* (Dublin, Fallons, 1929), tr. as *The Islandman* (Oxford, Oxford University Press, 1978 [1937]), and *Allagar na hInise/Island Cross-talk: Pages from a Diary,* tr. Tim Enright (Oxford, Oxford University Press, 1986 [1928]).

19. Bourke, "Women and Poultry," p. 295.

20. Former government minister Donnchadh Ó Gallchobhair in con-

versation with the author at Scoil Gheimhridh Merriman, in West-port, County Mayo, in January/February 1991. The proverb "a whistling woman and a crowing hen would raise the devil out of his den" is also found in the United States, but a corresponding one in Irish deplores *cearc ag glaoch, nó bean ag fiannaíocht:* "a crow-ing hen, or a woman telling hero-tales." *Fiannaíocht*—telling sto-ries of the hero Fionn mac Cumhaill and his band—was the most valued form of verbal art in Irish, and guaranteed its talented prac-titioners a respectful hearing.

21. Cormac Ó Gráda, *Ireland: A New Economic History* (Oxford, Ox-ford University Press, 1994), p. 215. By 1911, 27.3 percent of men and 24.9 percent of women aged between forty-five and fifty-four had never married.

22. This information is based on essays by special correspondents in the *Cork Examiner,* March 28, 29, 30, 1895, and the *Daily Express,* March 29, 1895, together with petitions written by Michael Cleary from prison. For married couples living apart because of obligations to elderly parents, see Robin Fox, *The Tory Islanders* (Notre Dame, University of Notre Dame Press, 1995).

23. I am grateful to Professor Mary E. Daly for pointing this out.

24. Cashel Poor Law Guardians, Minute Book No. 90, pp. 261–2.

25. Contemporary RIC photograph, National Archives, Dublin, CBS 9786/6, and author's observation.

26. Rena Lohan, *Guide to the Archives of the Office of Public Works* (Dublin, Government of Ireland Stationery Office, 1994), pp. 256–7.

27. Frank Mitchell and Michael Ryan, *Reading the Irish Landscape* (Dublin, Town House, 1997), pp. 254–61. See also F. H. A. Aalen, Kevin Whelan and Matthew Stout, *Atlas of the Irish Rural Landscape* (Cork, Cork University Press, 1997), pp. 44–9, 250–3; and Mat-thew Stout, *The Irish Ringfort* (Dublin, Four Courts Press, 1997).

28. Lady Gregory, "Irish Superstitions," *Spectator*, April 20, 1895.

29. *The Farm by Lough Gur* illustrates the class difference such stories marked, as Mary Fogarty asks her mother, "Why do you let the maids be so silly? . . . The nuns say we must never miss a chance of curing people of pagan superstition!" (Carbery, *Farm by Lough Gur,* pp. 161–2).

30. See Patricia Lysaght, "Fairylore from the Midlands of Ireland," in

Narváez, *The Good People,* p. 37, and cf. Angela Bourke, "The Virtual Reality of Irish Fairy Legend," *Éire–Ireland,* vol. 31, nos. 1 and 2 (Spring–Summer 1996) pp. 1–25 (pp. 12–13).

31. I owe this point to Professor Mary E. Daly.

32. *Cork Examiner,* March 29, 1895. The building referred to as a stable would not have been big enough to accommodate a horse, however.

4: Bridget Cleary Falls Ill

1. An exception is L. P. Curtis Jr, *Coercion and Conciliation in Ireland, 1880–1892: A Study in Conservative Unionism* (Princeton, Princeton University Press; London, Oxford University Press, 1963).

2. Curtis, *Coercion and Conciliation,* pp. 412–13.

3. National Archives, Dublin, CBS DCCI, Report of DC Alan Cameron.

4. Quoted in Lady Gregory's autobiography, *Seventy Years,* Colin Smythe (ed.), (Gerrards Cross, Colin Smythe, 1973). See also *Lady Gregory: Selected Writings,* Lucy McDiarmid and Maureen Waters (eds.), (London, Penguin, 1995), pp. 38–9.

5. National Archives, Dublin, CBS DCCI.

6. Patrick Bolger, *The Irish Co-operative Movement: Its History and Development* (Dublin, Institute of Public Administration, 1977).

7. *Daily Express,* March 18, 1895.

8. *Daily Express,* March 23, 1895.

9. *Dublin Evening Mail,* Editorial, March 27, 1895.

10. The *Cork Examiner* and *Daily Express* both give this information, but without naming Dunne. Johanna Burke names him at the July assizes (*Irish Times,* July 6, 1895), and the circumstantial evidence agrees that his was the house that Bridget Cleary visited.

11. Compare Erving Goffman, *Stigma: Notes on the Management of a Spoiled Identity* (Harmondsworth, Penguin, 1968 [1963]), and see Angela Bourke, "The Virtual Reality of Irish Fairy Legend," *Éire–Ireland,* vol. 31, nos. 1 and 2 (Spring–Summer 1996), pp. 1–25.

12. Eric Cross, *The Tailor and Ansty* (Cork, Mercier Press, 1942); Peadar Ó Ceannabháin (ed.), *Éamon a Búrc: Scéalta* (Dublin, An Clóchomhar, 1983).

13. For Peig Sayers and Sorcha Mhic Ghrianna, see *The Field Day Anthology of Irish Writing,* vol. iv (Cork: Cork University Press, forthcoming).

14. See Walter Ong, *Orality and Literacy: The Technologizing of the Word* (London, Methuen, 1982), and my "Virtual Reality."

15. Walter G. Skehan, *Cashel and Emly Heritage* (Abbey, 1993), p. 201.

16. In the barony of Middlethird in 1851, 396 males and 416 females aged 10–20 were bilingual, compared with 51 males and 75 females aged 1–10. The age groups 20–30 and 31–40, by contrast, had 626 males, 632 females and 704 males, 706 females respectively who were bilingual.

17. Author's interview with Patrick Power, Tullowcossaun, July 1997.

18. Charms were sometimes written on paper, folded small, and carried on the person. Compare Keith Thomas, *Religion and the Decline of Magic: Studies in Popular Beliefs in Sixteenth- and Seventeenth-Century England* (London, Penguin, 1973 [1971]), *passim.*

19. See Robert Wuthnow, *Meaning and Moral Order: Explorations in Cultural Analysis* (Berkeley, Los Angeles, London, University of California Press, 1987), pp. 97–144.

20. For attitudes to this substratum of religious thought and its demise in sixteenth-century England, see Thomas, *Religion and the Decline of Magic.* For its prevalence in Ireland, see S. J. Connolly, *Priests and People in Pre-Famine Ireland, 1780–1845* (Dublin, Gill and Macmillan 1982).

21. McDiarmid and Waters, *Lady Gregory: Selected Writings,* pp. 72, 79.

22. Peadar Ó Ceannabháin, *Éamon a Búrc, Scéalta,* p. 237. For a discussion of deformity of the legs as a motif in fairy and related traditions, see Diarmuid Ó Giolláin, "The Leipreachán and Fairies, Dwarfs and the Household Familiar: A Comparative Study," *Béaloideas,* vol. 52 (1984), pp. 75–150 (pp. 115–16).

23. See Ruth Barrington, *Health, Medicine and Politics in Ireland, 1900–1970* (Dublin, Institute of Public Administration, 1987); Mary E. Daly, *The Buffer State: The Historical Roots of the Department of the Environment* (Dublin, Institute of Public Administration, 1997); Brian Donnelly, "An Overview of the Development of Local Government in Ireland," *Irish Archives,* vol. 3, no. 2, new series (Autumn 1996), p. 9.

24. Crean: Cashel PLG Minute Book No. 98, p. 95; Heffernan: *ibid.,* pp. 14, 45 and *passim.*

25. National Archives, Dublin, Misc. 1618.910. Petition, July 1905. Johanna Burke's testimony corroborates Cleary's version of events.

26. Interview with Patrick Power.

27. Tony Butler, "The Burning of Bridget Cleary: The 100th Anniversary," *Nationalist,* March 25, 1995, p. 21.

28. National Archives, Dublin. Penal Record 1910/28, Convict No. C866, Michael Cleary. He weighed 189 pounds on release in 1910.

29. See Mary Lefkowitz, *Heroines and Hysterics* (London, Duckworth, 1981), pp. 12–25. For a discussion of the persistence of these ideas, see Germaine Greer, *The Female Eunuch* (London, Paladin, 1971 [1970]), pp. 48–9.

30. Cashel PLG Minute Book No. 98, p. 95.

31. Quoted in Barrington, *Health, Medicine and Politics,* p. 10.

32. In February 1999, "Liveline" on RTÉ Radio 1 in Ireland broadcast a spirited phone-in discussion on the powers of traditional healers, including seventh sons. For a first-person account of such a healer, who died in 1938, see Sean O'Sullivan, *Legends from Ireland* (London, B. T. Batsford, 1977), pp. 80–1, "The Seventh Son." Mary Carbery's *The Farm by Lough Gur: The Story of Mary Fogarty* (Cork, Mercier Press, 1973 [1937]), p. 14, tells of old people in County Limerick who "knew that if a sick person was not better by the eighth or ninth day of the moon he would hear *Ceolsidhe,* the fairy music" [an omen of death].

33. McDiarmid and Waters, *Lady Gregory: Selected Writings,* p. 60.

5: "Take It, You Witch!"

1. Except where otherwise stated, the following account of the events of March 14, including the quoted passages, is based on the *Cork Examiner,* April 8, 1895. The *Examiner's* reporter had visited the scene and interviewed William Simpson. His account is more comprehensive than that in any other newspaper.

2. For the use of beestings, see E. Estyn Evans, *Irish Folk Ways* (London, Routledge and Kegan Paul, 1957), pp. 303–4. Early Irish law texts mention *brothchán,* (cf. the modern *brachán,* porridge), a broth or porridge made of milk with oatmeal and herbs, as a special food for invalids, the ingredients for which were protected by law. One wisdom text, however, specifically counsels against giving beestings (*nús*) to invalids. See Fergus Kelly, *Early Irish Farming: A*

Study Based Mainly on the Law Texts of the Seventh and Eighth Centuries AD (Dublin, Dublin Institute for Advanced Studies, 1997), pp. 324, 349. I am grateful to Dr. Michael Doherty for help with this aspect of the story.

3. See Genevieve Brennan, "Yeats, Clodd, *Scatologic Rites* and the Clonmel Witch Burning," *Yeats Annual,* no. 4, Warwick Gould (ed.) (London, Macmillan, 1986), pp. 207–15.

4. Testimony of William Simpson, here and below, is taken from the *Clonmel Chronicle,* special supplement, "The Appalling Tragedy in Ballyvadlea," April 3, 1895.

5. Edmund Lenihan, *In Search of Biddy Early* (Cork, Mercier Press, 1987), p. 27. Lenihan points out a similarity between this story and the scene at the end of J. M. Synge's *The Playboy of the Western World,* when Pegeen Mike burns Christy Mahon's leg with a sod of turf from the fire.

6: "Bridgie Is Burned!"

1. For this kind of vernacular architecture, see Frank McDonald and Peigín Doyle, *Ireland's Earthen Houses,* with photographs by Hugh McConville (Dublin, A. and A. Farmar, 1997).

2. Richard Breen, "The Ritual Expression of Inter-Household Relationships in Ireland," *Cambridge Anthropology,* vol. 6, nos. 1 and 2 (1980), p. 37. Compare Kevin Danaher, *The Year in Ireland* (Cork, Mercier, 1972), p. 117. See also Conrad M. Arensberg, *The Irish Countryman: An Anthropological Study* (Garden City, NY, The Natural History Press, 1968 [1937]), pp. 174–8, and E. Estyn Evans, *Irish Folk Ways* (London, Routledge and Kegan Paul, 1957), pp. 295–306.

3. Pádraig Ó Héalaí, "Priest Versus Healer: The Legend of the Priest's Stricken Horse," *Béaloideas,* vols. 62–3 (1995), pp. 171–88, and "Cumhacht an tSagairt sa Bhéaloideas," in *Léachtaí Cholm Cille 8: Ár nDúchas Creidimh* (Maynooth, An Sagart, 1977), pp. 109–31. See also Edmund Lenihan, *In Search of Biddy Early* (Cork, Mercier Press, 1987), pp. 87–100, for stories about the "wise woman," a priest and his horse.

4. Thomas McGrath, "Fairy Faith and Changelings: The Burning of Bridget Cleary in 1895," *Studies,* Summer 1982, pp. 178–84

(p. 183). This short essay is a valuable study by a professional historian and native of the area. Fr. Power died in 1893, aged forty-six.

5. See, for instance, Michael J. F. McCarthy, *Five Years in Ireland: 1895–1900* (London, Simpkin, Marshall, Hamilton, Kent; Dublin, Hodges Figgis, 1901), pp. 177, 186–88.

6. Sir William Wilde, "A short account of the superstitions and popular practices relating to midwifery, and some of the diseases of women and children, in Ireland," *Monthly Journal of Medical Science,* New Series, vol. 35 (May, 1849), pp. 711–29, (p. 712).

7. Jo Murphy-Lawless, *Reading Birth and Death: A History of Obstetric Thinking* (Cork, Cork University Press, 1998), pp. 8–9; cf. pp. 256–60.

8. See Walter Ong, *Orality and Literacy: The Technologizing of the Word* (London, Methuen, 1982).

9. Mary Carbery, *The Farm by Lough Gur: The Story of Mary Fogarty* (Cork, Mercier Press, 1973 [1937]), pp. 157–66, devotes a chapter to "May-Eve." See also Danaher, *The Year in Ireland,* pp. 86–127, esp. pp. 109–19, and Éilís Ní Dhuibhne, "'The Old Woman as Hare': Structure and Meaning in an Irish Legend," *Folklore,* vol. 104, nos. 1 and 2 (1993), pp. 77–85. For another useful discussion, compare Richard P. Jenkins, "Witches and Fairies: Supernatural Aggression and Deviance among the Irish Peasantry," *Ulster Folklife,* vol. 23 (1977), pp. 33–56, revised in Peter Narváez (ed.), *The Good People: New Fairylore Essays* (New York, Garland, 1991), pp. 302–35.

10. Ní Dhuibhne, "Old Woman as Hare"; cf. Jacqueline Simpson, "Some Rationalized Motifs in Modern Urban Legends," *Folklore,* vol. 92 (1981), pp. 203–7.

11. Danaher, *The Year in Ireland,* p. 115.

12. For discussion of analogies between landscape and the human body as articulated in fairy legend and explored by contemporary women artists in Ireland, see my "Fairies and Anorexia: Nuala Ní Dhomhnaill's 'Amazing Grass,'" *Proceedings of the Harvard Celtic Colloquium,* vol. 13 (1993), pp. 25–38; "Language, Stories, Healing," in Anthony Bradley and Maryann Gialanella Valiulis (eds.), *Gender and Sexuality in Modern Ireland* (Amherst, University of Massachusetts Press, 1997), pp. 299–314, and "Exploring the Darkness: Gwen O'Dowd's *Uaimh,*" in Alston Conley and Jennifer Grinnell

(eds.), *Re/Dressing Cathleen* (Boston, McMullen Museum of Art, Boston College, 1997), pp. 69–73.

13. See Maud Ellmann, *The Hunger Artists: Starving, Writing and Imprisonment* (Cambridge, MA, Harvard University Press, 1993).

14. Compare reports of the South African Truth and Reconciliation Commission in 1998. A former commander of the notorious Vlakplaas, where state assassins were trained, testified before one of its hearings that "to burn a body to ashes takes about seven hours . . . It has to be turned frequently so all parts of the body burn away. It smells like a *braai* [barbecue]." Mary Braid, "Truth at the End of the Rainbow," *Independent on Sunday* magazine, June 14, 1998, pp. 4–6.

7: "Amongst Hottentots . . .": The Inquest and Inquiry

1. This was Fr. John Power, mentioned above, p. 106; see James O'Shea, *Priest, Politics and Society in Post-Famine Ireland: A Study of County Tipperary, 1850–1891* (Dublin, Wolfhound, 1983), p. 327.

2. Georges Cuvier, in P. Topinard, *Anthropology* (London, Chapman and Hall, 1878), p. 494, quoted in Stephen Jay Gould, *The Mismeasure of Man* (revised and expanded, London, Penguin, 1996 [1981]), p. 118.

3. See Thomas Pakenham, *The Scramble for Africa, 1876–1912* (London, Weidenfeld and Nicolson, 1991).

4. "Coroner Shee" appears as a sponsor in Fethard's baptismal register for November 19, 1884, as transcribed by Rev. Walter J. Skehan (notebook no. 70), and preserved in the Diocesan Archive, Thurles.

5. L. P. Curtis Jr, *Coercion and Conciliation in Ireland, 1880–1892: A Study in Conservative Unionism* (Princeton, NJ, Princeton University Press; and London, Oxford University Press, 1963), pp. 103–4.

6. Apart from the large house in River Street, where he lived in 1901, William Kickham Heffernan owned two other houses in Killenaule (including one occupied by a priest). He was still practicing as a physician and surgeon in Killenaule in 1911.

7. Michael J. F. McCarthy, *Five Years in Ireland: 1895–1900* (London, Simpkin, Marshall, Hamilton, Kent; Dublin, Hodges Figgis, 1901), p. 145; the author's remark about the parish priest is on p. 164.

8. See, for instance, Michel Foucault, *Discipline and Punish: The Birth of the Prison* (London, Penguin, 1991 [1977]), Chapter 2, "The Spectacle of the Scaffold."

9. According to George Henry Bassett's *The Book of County Tipperary* (Dublin, 1889), Grubb was lay president of the Clonmel YMCA in 1889.

10. Sir Joseph Ridgeway, Irish undersecretary to Prime Minister Balfour, February 23, 1888, quoted in Curtis, *Coercion and Conciliation,* p. 200.

11. He retired just as the Anglo-Irish War entered a particularly difficult phase in Cork, where he was then stationed. PRO HO184/45, p. 293 (No. 47734). I am grateful to Dr. Elizabeth Malcolm for generous help in finding and interpreting A. J. Wansbrough's service record.

12. This is not uncommon in colonial situations. Gayatri Chakravorty Spivak has characterized colonialism as a process of "white men saving brown women from brown men"—see "Can the Subaltern Speak?" in Patrick Williams and Laura Chrisman (eds.), *Colonial Discourse and Post-Colonial Theory: A Reader* (New York & London, Harvester Wheatsheaf, 1994), pp. 92–4. See also Rayna Green, "The Pocahontas Perplex: The Image of Indian Women in American Culture," *The Massachusetts Review,* Autumn 1975, pp. 698–714. For a discussion, see Angela Bourke, "Reading a Woman's Death: Colonial Text and Oral Tradition in Nineteenth-Century Ireland," *Feminist Studies,* vol. 21, no. 3 (Fall 1995), pp. 553–86.

13. See Stephen Jay Gould, *The Mismeasure of Man* (revised and expanded, London, Penguin, 1996 [1981]).

14. For Lamarck (1744–1829) and the adoption of his ideas by British anthropologists, see Henrika Kuklick, *The Savage Within: The Social History of British Anthropology, 1885–1945* (Cambridge, Cambridge University Press, 1991), Chapter 3.

15. W. B. Yeats, *Memoirs of W. B. Yeats: Autobiography and First-draft Journal,* transcribed and ed. Denis Donoghue (London, Macmillan, 1972), pp. 270–1.

16. Cf. Gould, *Mismeasure,* pp. 151–75, "The Ape In Some of Us: Criminal Anthropology."

17. "a dark continent": George Sims, *How the Poor Live* (1883), quoted in Kuklick, *The Savage Within,* p. 101; J. S. Mill, *Ibid.,* p. 107. See

also L. P. Curtis, *Apes and Angels: The Irishman in Victorian Caricature* (Washington and London, Smithsonian Institution, 1997 [1971]).

18. Kuklick, *The Savage Within,* pp. 114–16.

19. For a discussion of Lombroso's work, including its influence on Bram Stoker, see Gould, *Mismeasure,* pp. 151–75. Gould supplies this quotation, p.153, From I. Taylor, P. Walton and J. Young, *The New Criminology: For a Social Theory of Deviance* (London, Routledge and Kegan Paul, 1973), p. 41. Lombroso's *L'Homme Criminel* (Paris, Alcan), was published in 1887. Bram Stoker's *Dracula* appeared in 1897.

20. For Maamtrasna, see Jarlath Waldron, *Maamtrasna: The Murders and the Mystery* (Dublin, Edmund Burke, 1992). Five members of one family were murdered in a remote valley on the Galway–Mayo border in August 1882, in the third year of the Land War. Secret society involvement was suspected, and the accused were tried in Dublin, under coercion legislation, although most of them could not speak English, and prosecution witnesses were strongly suspected of perjury. Three men were hanged, and another five were still in prison by 1895. For unionists, Maamtrasna meant Irish savagery; for nationalists, British injustice.

21. Elaine Scarry, *The Body in Pain: The Making and Unmaking of the World* (New York and Oxford, Oxford University Press, 1985), p. 297. Scarry estimates that the events dealt with in product liability cases often encompass an action of between fifteen and ninety seconds.

8: A Funeral, Some Photographs, More Fairies

1. The use of "boycott" as a verb in *The Times* is interesting: it had been coined by Irish nationalists only fifteen years earlier.

2. Nina Witoszek, "Ireland: A Funerary Culture?," *Studies,* Summer 1987, pp. 206–15. See also Seán Ó Súilleabháin, *Irish Wake Amusements* (Cork, Mercier, 1967), and Gearóid Ó Crualaoich, "Contest in the Cosmology and the Ritual of the Irish 'Merry Wake,'" *Cosmos: The Yearbook of the Traditional Cosmology Society,* vol. 6 (1990), pp. 145–60.

3. Michael J. F. McCarthy, *Five Years in Ireland, 1895–1900* (London, Simpkin, Marshall, Hamilton, Kent; Dublin, Hodges Figgis, 1901), p. 171.

4. A. E. S. Heard, Divisional Commissioner, Kilkenny, confidential

monthly report for September 1894. National Archives, Dublin, CBS DCCI, 3/715, box 5.

5. National Archives, Dublin, CBS, 1895, 9786/S.

6. Ashis Nandy, *The Intimate Enemy: Loss and Recovery of Self Under Colonialism* (Delhi, Oxford University Press, 1983), p. 82.

7. Ashis Nandy, "Sati: A Nineteenth-Century Tale of Women, Violence and Protest," in V. C. Joshi (ed.), *Rammohun Roy and the Process of Modernization in India* (New Delhi, Vikas Publishing House, 1975), p. 68. Quoted in Gayatri Chakravorty Spivak, "Can the Subaltern Speak?" in Patrick William and Laura Chrisman (eds.), *Colonial Discourse and Post-Colonial Theory: A Reader* (New York and London, Harvester Wheatsheaf, 1994), p. 94.

8. *Cork Examiner,* March 30, 1895.

9. Hubert Butler, "The Eggman and the Fairies," *Escape from the Anthill,* with a foreword by Maurice Craig (Mullingar, Lilliput, 1985), pp. 63–74.

10. John Dunne, "The Fenian Traditions of Sliabh na mBan," *Transactions of the Kilkenny Archaeological Society,* vol. 1, no. 3 (1851), pp. 333–62. For the legend of the fairy women and the spinner(s), see Áine O'Neill, "'The Fairy Hill is on Fire!' (MLSIT 6071): A Panorama of Multiple Functions," *Béaloideas,* vol. 59 (1991), pp. 189–96.

11. Osborn Bergin and R. I. Best, "Tochmarc Étaíne," *Eriu,* vol. 12, no. 2 (1938), pp. 137–96.

12. See James Carney, *The Playboy and the Yellow Lady* (Dublin, Poolbeg, 1986).

13. See R. F. Foster, *W. B. Yeats: A Life,* Part 1, *The Apprentice Mage* (Oxford, Oxford University Press, 1997), pp. 145, 186. WBY singled out "The Gifts of Aodh and Una" from *Ballads in Prose,* in *Bookman,* August 1895.

14. *Bookman,* November 1893. I am indebted to George Bornstein for this reference.

15. W. B. Yeats, *The Celtic Twilight* (1982 [1893]), pp. 73–4.

16. See Mary Helen Thuente, *W. B. Yeats and Irish Folklore* (Dublin, Gill and Macmillan, 1981; Totowa, NJ, Barnes and Noble, 1981), p. 131.

17. See, for example, Énrí Ó Muirgheasa, *Dhá Chéad de Cheoltaibh Uladh* (Dublin, Government Publications, 1974 [1934]), pp. 372–6.

18. John P. Frayne and Colton Johnson (eds.), *Uncollected Prose by W. B. Yeats,* vol. 2 (London, Macmillan, 1975), p. 277.

19. Genevieve Brennan, "Yeats, Clodd, *Scatalogic Rites* and the Clonmel Witch Burning," *Yeats Annual,* no. 4 (1986), ed. Warwick Gould, pp. 207–15, 212. Thanks to Liz Butler Cullingford for this reference. Hartland's *The Science of Fairy Tales: An Inquiry into Fairy Mythology* had included an account of the killing in Clonmel of the child Philip Dillon, quoted in Chapter 2.

20. Anon., "The 'Witch-burning' at Clonmel," *Folk-Lore,* vol. 6, no. 4 (1895), p. 378, n.1. Duncan's own account of the traditions he gathered in the parish of Kiltubbrid appeared in vol. 7 (1896), pp. 160–83, as "Fairy Beliefs and Other Folklore Notes from County Leitrim."

21. *Folk-Lore,* vol. 7 (1896), p. 164.

22. *Folk-Lore,* vol. 7 (1896), pp. 171–2.

23. *Daily Express,* March 30, 1895. There were two creameries in Fethard, one owned by Michael Coffey (who also owned one in Drangan), the other by William Dwyer.

24. See Joanna Bourke, *Husbandry to Housewifery: Women, Economic Change, and Housework in Ireland, 1890–1914* (Oxford, Oxford University Press, 1993), Chapter 3, "Dairymaids," pp. 80–108.

25. The song was written by Charles K. Harris. Thanks to Kevin Hough for this information. The fame of popular artists spread after Thomas Edison invented the phonograph in 1877. The *Dublin Evening Telegraph* picked up a story from the *New York World,* datelined Chicago, March 23, 1895, which reported that "Fully one thousand women went on an emotional spree this afternoon at the Auditorium, when it was announced that Jean de Reszke would not appear in [Meyerbeer's opera] 'Les Huguenots.' Some wept, others had hysterics, and all lost control of themselves . . . When the ushers inspected the scene of the tumult they found fifty-eight veils, twenty combs, two purses, four bags of cosmetics, one pair of garters, and a lot of ribbons."

The telephone was sufficiently widespread for the *Cork Examiner* to publish a joke about it on April 6, under the heading "A Noble Aim": "Parker: 'Poor old Brownley! He's become insane, I hear, working on that telephone invention of his.' Barker: 'What was he trying to invent?' Parker: 'A device for preventing people from calling you up when you don't want to talk with them.'"

26. *Nationalist,* September 25 and 28, 1895. I am grateful to Mary Darmody, Tipperary County Library, Thurles, for these references.

9: Two Courtrooms

1. The following account is based on Richard Ellmann's incomparable biography, *Oscar Wilde* (New York, Vintage, 1988), with additional material from H. Montgomery Hyde, *The Trials of Oscar Wilde* (New York, Dover, 1973 [1962]), Davis Coakley, *Oscar Wilde: The Importance of Being Irish* (Dublin, Town House, 1994), and contemporary newspapers.

2. Ellmann, *Oscar Wilde*, p. 427.

3. Hyde, *Trials of Oscar Wilde*, p. 91.

4. John Dillon, MP for Mayo East, who had been among those invited to attend the nationalist protest at the Mitchelstown trial, was also present in the House of Commons on April 2. See L. P. Curtis Jr, *Coercion and Conciliation in Ireland, 1880–1892: A Study in Conservative Unionism* (Princeton, Princeton University Press; London, Oxford University Press, 1963), pp. 197–9.

5. *United Ireland,* April 6, 1895, p. 3.

6. Alan O'Day, *Irish Home Rule 1867–1921* (Manchester, Manchester University Press, 1998) devotes less than one page to John Morley's two attempts to introduce land legislation.

7. *Irish Times,* July 5, 1895.

8. Michael J. F. McCarthy, *Five Years in Ireland, 1895–1900* (London, Simpkin, Marshall, Hamilton, Kent; Dublin, Hodges Figgis, 1901), pp. 167–71, (p. 168).

9. The document to which this entry refers could not be traced in the National Archives.

10. CSORP 1895, no. 6695.

11. McCarthy, *Five Years,* p. 159.

12. Patricia Lysaght, "Fairy Lore from the Midlands of Ireland," in Peter Narváez (ed.), *The Good People: New Fairylore Essays* (New York, Garland, 1991), pp. 22–46. This essay is a valuable discussion of the importance of the storyteller's own skepticism as a catalyst for her verbal art.

13. *Ibid.,* p. 38.

14. David Blackbourn, *The Marpingen Visions: Rationalism, Religion and the Rise of Modern Germany* (Oxford, Oxford University Press, 1993), p. 290. Robert Koch identified the anthrax bacillus in 1878, the cholera bacillus in 1885.

15. Peter Narváez, "Newfoundland Berry Pickers 'In the Fairies':

Maintaining Spatial, Temporal, and Moral Boundaries through Legendry," in his (ed.) *The Good People,* pp. 336, 360 n. For a fuller discussion of this question, see my "Hunting out the Fairies: E. F. Benson, Oscar Wilde and the Burning of Bridget Cleary," in Jerusha McCormack (ed.), *Wilde the Irishman* (New Haven and London, Yale University Press, 1998), pp. 36–46.

16. For the importance of dissection after the French Revolution and the privileging of the medical gaze, see Michel Foucault, *The Birth of the Clinic: An Archaeology of Medical Perception* (New York, Vintage, 1994 [1973]).

17. See, for instance, the *Report of the Working Party on the Legal and Judicial Process for Victims of Sexual and Other Crimes of Violence Against Women and Children* (Dublin, National Women's Council of Ireland, 1996), which notes (p. 33) that although "[i]n most adult men's experience of crime, the perpetrator is a stranger . . . for women, the greatest potential of sexual or physical danger comes from known men within a so-called safe environment such as the family home."

18. Patrick Boland's home was some eleven miles from Clonmel courthouse. He may have meant that he lived within half a mile of Cloneen RIC barracks.

19. This remark was the inspiration for Hubert Butler's essay "The Eggman and the Fairies," see n. 9, p. 263.

20. This may mean that Michael Kennedy had been a soldier. I can find no other reference to his having been abroad.

21. Brian Masters, *The Life of E. F. Benson* (London, Pimlico, 1991), p. 115. See also Geoffrey Palmer and Noel Lloyd, *E. F. Benson As He Was* (Luton, 1988).

22. See my "Hunting Out the Fairies," pp. 36–46.

23. Anon., "The 'Witch-Burning' at Clonmel," *Folk-Lore,* vol. 6, no. 4 (1895), pp. 373–84.

10: Trial and Imprisonment

1. One outcome of the murders of Lord Frederick Cavendish and T. H. Burke was the three-year Prevention of Crime Act, a draconian piece of legislation through which, in the words of one historian, "Many Irishmen had firsthand experience of what amounted to martial law." (L. P. Curtis Jr, *Coercion and Conciliation*

in Ireland, 1880–1892: A Study in Conservative Unionism (Princeton, Princeton University Press; London, Oxford University Press, 1963), p. 15).

2. Speech at Lambeth Baths, *Evening Telegraph,* April 4, 1895. The *Irish Times* reported, April 2, that white gloves had been presented to the judge at the Mayo Criminal Quarter Sessions in Castlebar on the previous day, in celebration of there being no cases to be heard.

3. Richard Ellmann, *Oscar Wilde* (New York, Vintage, 1988), pp. 503–4.

4. Thanks to my friend and colleague, Dr. Lee Komito, for this insight.

5. William O'Brien was twenty-seven when he entered the King's Inns in Dublin in 1855. I am indebted to Professor Nial Osborough for this information.

6. *Clonmel Chronicle,* July 6, 1895; Michael J. F. McCarthy, *Five Years in Ireland, 1895–1900* (London, Simpkin, Marshall, Hamilton, Kent; Dublin, Hodges Figgis, 1901), p. 173.

7. *Clonmel Chronicle,* July 6, 1895.

8. From "The Ballad of Reading Gaol," *Collected Works of Oscar Wilde,* p. 753.

9. See Michel Foucault, *Discipline and Punish: The Birth of the Prison* (London, Penguin, 1991 [1977]), p. 143: "Disciplinary space tends to be divided into as many sections as there are bodies or elements to be distributed. One must eliminate the effects of imprecise distributions, the uncontrolled disappearance of individuals, their diffuse circulation, their unusable and dangerous coagulation; [partitioning] was a tactic of anti-desertion, anti-vagabondage, anti-concentration. Its aim was to establish presences and absences, to know where and how to locate individuals, to set up useful communications, to interrupt others, to be able at each moment to supervise the conduct of each individual, to assess it, to judge it, to calculate its qualities or merits. It was a procedure, therefore, aimed at knowing, mastering and using. Discipline organizes an analytical space." For the control of space and of individual bodies in Irish schools, see Tom Inglis, *Moral Monopoly: The Rise and Fall of the Catholic Church in Modern Ireland* (2nd ed., Dublin, University College Dublin Press, 1998), pp. 151–8.

10. National Archives, Dublin, Convict Records Misc. 1619/10. The

judge's report becomes almost indecipherable at the end, so that the civil servant who annotated the file quotes only the middle of it in his summary. My transcription of the last sentence is based to some extent on guesswork.

11. "*H[austus] Oleosis*" (a draught of castor oil), a powerful laxative, was prescribed repeatedly, according to prison medical records. I am grateful to Dr. John Fleetwood Sr. for help in interpreting them.

12. His age on admission to prison was given as fifty-five, but in his first petition a year later, he said he was over sixty.

13. James Carney, *The Playboy and the Yellow Lady* (Dublin, Poolbeg, 1986), pp. 131–49.

14. Carney, *The Playboy and the Yellow Lady*, pp. 150–6. James Lynchehaun was the subject of a famous extradition case in Indianapolis in 1904.

15. The letter he received on December 25, 1895 was sent by "Pat" Boland, Cloneen, Fethard, County Tipperary. This may have been his father-in-law, released from prison a week earlier; illiteracy had not prevented Jack Dunne and Patrick Kennedy from sending letters when they were in prison.

Epilogue: When Does a True Story End?

1. See Richard P. Jenkins, "Witches and Fairies: Supernatural Aggression and Deviance among the Irish Peasantry," *Ulster Folklife*, vol. 23 (1977), pp. 33–56, revised in Peter Narváez (ed.), *The Good People: New Fairylore Essays* (New York, Garland, 1991), pp. 302–35.

2. See John Putnam Demos, *Entertaining Satan: Witchcraft and the Culture of Early New England* (Oxford and New York, Oxford University Press, 1982), and Paul Boyer and Stephen Nissenbaum, *Salem Possessed: The Social Origins of Witchcraft* (Cambridge, MA, and London, Harvard University Press, 1974).

3. Cormac Ó Gráda, *Ireland: A New Economic History* (Oxford, Oxford University Press, 1994), pp. 218–24. See also Timothy W. Guinnane, *The Vanishing Irish: Households, Migration, and the Rural Economy in Ireland, 1850–1914* (Princeton, Princeton University Press, 1997), pp. 263–71. Both authors correct the long-held belief that family size in Ireland did not begin to fall until the 1920s, but Ó Gráda (p. 222) finds that urban, middle-class couples were more

likely to limit their families than the rural working class; Guinnane (p. 267) contrasts the situation in industrialized areas of Europe where child rearing had to compete with factory work, with that in rural Ireland where a lack of paid employment outside the home made children relatively cheap in terms of the use of women's time.

4. Erving Goffman, *Stigma: Notes on the Management of a Spoiled Identity* (Harmondsworth, Penguin, 1968 [1963]), p. 15.

5. In addition to works already mentioned, see Patrick Galvin's play *The Last Burning,* in Patrick Galvin, *Three Plays* (Belfast, Threshold, 1976), pp. 5–58; Host's record album, *Tryal* (London, Aura Records Ltd, 1982—thanks to Deborah Pogson for this reference); William Kennedy's novel, *Very Old Bones* (New York, Viking, 1992); Carlo Gébler's novel *The Cure* (London, Hamish Hamilton, 1994); Pat Feely's documentary "The Burning of Bridget Cleary," Radio Teilifís Éireann, Radio 1, April 5, 1995 (thanks to Ian Lee, RTÉ Sound Archive); Sharron FitzGerald's essay "The Burning of Bridget Cleary: A Community on Guard," in Ullrich Kockel (ed.), *Landscape, Heritage and Identity: Case Studies in Irish Ethnography* (Liverpool, Liverpool University Press, 1995), pp. 117–34.

INDEX

FOR THE BEST IN PAPERBACKS, LOOK FOR THE

In every corner of the world, on every subject under the sun, Penguin represents quality and variety—the very best in publishing today.

For complete information about books available from Penguin—including Puffins, Penguin Classics, and Compass—and how to order them, write to us at the appropriate address below. Please note that for copyright reasons the selection of books varies from country to country.

In the United Kingdom: Please write to *Dept. EP, Penguin Books Ltd, Bath Road, Harmondsworth, West Drayton, Middlesex UB7 0DA.*

In the United States: Please write to *Penguin Putnam Inc., P.O. Box 12289 Dept. B, Newark, New Jersey 07101-5289* or call 1-800-788-6262.

In Canada: Please write to *Penguin Books Canada Ltd, 10 Alcorn Avenue, Suite 300, Toronto, Ontario M4V 3B2.*

In Australia: Please write to *Penguin Books Australia Ltd, P.O. Box 257, Ringwood, Victoria 3134.*

In New Zealand: Please write to *Penguin Books (NZ) Ltd, Private Bag 102902, North Shore Mail Centre, Auckland 10.*

In India: Please write to *Penguin Books India Pvt Ltd, 11 Panchsheel Shopping Centre, Panchsheel Park, New Delhi 110 017.*

In the Netherlands: Please write to *Penguin Books Netherlands bv, Postbus 3507, NL-1001 AH Amsterdam.*

In Germany: Please write to *Penguin Books Deutschland GmbH, Metzlerstrasse 26, 60594 Frankfurt am Main.*

In Spain: Please write to *Penguin Books S. A., Bravo Murillo 19, 1° B, 28015 Madrid.*

In Italy: Please write to *Penguin Italia s.r.l., Via Benedetto Croce 2, 20094 Corsico, Milano.*

In France: Please write to *Penguin France, Le Carré Wilson, 62 rue Benjamin Baillaud, 31500 Toulouse.*

In Japan: Please write to *Penguin Books Japan Ltd, Kaneko Building, 2-3-25 Koraku, Bunkyo-Ku, Tokyo 112.*

In South Africa: Please write to *Penguin Books South Africa (Pty) Ltd, Private Bag X14, Parkview, 2122 Johannesburg.*